CRACKNELL'S STATUTES

Succession:
THE LAW OF WILLS AND ESTATES

Fifth Edition

D G CRACKNELL
LLB, of the Middle Temple, Barrister

OLD BAILEY PRESS

OLD BAILEY PRESS
at Holborn College, Woolwich Road,
Charlton, London SE7 8LN

First published 1994
Fifth edition 2004

ISBN 1 85836 570 8

British Library Cataloguing-in-Publication Data

A catalogue record for this book is available from the
British Library.

Printed and bound in Great Britain.

CONTENTS

Contents

PREFACE

THIS book sets out, in their amended form, in whole or in part, the provisions of forty-one statutes to which students will need to refer as they prepare for their Succession examination.

Of course, the relevant sections of the Wills Act 1837, the Administration of Estates Act 1925 and the Inheritance (Provision for Family and Dependants) Act 1975 are included, but all of the other provisions (not least those relating to taxation) have an important bearing on particular aspects of the whole subject. This edition covers the important changes made by, amongst other statutes or statutory instruments, the Finance Acts 2001, 2002 and 2003.

Insertions, repeals or substitutions made and brought into force on or before 1 May 2004 have been taken into account and a note at the end of the particular statute indicates the source of any changes.

The provisions of the Administration of Justice Act 1982 relating to international wills were not in force on 1 May 2004 but, because of their significance, they have been included in the Appendix. These provisions include the Annex to the Convention on International Wills.

Suggestions as to statutes, or provisions of statutes, which could helpfully be included in future editions would always be most gratefully received.

ALPHABETICAL TABLE OF STATUTES

STAMP ACT 1815
(35 Geo 3 c 184)

37 Penalty for administering effects of a deceased person without proving the will or taking out letters of administration within a given time

If any person shall take possession of and in any manner administer any part of the estate and effects of any person deceased without obtaining probate of the will or letters of administration of the estate and effects of the deceased within six calendar months after his or her decease or within two calendar months after the termination of any suit or dispute respecting the will or the right to letters of administration, if there shall be any such which shall not be ended within four calendar months after the death of the deceased, every person so offending shall forfeit the sum of one hundred pounds.

As amended by the Statute Law Revision (No 2) Act 1890; Finance Act 1975, ss52(2), (3), 59(5), Schedule 13, Pt I.

WILLS ACT 1837
(7 Will 4 & 1 Vict c 26)

1   Meaning of certain words in this Act

The words and expressions hereinafter mentioned, which in their ordinary signification have a more confined or a different meaning, shall in this Act, except where the nature of the provision or the context of the Act shall exclude such construction, be interpreted as follows: (that is to say,) the word 'will' shall extend to a testament, and to a codicil, and to an appointment by will or by writing in the nature of a will in exercise of a power, and also to an appointment by will of a guardian of a child, and to any other testamentary disposition; and the words 'real estate' shall extend to manors, advowsons, messuages, lands, tithes, rents, and hereditaments, whether freehold, customary freehold, tenant right, customary or copyhold, or of any other tenure, and whether corporeal, incorporeal, or personal, and to any estate, right, or interest (other than a chattel interest) therein; and the words 'personal estate' shall extend to leasehold estates, and other chattels real, and also to moneys, shares of government and other funds, securities for money (being not real estates), debts, choses in action, rights, credits, goods, and all other property whatsoever, which by law devolves upon the executor or administrator, and to any share or interest therein; and every word importing the singular number only shall extend and be applied to several persons or things as well as one person or thing; and every word importing the masculine gender only shall extend and be applied to a female as well as a male.

3   All property may be disposed of by will

It shall be lawful for every person to devise, bequeath, or dispose of, by his will executed in manner hereinafter required, all real estate and all personal estate which he shall be entitled to, either at law or in equity, at the time of his death, and which, if not so devised, bequeathed, and disposed of, would devolve upon his executor or administrator; and the power hereby given shall extend to all contingent, executory or other future interests in any real or personal estate, whether the testator may or may not be ascertained as the person or one of the persons in whom the same respectively may become vested, and whether he may be entitled thereto under the instrument by which the same respectively were created, or under any disposition thereof by deed or will; and also to all rights of entry for conditions broken, and other rights of entry; and also to such of the same estates, interests, and rights respectively, and other real and personal estate, as the testator may be entitled to at the time of his death, notwithstanding that he may become entitled to the same subsequently to the execution of his will.

7   No will of a person under age valid

No will made by any person under the age of eighteen years shall be valid.

9   Signing and attestation of wills

No will shall be valid unless –

(a) it is in writing, and signed by the testator, or by some other person in his presence and by his direction; and

(b) it appears that the testator intended by his signature to give effect to the will; and

(c) the signature is made or acknowledged by the testator in the presence of two or more witnesses present at the same time; and

(d) each witness either –

(i) attests and signs the will; or

(ii) acknowledges his signature,

in the presence of the testator (but not necessarily in the presence of any other witness),

but no form of attestation shall be necessary.

10   Appointments by will to be executed like other wills, and to be valid, although other required solemnities are not observed

No appointment made by will, in exercise of any power, shall be valid, unless the same be executed in manner hereinbefore required; and every will executed in manner hereinbefore required shall, so far as respects the execution and attestation thereof, be a valid execution of a power of appointment by will, notwithstanding it shall have been expressly required that a will made in exercise of such power should be executed with some additional or other form of execution or solemnity.

11   Soldiers' and mariners' wills excepted

Provided always, that any soldier being in actual military service, or any mariner or seaman being at sea, may dispose of his personal estate as he might have done before the making of this Act.

13   Publication not to be requisite

Every will executed in manner hereinbefore required shall be valid without any other publication thereof.

14   Will not to be void on account of incompetency of attesting witness

If any person who shall attest the execution of a will shall at the time of the execution thereof or at any time afterwards be incompetent to be admitted a witness to prove the execution thereof, such will shall not on that account be invalid.

15   Gifts to an attesting witness to be void

If any person shall attest the execution of any will to whom or to whose wife or husband any beneficial devise, legacy, estate, interest, gift, or appointment, of or affecting any real or personal estate (other than and except charges and directions for the payment of any debt or debts), shall be thereby given or made, such devise, legacy, estate, gift, or appointment shall, so far only as concerns such person attesting the execution of such will, or the wife or husband of such person, or any person claiming under such person or wife, or husband, be utterly null and void, and such person so attesting shall be admitted as a witness to prove the execution of such will, or to prove the validity or invalidity thereof, notwithstanding such devise, legacy, estate, interest, gift, or appointment mentioned in such will.

16   Creditor attesting to be admitted a witness

In case by any will any real or personal estate shall be charged with any debt or debts, and any creditor, or the wife or husband of any creditor, whose debt is so charged, shall attest the execution of such will, such creditor notwithstanding such charge shall be admitted a witness to prove the execution of such will, or to prove the validity or invalidity thereof.

17   Executor to be admitted a witness

No person shall, on account of his being an executor of a will, be incompetent to be admitted a witness to prove the execution of such will, or a witness to prove the validity or invalidity thereof.

18   Will to be revoked by marriage

(1) Subject to subsections (2) to (4) below, a will shall be revoked by the testator's marriage.

(2) A disposition in a will in exercise of a power of appointment shall take effect notwithstanding the testator's subsequent marriage unless the property so appointed would in default of appointment pass to his personal representatives.

(3) Where it appears from a will that at the time it was made the testator was expecting to be married to a particular person and that he intended that the will should not be revoked by the marriage, the will shall not be revoked by his marriage to that person.

(4) Where it appears from a will that at the time it was made the testator was expecting to be married to a particular person and that he intended that a disposition in the will should not be revoked by his marriage to that person –

  (a) that disposition shall take effect notwithstanding the marriage; and

  (b) any other disposition in the will shall take effect also, unless it appears from the will that the testator intended the disposition to be revoked by the marriage.

18A Effect of dissolution or annulment of marriage on wills

(1) Where, after a testator has made a will, a decree of a court of civil jurisdiction in England and Wales dissolves or annuls his marriage or his marriage is dissolved or annulled and the divorce or annulment is entitled to recognition in England and Wales by virtue of Part II of the Family Law Act 1986, –

  (a) provisions of the will appointing executors or trustees or conferring a power of appointment, if they appoint or confer the power on the former spouse, shall take effect as if the former spouse had died on the date on which the marriage is dissolved or annulled, and

  (b) any property which, or an interest in which, is devised or bequeathed to the former spouse shall pass as if the former spouse had died on that date,

except in so far as a contrary intention appears by the will.

(2) Subsection (1)(b) above is without prejudice to any right of the former spouse to apply for financial provision under the Inheritance (Provision for Family and Dependants) Act 1975.

19   No will to be revoked by presumption

No will shall be revoked by any presumption of an intention on the ground of an alteration in circumstances.

20   No will to be revoked otherwise than by another will or codicil, or by a writing executed like a will, or by destruction

No will or codicil, or any part thereof, shall be revoked otherwise than as aforesaid, or by another will or codicil executed in manner hereinbefore required, or by some writing declaring an intention to revoke the same, and executed in the manner in which a will is hereinbefore required to be executed, or by the burning, tearing, or otherwise destroying the same by the testator, or by some person in his presence and by his direction, with the intention of revoking the same.

21   No alteration in a will shall have any effect unless executed as a will

No obliteration, interlineation, or other alteration made in any will after the execution thereof shall be valid or have any effect, except so far as the words or effect of the will before such alteration shall not be apparent, unless such alteration shall be executed in like manner as hereinbefore is required for the execution of the will; but the will, with such alteration as part thereof, shall be deemed to be duly executed if the signature of the testator and the subscription of the witnesses be made in the margin or on some other part of the will opposite or near to such alteration, or at the foot or end of or opposite to a memorandum referring to such alteration, and written at the end or some other part of the will.

22   No will revoked to be revived otherwise than by re-execution or a codicil to revive it

No will or codicil, or any part thereof, which shall be in any manner revoked, shall be revived otherwise than by the re-execution thereof, or by a codicil executed in manner hereinbefore required, and showing an intention to revive the same; and when any will or codicil which shall be partly revoked, and afterwards wholly revoked, shall be revived, such revival shall not extend to so much thereof as shall have been revoked before the revocation of the whole thereof, unless an intention to the contrary shall be shown.

23 A devise not to be rendered inoperative by any subsequent conveyance or act

No conveyance or other act made or done subsequently to the execution of a will of or relating to any real or personal estate therein comprised, except an act by which such will shall be revoked as aforesaid, shall prevent the operation of the will with respect to such estate or interest in such real or personal estate as the testator shall have power to dispose of by will at the time of his death.

24 A will shall be construed to speak from the death of the testator

Every will shall be construed, with reference to the real estate and personal estate comprised in it, to speak and take effect as if it had been executed immediately before the death of the testator, unless a contrary intention shall appear by the will.

25 A residuary devise shall include estates comprised in lapsed and void devises

Unless a contrary intention shall appear by the will, such real estate or interest therein as shall be comprised or intended to be comprised in any devise in such will contained, which shall fail or be void by reason of the death of the devisee in the lifetime of the testator, or by reason of such devise being contrary to law or otherwise incapable of taking effect, shall be included in the residuary devise (if any) contained in such will.

26 A general devise of the testator's lands shall include leasehold as well as freehold lands

A devise of the land of the testator, or of the land of the testator in any place or in the occupation of any person mentioned in his will, or otherwise described in a general manner, and any other general devise which would describe a leasehold estate if the testator had no freehold estate which could be described by it, shall be construed to include the leasehold estates of the testator, or any of them, to which such description shall extend, as the case may be, as well as freehold estates, unless a contrary intention shall appear by the will.

27   A general gift shall include estates over which the testator has a general power of appointment

A general devise of the real estate of the testator, or of the real estate of the testator in any place or in the occupation of any person mentioned in his will, or otherwise described in a general manner, shall be construed to include any real estate, or any real estate to which such description shall extend (as the case may be), which he may have power to appoint in any manner he may think proper, and shall operate as an execution of such power, unless a contrary intention shall appear by the will; and in like manner a bequest of the personal estate of the testator, or any bequest of personal property described in a general manner, shall be construed to include any personal estate, or any personal estate to which such description shall extend (as the case may be), which he may have power to appoint in any manner he may think proper, and shall operate as an execution of such power, unless a contrary intention shall appear by the will.

28   A devise without any words of limitation shall be construed to pass the fee

Where any real estate shall be devised to any person without any words of limitation, such devise shall be construed to pass the fee simple, or other the whole estate or interest which the testator had power to dispose of by will in such real estate, unless a contrary intention shall appear by the will.

29   The words 'die without issue', or 'die without leaving issue', shall be construed to mean die without issue living at the death

In any devise or bequest of real or personal estate the words 'die without issue' or 'die without leaving issue', or 'have no issue', or any other words which may import either a want or failure of issue of any person in his lifetime or at the time of his death, or an indefinite failure of his issue, shall be construed to mean a want or failure of issue in the lifetime or at the time of the death of such person, and not an indefinite failure of his issue, unless a contrary intention shall appear by the will, by reason of such person having a prior estate tail, or of a preceding gift, being, without any implication arising from such words, a limitation of an estate tail to such person or issue, or otherwise: Provided, that this Act shall not extend to cases where such words as aforesaid import if no issue described in a preceding gift shall be born, or if there shall be no issue who shall live to attain the age or otherwise answer the description required for obtaining a vested estate by a preceding gift to such issue.

33 Gifts to children or other issue who leave issue living at the testator's death shall not lapse

(1) Where –

(a) a will contains a devise or bequest to a child or remoter descendant of the testator; and

(b) the intended beneficiary dies before the testator, leaving issue; and

(c) issue of the intended beneficiary are living at the testator's death,

then, unless a contrary intention appears by the will, the devise or bequest shall take effect as a devise or bequest to the issue living at the testator's death.

(2) Where –

(a) a will contains a devise or bequest to a class of person consisting of children or remoter descendants of the testator; and

(b) a member of the class dies before the testator, leaving issue, and

(c) issue of that member are living at the testator's death,

then, unless a contrary intention appears by the will, the devise or bequest shall take effect as if the class included the issue of its deceased member living at the testator's death.

(3) Issue shall take under this section through all degrees, according to their stock, in equal shares if more than one, any gift or share which their parent would have taken and so that no issue shall take whose parent is living at the testator's death and that no issue shall take whose parent is living at the testator's death and so capable of taking.

(4) For the purposes of this section –

(a) the illegitimacy of any person is to be disregarded; and

(b) a person conceived before the testator's death and born living thereafter is to be taken to have been living at the testator's death.

34 Act not to extend to wills made before 1838, or to estates pur autre vie of persons who die before 1838

This Act shall not extend to any will made before the first day of January one thousand eight hundred and thirty-eight, and every will re-executed or republished, or revived by any codicil, shall for the purposes of this Act be deemed to have been made at the time at which the same shall be so re-executed, republished, or revived; and this Act shall not extend to any estate pur autre vie of any person who shall die before the first day of January one thousand eight hundred and thirty-eight.

As amended by the Statute Law Revision (No 2) Act 1888; Statute Law Revision Act 1893; Statute Law (Repeals) Act 1969; Family Law Reform Act 1969, s3(1)(a); Administration of Justice Act 1982, ss17, 18(1), (2), 19; Family Law Act 1986, s53; Children Act 1989, s108(5), Schedule 13, para 1; Law Reform (Succession) Act 1995, ss3, 5, Schedule; Trusts of Land and Appointment of Trustees Act 1996, s25(2), Schedule 4.

APPORTIONMENT ACT 1870
(33 & 34 Vict c 35)

2 Rents, etc to be apportionable in respect of time

All rents, annuities, dividends, and other periodical payments in the nature of income (whether reserved or made payable under an instrument in writing or otherwise) shall, like interest on money lent, be considered as accruing from day to day, and shall be apportionable in respect of time accordingly.

3 Apportioned part of rent, etc to be payable when the next entire portion shall have become due

The apportioned part of any such rent, annuity, dividend, or other payment shall be payable or recoverable in the case of a continuing rent, annuity, or other such payment when the entire portion of which such apportioned part shall form part shall become due and payable, and not before, and in the case of a rent, annuity, or other such payment determined by re-entry, death, or otherwise when the next entire portion of the same would have been payable if the same had not so determined, and not before.

7 Nor where stipulation made to the contrary

The provisions of this Act shall not extend to any case in which it is or shall be expressly stipulated that no apportionment shall take place.

As amended by the Statute Law Revision (No 2) Act 1893.

REVENUE ACT 1884
(47 & 48 Vict c 62)

11   Representation in the United Kingdom to constitute the title to assets therein situate

Notwithstanding any provision to the contrary contained in any local or private Act of Parliament, the production of a grant of representation from a court in the United Kingdom by probate or letters of administration or confirmation shall be necessary to establish the right to recover or receive any part of the personal estate and effects of any deceased person situated in the United Kingdom. Provided that where a policy of life assurance has been effected with any insurance company by a person who shall die domiciled elsewhere than in the United Kingdom, the production of a grant of representation from a court in the United Kingdom shall not be necessary to establish the right to receive the money payable in respect of such policy.

As amended by the Revenue Act 1889, s19.

PARTNERSHIP ACT 1890
(53 & 54 Vict c 39)

2 Rules for determining existence of partnership

In determining whether a partnership does or does not exist, regard shall be had to the following rules: ...

(3) The receipt by a person of a share of the profits of a business is prima facie evidence that he is a partner in the business, but receipt of such a share, or of a payment contingent on or varying with the profits of a business, does not of itself make him a partner in the business; and in particular ...

(d) The advance of money by way of loan to a person engaged or about to engage in any business on a contract with that person that the lender shall receive a rate of interest varying with the profits, or shall receive a share of the profits arising from carrying on the business, does not of itself make the lender a partner with the person or persons carrying on the business or liable as such. Provided that the contract is in writing, and signed by or on behalf of all the parties thereto: ...

3 Postponement of rights of person lending or selling in consideration of share of profits in case of insolvency

In the event of any person to whom money has been advanced by way of loan upon such a contract as is mentioned in the last foregoing section, or of any buyer of a goodwill in consideration of a share of the profits of the business, being adjudged a bankrupt, entering into an arrangement to pay his creditors less than 100p in the pound, or dying in insolvent circumstances, the lender of the loan shall not be entitled to recover anything in respect of his loan, and the seller of the goodwill shall not be entitled to recover anything in respect of the share of profits contracted for, until the claims of the other creditors of the borrower or buyer for valuable consideration in money or money's worth have been satisfied.

As amended by the Decimal Currency Act 1969, s10(1).

WILLS (SOLDIERS AND SAILORS) ACT 1918

(7 & 8 Geo 5 c 58)

1 Explanation of s11 of Wills Act 1837

In order to remove doubts as to the construction of the Wills Act 1837, it is hereby declared and enacted that section 11 of that Act authorises and always has authorised any soldier being in actual military service, or any mariner or seaman being at sea, to dispose of his personal estate as he might have done before the passing of that Act, though under the age of eighteen years.

2 Extension of s11 of the Wills Act 1837

Section 11 of the Wills Act 1837 shall extend to any member of His Majesty's naval or marine forces not only when he is at sea but also when he is so circumstanced that if he were a soldier he would be in actual military service within the meaning of that section.

3 Validity of testamentary dispositions of real property made by soldiers and sailors

(1) A testamentary disposition of any real estate in England or Ireland made by a person to whom section 11 of the Wills Act 1837, applies, and who dies after the passing of this Act, shall, notwithstanding that the person making the disposition was at the time of making it under eighteen years of age or that the disposition has not been made in such manner or form as was at the passing of this Act required by law, be valid in any case where the person making the disposition was of such age and the disposition has been made in such manner and form that if the disposition had been a disposition of personal estate made by such a person domiciled in England or Ireland it would have been valid.

4   Power to appoint testamentary guardians

Where any person dies after the passing of this Act having made a will which is, or which, if it had been a disposition of property, would have been rendered valid by s11 of the Wills Act 1837, any appointment contained in that will of any person as guardian of the infant children of the testator shall be of full force and effect.

5   Short title and interpretation

(2) For the purposes of section 11 of the Wills Act 1837 and this Act the expression 'soldier' includes a member of the Air Force, and references in this Act to the said section 11 include a reference to that section as explained and extended by this Act.

As amended by the Family Law Reform Act 1969, s3(1)(b).

TRUSTEE ACT 1925
(15 & 16 Geo 5 c 19)

14 Power of trustees to give receipts

(1) The receipt in writing of a trustee for any money, securities, investments or other personal property or effects payable, transferable, or deliverable to him under any trust or power shall be a sufficient discharge to the person paying, transferring, or delivering the same and shall effectual exonerate him from seeing to the application or being answerable for any loss or misapplication thereof.

(2) This section does not, except where the trustee is a trust corporation, enable a sole trustee to give a valid receipt for –

    (a) the proceeds of sale or other capital money arising under a trust of land;

    (b) capital money arising under the Settled Land Act 1925.

(3) This section applies notwithstanding anything to the contrary in the instrument, if any, creating the trust.

15 Power to compound liabilities

A personal representative, or two or more trustees acting together, or, subject to the restrictions imposed in regard to receipts by a sole trustee not being a trust corporation, a sole acting trustee where by the instrument, if any, creating the trust, or by statute, a sole trustee is authorised to execute the trusts and powers reposed in him, may, if and as he or they think fit –

    (a) accept any property, real or personal, before the time at which it is made transferable or payable; or

    (b) sever and apportion any blended trust funds or property; or

    (c) pay or allow any debt or claim on any evidence that he or they think sufficient; or

    (d) accept any composition or any security, real or personal, for any debt or for any property, real or personal, claimed; or

(e) allow any time for payment of any debt; or

(f) compromise, compound, abandon, submit to arbitration, or otherwise settle any debt, account, claim or thing whatever relating to the testator's or intestate's estate or to the trust;

and for any of those purposes may enter into, give, execute, and do such agreements, instruments of composition or arrangements, releases, and other things as to him or them seem expedient, without being responsible for any loss occasioned by any act or thing so done by him or them if he has or they have discharged the duty of care set out in section 1(1) of the Trustee Act 2000.

18 Devolution of powers or trusts

(1) Where a power or trust is given to or imposed on two or more trustees jointly, the same may be exercised or performed by the survivors or survivor of them for the time being.

(2) Until the appointment of new trustees, the personal representatives or representative for the time being of a sole trustee, or, where there were two or more trustees of the last surviving or continuing trustee, shall be capable of exercising or performing any power or trust which was given to, or capable of being exercised by, the sole or last surviving or continuing trustee, or other the trustees or trustee for the time being of the trust.

(3) This section takes effect subject to the restrictions imposed in regard to receipts by a sole trustee, not being a trust corporation.

(4) In this section 'personal representative' does not include an executor who has renounced or has not proved.

26 Protection against liability in respect of rents and covenants

(1) Where a personal representative or trustee liable as such for –

(a) any rent, covenant, or agreement reserved by or contained in any lease; or

(b) any rent, covenant or agreement payable under or contained in any grant made in consideration of a rentcharge; or

(c) any indemnity given in respect of any rent, covenant or agreement referred to in either of the foregoing paragraphs;

satisfies all liabilities under the lease or grant which may have accrued, and been claimed, up to the date of the conveyance hereinafter mentioned, and, where necessary, sets apart a sufficient fund to answer any future claim that may be made in respect of any fixed and ascertained sum which the lessee or grantee agreed to lay out on the property demised or granted, although the period for laying out the same may not have arrived, then and in any such case the personal representative or trustee may convey the property demised or granted to a purchaser, legatee, devisee, or other person entitled to call for a conveyance thereof and thereafter –

(i) he may distribute the residuary real and personal estate of the deceased testator or intestate or, as the case may be, the trust estate (other than the fund, if any, set apart as aforesaid) to or amongst the persons entitled thereto, without appropriating any part, or any further part, as the case may be, of the estate of the deceased or of the trust estate to meet any future liability under the said lease or grant;

(ii) notwithstanding such distribution, he shall not be personally liable in respect of any subsequent claim under the said lease or grant.

(1A) Where a personal representative or trustee has as such entered into, or may as such be required to enter into, an authorised guarantee agreement with respect to any lease compromised in the estate of a deceased testator or intestate or a trust estate (and, in a case where he has entered into such an agreement, he has satisfied all liabilities under it which may have accrued and been claimed up to the date of distribution) –

(a) he may distribute the residuary real and personal estate of the deceased testator or intestate, or the trust estate, to or amongst the persons entitled thereto –

(i) without appropriating any part of the estate of the deceased, or the trust estate, to meet any future liability (or, as the case may be, any liability) under any such agreement, and

(ii) notwithstanding any potential liability of his to enter into any such agreement; and

(b) notwithstanding such distribution, he shall not be personally liable in respect of any subsequent claim (or, as the case may be, any claim) under any such agreement.

In this subsection 'authorised guarantee agreement' has the same meaning as in the Landlord and Tenant (Covenants) Act 1995.

(2) This section operates without prejudice to the right of the lessor or grantor, or the persons deriving title under the lessor or grantor, to follow the assets of the deceased or the trust property into the hands of the persons amongst whom the same may have been respectively distributed, and applies notwithstanding anything to the contrary in the will or other instrument, if any, creating the trust.

additional trustee, unless the instrument, if any, creating the trust, or any statutory enactment provides to the contrary, nor shall the number of trustees be increased beyond four by virtue of any such appointment.

(6A) A person who is either –

(a) both a trustee and attorney for the other trustee (if one other), or for both of the other trustees (if two others), under a registered power; or

(b) attorney under a registered power for the trustee (if one) or for both or each of the trustees (if two or three),

may, if subsection (6B) of this section is satisfied in relation to him, make an appointment under subsection (6)(b) of this section on behalf of the trustee or trustees.

(6B) This subsection is satisfied in relation to an attorney under a registered power for one or more trustees if (as attorney under the power) –

(a) he intends to exercise any function of the trustee or trustees by virtue of section 1(1) of the Trustee Delegation Act 1999; or

(b) he intends to exercise any function of the trustee or trustees in relation to any land, capital proceeds of a conveyance of land or income from land by virtue of its delegation to him under section 25 of this Act or the instrument (if any) creating the trust.

(6C) In subsections (6A) and (6B) of this section 'registered power' means a power of attorney created by an instrument which is for the time being registered under section 6 of the Enduring Powers of Attorney Act 1985.

(6D) Subsection (6A) of this section –

(a) applies only if and so far as a contrary intention is not expressed in the instrument creating the power of attorney (or, where more than one, any of them) or the instrument (if any) creating the trust; and

(b) has effect subject to the terms of those instruments.

(7) Every new trustee appointed under this section as well before as after all the trust property becomes by law, or by assurance, or otherwise, vested in him, shall have the same powers, authorities, and discretions, and may in all respects act as if he had been originally appointed a trustee by the instrument, if any, creating the trust.

(8) The provisions of this section relating to a trustee who is dead include the case of a person nominated trustee in a will but dying before the testator, and those relative to a continuing trustee include a refusing or retiring trustee, if willing to act in the execution of the provisions of this section. ...

57 Power of court to authorise dealings with trust property

(1) Where in the management or administration of any property vested in trustees, any sale, lease, mortgage, surrender, release, or other disposition, or any purchase, investment, acquisition, expenditure, or other transaction, is in the opinion of the court expedient, but the same cannot be effected by reason of the absence of any power for that purpose vested in the trustees by the trust instrument, if any, or by law, the court may by order confer upon the trustees, either generally or in any particular instance, the necessary power for the purpose, on such terms, and subject to such provisions and conditions, if any, as the court may think fit and may direct in what manner any money authorised to be expended, and the costs of any transaction, are to be paid or borne as between capital and income.

(2) The court may, from time to time, rescind or vary any order made under this section, or may make any new or further order.

(3) An application to the court under this section may be made by the trustees, or by any of them, or by any person beneficially interested under the trust.

(4) This section does not apply to trustees of a settlement for the purposes of the Settled Land Act 1925.

61 Power to relieve trustee from personal liability

If it appears to the court that a trustee, whether appointed by the court or otherwise, is or may be personally liable for any breach of trust, whether the transaction alleged to be a breach of trust occurred before or after the commencement of this Act, but has acted honestly and reasonably, and ought fairly to be excused for the breach of trust and for omitting to obtain the directions of the court in the matter in which he committed such breach, then the court may relieve him either wholly or partly from personal liability for the same.

62 Power to make beneficiary indemnify for breach of trust

(1) Where a trustee commits a breach of trust at the instigation or request or with the consent in writing of a beneficiary, the court may, if it thinks fit, make such order as to the court seems just, for impounding all or any part of the interest of the beneficiary in the trust estate by way of indemnity to the trustee or persons claiming through him.

68 Definitions

In this Act, unless the context otherwise requires, the following expressions have the meanings hereby assigned to them respectively, that is to say – ...

(4) 'Gazette' means the London Gazette; ...

(9) 'Personal representative' means the executor, original or by representation, or administrator for the time being of a deceased person;

(17) 'Trust' does not include the duties incident to an estate conveyed by way of mortgage, but with this exception the expressions 'trust' and 'trustee' extend to implied and constructive trusts, and to cases where the trustee has a beneficial interest in the trust property, and to the duties incident to the office of a personal representative, and 'trustee' where the context admits, includes a personal representative, and 'new trustee' includes an additional trustee; ...

As amended by the Law of Property (Amendment) Act 1926, ss7, 8(2), Schedule; Married Women (Restraint upon Anticipation) Act 1949, s1(4), Schedule 2; Landlord and Tenant (Covenants) Act 1995, s30(1), Schedule 1, para 1; Trusts of land and Appointment of Trustees Act 1996, s25(1), Schedule 3, para 3(1), (3), (7), (11); Trustee Delegation Act 1999, s8; Trustee Act 2000, s40, Schedule 2, paras 19, 20, 23, 24, Schedule 4, Pt II.

LAW OF PROPERTY ACT 1925
(15 & 16 Geo 5 c 20)

PART I

GENERAL PRINCIPLES AS TO LEGAL ESTATES, EQUITABLE
INTERESTS AND POWERS

33 Application of Part I to personal representatives

The provisions of this Part of this Act relating to trustees of land apply to personal representatives holding land in trust, but without prejudice to their rights and powers for purposes of administration.

PART X

WILLS

175 Contingent and future testamentary gifts to carry the intermediate income

(1) A contingent or future specific devise or bequest of property, whether real or personal, and a contingent residuary devise of freehold land, and a specific or residuary devise of freehold land to trustees upon trust for persons whose interests are contingent or executory shall, subject to the statutory provisions relating to accumulations, carry the intermediate income of that property from the death of the testator, except so far as such income, or any part thereof, may be otherwise expressly disposed of.

176 Power for tenant in tail in possession to dispose of property by specific devise or bequest

(1) A tenant in tail of full age shall have power to dispose by will, by means of a devise or bequest referring specifically either to the property or to the instrument under which it was acquired or to entailed property generally –

    (a) of all property of which he is tenant in tail in possession at his death; and

(b) of money (including the proceeds of property directed to be sold) subject to be invested in the purchase of property, of which if it had been so invested he would have been tenant in tail in possession at his death;

in like manner as if, after barring the entail, he had been tenant in fee simple or absolute owner thereof for an equitable interest at his death, but, subject to and in default of any such disposition by will, such property shall devolve in the same manner as if this section had not been passed.

(2) This section applies to entailed interests authorised to be created by this Act as well as to estates tail created before the commencement of this Act, but does not extend to a tenant in tail who is by statute restrained from barring or defeating his estate tail, whether the land or property in respect whereof he is so restrained was purchased with money provided by Parliament in consideration of public services or not, or to a tenant in tail after possibility of issue extinct, and does not render any interest which is not disposed of by the will of the tenant in tail liable for his debts or other liabilities.

(3) In this section 'tenant in tail' includes an owner of a base fee in possession who has power to enlarge the base fee into a fee simple without the concurrence of any other person.

179 Prescribed forms for reference in wills

The Lord Chancellor may from time to time prescribe and publish forms to which a testator may refer in his will, and give directions as to the manner in which they may be referred to, but, unless so referred to, such forms shall not be deemed to be incorporated in a will.

205 General definitions

(1) In this Act unless the context otherwise requires, the following expressions have the meanings hereby assigned to them respectively, that is to say ...

(ii) 'Conveyance' includes a mortgage, charge, lease, assent, vesting declaration, vesting instrument, disclaimer, release and every other assurance of property or of an interest therein by any instrument, except a will; 'convey' has a corresponding meaning; and 'disposition' includes a conveyance and also a devise, bequest, or an appointment of property contained in a will; and 'dispose of' has a corresponding meaning; ...

(viii) 'Instrument' does not include a statute, unless the statute creates a settlement;

(ix) 'Land' includes land of any tenure, and mines and minerals, whether or not held apart from the surface, buildings or parts of buildings (whether the division is horizontal, vertical or made in any other way) and other corporeal hereditaments; also a manor, an advowson, and a rent and other incorporeal hereditaments, and an easement, right, privilege, or benefit in, over, or derived from land; and 'mines and minerals' include any strata or seam of minerals or substances in or under any land, and powers of working and getting the same; and 'manor' includes a lordship, and reputed manor or lordship; and 'hereditament' means any real property which on an intestacy occurring before the commencement of this Act might have devolved upon an heir;

(x) 'Legal estates' means the estates, interests and charges, in or over land (subsisting or created at law) which are by this Act authorised to subsist or to be created as legal estates; 'equitable interests' means all the other interests and charges in or over land; an equitable interest 'capable of subsisting as a legal estate' means such as could validly subsist or be created as a legal estate under this Act; ...

(xviii) 'Personal representative' means the executor, original or by representation, or administrator for the time being of a deceased person, and as regards any liability for the payment of death duties includes any person who takes possession of or intermeddles with the property of a deceased person without the authority of the personal representatives or the court;

(xix) 'Possession' includes receipt of rents and profits or the right to receive the same, if any; and 'income' includes rents and profits;

(xx) 'Property' includes any thing in action, and any interest in real or personal property;

(xxi) 'Purchaser' means a purchaser in good faith for valuable consideration and includes a lessee, mortgagee or other person who for valuable consideration acquires an interest in property except that in Part I of this Act and elsewhere where so expressly provided 'purchaser' only means a person who acquires an interest in or charge on property for money or money's worth; and in reference to a legal estate includes a chargee by way of legal mortgage; and where the context so requires 'purchaser' includes an intending purchaser; 'purchase' has a meaning corresponding with that of 'purchaser'; and 'valuable consideration' includes marriage but does not include a nominal consideration in money; ...

(xxix) 'Trust for sale', in relation to land, means an immediate trust for sale, whether or not exercisable at the request or with the consent of any person; 'trustees for sale' means the persons (including a personal representative) holding land on trust for sale; ...

(xxxi) 'Will' includes codicil ...

(2) Where an equitable interest in or power over property arises by statute or operation of law, references to the creation of an interest or power include references to any interest or power so arising.

As amended by the Trusts of Land and Appointment of Trustees Act 1996, s25(1), (2), Schedule 3, para 4(1), (9), Schedule 4.

ADMINISTRATION OF ESTATES ACT 1925
(15 & 16 Geo 5 c 23)

PART I

DEVOLUTION OF REAL ESTATE

1 Devolution of real estate on personal representative

(1) Real estate to which a deceased person was entitled for an interest not ceasing on his death shall on his death, and notwithstanding any testamentary disposition thereof, devolve from time to time on the personal representative of the deceased, in like manner as before the commencement of this Act chattels real devolved on the personal representative from time to time of a deceased person.

(2) The personal representatives for the time being of a deceased person are deemed in law his heirs and assigns within the meaning of all trusts and powers.

(3) The personal representatives shall be the representatives of the deceased in regard to his real estate to which he was entitled for an interest not ceasing on his death as well as in regard to his personal estate.

2 Application to real estate of law affecting chattels real

(1) Subject to the provisions of this Act, all enactments and rules of law, and all jurisdiction of any court with respect to the appointment of administrators or to probate or letters of administration, or to dealings before probate in the case of chattels real, and with respect to costs and other matters in the administration of personal estate, in force before the commencement of this Act, and all powers, duties, rights, equities, obligations, and liabilities of a personal representative in force at the commencement of this Act with respect to chattels real, shall apply and attach to the personal representative and shall have effect with respect to real estate vested in him, and in particular all such powers of disposition and dealing as were before the commencement of this Act exercisable as respects chattels real by the survivor or survivors of two or more personal

representatives, as well as by a single personal representative, or by all the personal representatives together, shall be exercisable by the personal representatives or representative of the deceased with respect to his real estate.

(2) Where as respects real estate there are two or more personal representatives, a conveyance of real estate devolving under this Part of this Act or a contract for such a conveyance shall not be made without the concurrence therein of all such representatives or an order of the court, but where probate is granted to one or some of two or more persons named as executors, whether or not power is reserved to the other or others to prove, any conveyance of the real estate or contract for such a conveyance may be made by the proving executor or executors for the time being, without an order of the court, and shall be as effectual as if all the persons named as executors had concurred therein.

3   Interpretation of Part I

(1) In this Part of this Act 'real estate' includes –

(i) chattels real, and land in possession, remainder, or reversion, and every interest in or over land to which a deceased person was entitled at the time of his death; and

(ii) real estate held on trust (including settled land) or by way of mortgage or security, but not money secured or charged on land.

(2) A testator shall be deemed to have been entitled at his death to any interest in real estate passing under any gift contained in his will which operates as an appointment under a general power to appoint by will, or operates under the testamentary power conferred by statute to dispose of an entailed interest.

(3) An entailed interest of a deceased person shall (unless disposed of under the testamentary power conferred by statute) be deemed an interest ceasing on his death, but any further or other interest of the deceased in the same property in remainder or reversion which is capable of being disposed of by his will shall not be deemed to be an interest so ceasing.

(4) The interest of a deceased person under a joint tenancy where another tenant survives the deceased is an interest ceasing on his death. ...

PART II

EXECUTORS AND ADMINISTRATORS

5   Cesser of right of executor to prove

Where a person appointed executor by a will –

(i) survives the testator but dies without having taken out probate of the will; or

(ii) is cited to take out probate of the will and does not appear to the citation; or

(iii) renounces probate of the will;

his rights in respect of the executorship shall wholly cease, and the representation to the testator and the administration of his real and personal estate shall devolve and be committed in like manner as if that person had not been appointed executor.

6   Withdrawal of renunciation

(1) Where an executor who has renounced probate has been permitted, whether before or after the commencement of this Act, to withdraw the renunciation and prove the will, the probate shall take effect and be deemed always to have taken effect without prejudice to the previous acts and dealings of and notices to any other personal representative who has previously proved the will or taken out letters of administration, and a memorandum of the subsequent probate shall be endorsed on the original probate or letters of administration.

(2) This section applies whether the testator died before or after the commencement of this Act.

7   Executor of executor represents original testator

(1) An executor of a sole or last surviving executor of a testator is the executor of that testator.

This provision shall not apply to an executor who does not prove the will of his testator, and in the case of an executor who on his death leaves surviving him some other executor of his testator who afterwards proves the will of that testator, it shall cease to apply on such probate being granted.

(2) So long as the chain of such representation is unbroken, the last executor in the chain is the executor of every preceding testator.

(3) The chain of such representation is broken by –

(a) an intestacy; or

(b) the failure of a testator to appoint an executor; or

(c) the failure to obtain probate of a will;

but is not broken by a temporary grant of administration if probate is subsequently granted.

(4) Every person in the chain of representation to a testator –

(a) has the same rights in respect of the real and personal estate of that testator as the original executor would have had if living; and

(b) is, to the extent to which the estate whether real or personal of that testator has come to his hands, answerable as if he were an original executor.

8   Right of proving executors to exercise powers

(1) Where probate is granted to one or some of two or more persons named as executors, whether or not power is reserved to the others or other to prove, all the powers which are by law conferred on the personal representative may be exercised by the proving executor or executors for the time being and shall be as effectual as if all the persons named as executors had concurred therein.

(2) This section applies whether the testator died before or after the commencement of this Act.

9   Vesting of estate in Public Trustee where intestacy or lack of executors

(1) Where a person dies intestate, his real and personal estate shall vest in the Public Trustee until the grant of administration.

(2) Where a testator dies and –

(a) at the time of his death there is no executor with power to obtain probate of the will, or

(b) at any time before probate of the will is granted there ceases to be any executor with power to obtain probate,

the real and personal estate of which he disposes by the will shall vest in the Public Trustee until the grant of representation.

(3) The vesting of real or personal estate in the Public Trustee by virtue of

this section does not confer on him any beneficial interest in, or impose on him any duty, obligation or liability in respect of, the property.

15 Executor not to act while administration is in force

Where administration has been granted in respect of any real or personal estate of a deceased person, no person shall have power to bring any action or otherwise act as executor of the deceased person in respect of the estate comprised in or affected by the grant until the grant has been recalled or revoked.

17 Continuance of legal proceedings after revocation of temporary administration

(1) If, while any legal proceeding is pending in any court by or against an administrator to whom a temporary administration has been granted, that administration is revoked, that court may order that the proceeding be continued by or against the new personal representative in like manner as if the same had been originally commenced by or against him, but subject to such conditions and variations, if any, as that court directs.

(2) The county court has jurisdiction under this section where the proceedings are pending in that court.

21 Rights and liabilities of administrator

Every person to whom administration of the real and personal estate of a deceased person is granted shall, subject to the limitations contained in the grant, have the same rights and liabilities and be accountable in like manner as if he were the executor of the deceased.

21A Debtor who becomes creditor's executor by representation or administrator to account for debt to estate

(1) Subject to subsection (2) of this section, where a debtor becomes his deceased creditor's executor by representation or administrator –

(a) his debt shall thereupon be extinguished; but

(b) he shall be accountable for the amount of the debt as part of the creditor's estate in any case where he would be so accountable if he had been appointed as an executor by the creditor's will.

(2) Subsection (1) of this section does not apply where the debtor's authority to act as executor or administrator is limited to part only of the creditor's

estate which does not include the debt; and a debtor whose debt is extinguished by virtue of paragraph (a) shall not be accountable for its amount by virtue of paragraph (b) of that subsection in any case where the debt was barred by the Limitation Act 1939 before he became the creditor's executor or administrator.

(3) In this section 'debt' includes any liability, and 'debtor' and 'creditor' shall be construed accordingly.

22 Special executors as respects settled land

(1) A testator may appoint, and in default of such express appointment shall be deemed to have appointed, as his special executors in regard to settled land, the persons, if any, who are at his death the trustees of the settlement thereof, and probate may be granted to such trustees specially limited to the settled land.

In this subsection 'settled land' means land vested in the testator which was settled previously to his death and not by his will.

(2) A testator may appoint other persons either with or without such trustees as aforesaid or any of them to be his general executors in regard to his other property and assets.

23 Provisions where, as respects settled land, representation is not granted to the trustees of the settlement

(1) Where settled land becomes vested in a personal representative, not being a trustee of the settlement, upon trust to convey the land to or assent to the vesting thereof in the tenant for life or statutory owner in order to give effect to a settlement created before the death of the deceased and not by his will, or would, on the grant of representation to him, have become so vested, such representative may –

(a) before representation has been granted, renounce his office in regard only to such settled land without renouncing it in regard to other property;

(b) after representation has been granted, apply to the court for revocation of the grant in regard to the settled land without applying in regard to other property.

(2) Whether such renunciation or revocation is made or not, the trustees of the settlement, or any person beneficially interested thereunder, may apply to the High Court for an order appointing a special or additional personal representative in respect of the settled land, and a special or additional

personal representative, if and when appointed under the order, shall be in the same position as if representation had originally been granted to him alone in place of the original personal representative, if any, or to him jointly with the original personal representative, as the case may be, limited to the settled land, but without prejudice to the previous acts and dealings, if any, of the personal representative originally constituted or the effect of notices given to such personal representative.

(3) The court may make such order as aforesaid subject to such security, if any, being given by or on behalf of the special or additional personal representative, as the court may direct, and shall, unless the court considers that special considerations apply, appoint such persons as may be necessary to secure that the persons to act as representatives in respect of the settled land shall, if willing to act, be the same persons as are the trustees of the settlement, and an office copy of the order when made shall be furnished to the principal registry of the Family Division of the High Court for entry, and a memorandum of the order shall be endorsed on the probate or administration.

(4) The person applying for the appointment of a special or additional personal representative shall give notice of the application to the principal registry of the Family Division of the High Court in the manner prescribed.

(5) Rules of court may be made for prescribing for all matters required for giving effect to the provisions of this section, and in particular –

    (a) for notice of any application being given to the proper officer;

    (b) for production of orders, probates, and administration to the registry;

    (c) for the endorsement on a probate or administration of a memorandum of an order, subject or not to any exceptions;

    (d) for the manner in which the costs are to be borne;

    (e) for protecting purchasers and trustees and other persons in a fiduciary position, dealing in good faith with or giving notices to a personal representative before notice of any order has been endorsed on the probate or administration or a pending action has been registered in respect of the proceedings.

24 Power for special personal representatives to dispose of settled land

(1) The special personal representatives may dispose of the settled land without the concurrence of the general personal representatives, who may likewise dispose of the other property and assets of the deceased without the concurrence of the special personal representatives.

(2) In this section the expression 'special personal representatives' means the representatives appointed to act for the purposes of settled land and includes any original personal representative who is to act with an additional personal representative for those purposes.

25 Duty of personal representatives

The personal representative of a deceased person shall be under a duty to –

(a) collect and get in the real and personal estate of the deceased and administer it according to law;

(b) when required to do so by the court, exhibit on oath in the court a full inventory of the estate and when so required render an account of the administration of the estate to the court;

(c) when required to do so by the High Court, deliver up the grant of probate or administration to that court.

26 Right of personal representative to distrain for arrears of a rentcharge or rent

(3) A personal representative may distrain for arrears of a rentcharge due or accruing to the deceased in his lifetime on the land affected or charged therewith, so long as the land remains in the possession of the person liable to pay the rentcharge or of the persons deriving title under him, and in like manner as the deceased might have done had he been living.

(4) A personal representative may distrain upon land for arrears of rent due or accruing to the deceased in like manner as the deceased might have done had he been living.

Such arrears may be distrained for after the termination of the lease or tenancy as if the term or interest had not determined, if the distress is made –

(a) within six months after the termination of the lease or tenancy;

(b) during the continuance of the possession of the lessee or tenant from whom the arrears were due.

The statutory enactments relating to distress for rent apply to any distress made pursuant to this subsection.

27 Protection of persons acting on probate or administration

(1) Every person making or permitting to be made any payment or disposition in good faith under a representation shall be indemnified and

protected in so doing, notwithstanding any defect or circumstance whatsoever affecting the validity of the representation.

(2) Where a representation is revoked, all payments and dispositions made in good faith to a personal representative under the representation before the revocation thereof are a valid discharge to the person making the same; and the personal representative who acted under the revoked representation may retain and reimburse himself in respect of any payments or dispositions made by him which the person to whom representation is afterwards granted might have properly made.

28 Liability of person fraudulently obtaining or retaining estate of deceased

If any person, to the defrauding of creditors or without full valuable consideration, obtains, receives or holds any real or personal estate of a deceased person or effects the release of any debt or liability due to the estate of the deceased, he shall be charged as executor in his own wrong to the extent of the real and personal estate received or coming to his hands, or the debt or liability released, after deducting –

(a) any debt for valuable consideration and without fraud due to him from the deceased person at the time of his death; and

(b) any payment made by him which might properly be made by a personal representative.

29 Liability of estate of personal representative

Where a person as personal representative of a deceased person (including an executor in his own wrong) wastes or converts to his own use any part of the real or personal estate of the deceased, and dies, his personal representative shall to the extent of the available assets of the defaulter be liable and chargeable in respect of such waste or conversion in the same manner as the defaulter would have been if living.

PART III

ADMINISTRATION OF ASSETS

32 Real and personal estate of deceased are assets for payments of debts

(1) The real and personal estate, whether legal or equitable, of a deceased person, to the extent of his beneficial interest therein, and the real and

personal estate of which a deceased person in pursuance of any general power (including the statutory power to dispose of entailed interests) disposes by his will, are assets for payment of his debts (whether by specialty or simple contract) and liabilities, and any disposition by will inconsistent with this enactment is void as against the creditors, and the court shall, if necessary, administer the property for the purposes of the payment of the debts and liabilities.

This subsection takes effect without prejudice to the rights of incumbrancers.

(2) If any person to whom any such beneficial interest devolves or is given, or in whom any such interest vests, disposes thereof in good faith before an action is brought or process is sued out against him, he shall be personally liable for the value of the interest so disposed of by him, but that interest shall not be liable to be taken in execution in the action or under the process.

33 Trust for sale

(1) On the death of a person intestate as to any real or personal estate, that estate shall be held in trust by his personal representatives with the power to sell it.

(2) The personal representatives shall pay out of –

(a) the ready money of the deceased (so far as not disposed of by his will, if any); and

(b) any net money arising from disposing of any other part of his estate (after payment of costs),

all such funeral, testamentary and administration expenses, debts and other liabilities as are properly payable thereout having regard to the rules of administration contained in this Part of this Act, and out of the residue of the said money the personal representative shall set aside a fund sufficient to provide for any pecuniary legacies bequeathed by the will (if any) of the deceased.

(3) During the minority of any beneficiary or the subsistence of any life interest and pending the distribution of the whole or any part of the estate of the deceased, the personal representatives may invest the residue of the said money, or so much thereof as may not have been distributed, under the Trustee Act 2000.

(4) The residue of the said money and any investments for the time being representing the same, and any part of the estate of the deceased which remains unsold and is not required for the administration purposes aforesaid, is in this Act referred to as 'the residuary estate of the intestate'.

(5) The income (including net rents and profits of real estate and chattels real after payment of rates, taxes, rent, costs of insurance, repairs and other outgoings properly attributable to income) of so much of the real and personal estate of the deceased as may not be disposed of by his will, if any, or may not be required for the administration purposes aforesaid, may, however such estate is invested, as from the death of the deceased, be treated and applied as income, and for that purpose any necessary apportionment may be made between tenant for life and remainderman.

(6) Nothing in this section affects the rights of any creditor of the deceased or the rights of the Crown in respect of death duties.

(7) Where the deceased leaves a will, this section has effect subject to the provisions contained in the will.

34 Administration of assets

(3) Where the estate of a deceased person is solvent his real and personal estate shall, subject to rules of court and the provisions hereinafter contained as to charges on property of the deceased, and to the provisions, if any, contained in his will, be applicable towards the discharge of the funeral, testamentary and administration expenses, debts and liabilities payable thereout in the order mentioned in Part II of the First Schedule to this Act.

35 Charges on property of deceased to be paid primarily out of the property charged

(1) Where a person dies possessed of, or entitled to, or, under a general power of appointment (including the statutory power to dispose of entailed interest) by his will disposes of, an interest in property, which at the time of his death is charged with the payment of money, whether by way of legal mortgage, equitable charge or otherwise (including a lien for unpaid purchase money), and the deceased has not by will deed or other document signified a contrary or other intention, the interest so charged shall, as between the different persons claiming through the deceased, be primarily liable for the payment of the charge; and every part of the said interest, according to its value, shall bear a proportionate part of the charge on the whole thereof.

(2) Such contrary or other intention shall not be deemed to be signified –

(a) by a general direction for the payment of debts or of all the debts of the testator out of his personal estate, or his residuary real and personal estate, or his residuary real estate; or

(b) by a charge of debts upon any such estate;

unless such intention is further signified by words expressly or by necessary implication referring to all or some part of the charge.

(3) Nothing in this section affects the right of a person entitled to the charge to obtain payment or satisfaction thereof either out of the other assets of the deceased or otherwise.

36 Effect of assent or conveyance by personal representative

(1) A personal representative may assent to the vesting, in any person who (whether by devise, bequest, devolution, appropriation or otherwise) may be entitled thereto, either beneficially or as a trustee or personal representative, of any estate or interest in real estate to which the testator or intestate was entitled or over which he exercised a general power of appointment by his will, including the statutory power to dispose of entailed interests, and which devolved upon the personal representative.

(2) The assent shall operate to vest in that person the estate or interest to which the assent relates, and, unless a contrary intention appears, the assent shall relate back to the death of the deceased.

(4) An assent to the vesting of a legal estate shall be in writing, signed by the personal representative, and shall name the person in whose favour it is given and shall operate to vest in that person the legal estate to which it relates; and an assent not in writing or not in favour of a named person shall not be effectual to pass a legal estate.

(5) Any person in whose favour an assent or conveyance of a legal estate is made by a personal representative may require that notice of the assent or conveyance be written or endorsed on or permanently annexed to the probate or letters of administration, at the cost of the estate of the deceased, and that the probate or letters of administration be produced, at the like cost, to prove that the notice has been placed thereon or annexed thereto.

(6) A statement in writing by a personal representative that he has not given or made an assent or conveyance in respect of a legal estate, shall, in favour of a purchaser, but without prejudice to any previous disposition made in favour of another purchaser deriving title mediately or immediately under the personal representative, be sufficient evidence that an assent or conveyance has not been given or made in respect of the legal estate to which the statement relates, unless notice of a previous assent or conveyance affecting that estate has been placed on or annexed to the probate or administration.

A conveyance by a personal representative of a legal estate to a purchaser accepted in the faith of such a statement shall (without prejudice as aforesaid and unless notice of a previous assent or conveyance affecting that estate has been placed on or annexed to the probate or administration) operate to transfer or create the legal estate expressed to be conveyed in like manner as if no previous assent or conveyance had been made by the personal representative.

A personal representative making a false statement, in regard to any such matter, shall be liable in like manner as if the statement had been contained in a statutory declaration.

(7) An assent or conveyance by a personal representative in respect of a legal estate shall, in favour of a purchaser, unless notice of a previous assent or conveyance affecting that legal estate has been placed on or annexed to the probate or administration, be taken as sufficient evidence that the person in whose favour the assent or conveyance is given or made is the person entitled to have the legal estate conveyed to him, and upon the proper trusts, if any, but shall not otherwise prejudicially affect the claim of any person rightfully entitled to the estate vested or conveyed or any charge thereon.

(8) A conveyance of a legal estate by a personal representative to a purchaser shall not be invalidated by reason only that the purchaser may have notice that all the debts, liabilities, funeral, and testamentary or administration expenses, duties and legacies of the deceased have been discharged or provided for.

(9) An assent or conveyance given or made by a personal representative shall not, except in favour of a purchaser of a legal estate, prejudice the right of the personal representative or any other person to recover the estate or interest to which the assent or conveyance relates, or to be indemnified out of such estate or interest against any duties, debt or liability to which such estate or interest would have been subject if there had not been any assent or conveyance.

(10) A personal representative may, as a condition of giving an assent or making a conveyance, require security for the discharge of any such duties, debt, or liability, but shall not be entitled to postpone the giving of an assent merely by reason of the subsistence of any such duties, debt or liability if reasonable arrangements have been made for discharging the same; and an assent may be given subject to any legal estate or charge by way of legal mortgage.

(11) This section shall not operate to impose any stamp duty in respect of an assent, and in this section 'purchaser' means a purchaser for money or money's worth.

(12) This section applies to assents and conveyances made after the commencement of this Act, whether the testator or intestate died before or after such commencement.

37 Validity of conveyance not affected by revocation of representation

(1) All conveyances of any interest in real or personal estate made to a purchaser either before or after the commencement of this Act by a person to whom probate or letters of administration have been granted are valid, notwithstanding any subsequent revocation or variation, either before or after the commencement of this Act, of the probate or administration.

(2) This section takes effect without prejudice to any order of the court made before the commencement of this Act, and applies whether the testator or intestate died before or after such commencement.

38 Right to follow property and powers of the court in relation thereto

(1) An assent or conveyance by a personal representative to a person other than a purchaser does not prejudice the rights of any person to follow the property to which the assent or conveyance relates, or any property representing the same, into the hands of the person in whom it is vested by the assent or conveyance, or of any other person (not being a purchaser) who may have received the same or in whom it may be vested.

(2) Notwithstanding any such assent or conveyance the court may, on the application of any creditor or other person interested –

(a) order a sale, exchange, mortgage, charge, lease, payment, transfer or other transaction to be carried out which the court considers requisite for the purpose of giving effect to the rights of the persons interested;

(b) declare that the person, not being a purchaser, in whom the property is vested is a trustee for those purposes;

(c) give directions respecting the preparation and execution of any conveyance or other instrument or as to any other matter required for giving effect to the order;

(d) make any vesting order, or appoint a person to convey in accordance with the provisions of the Trustee Act 1925.

(3) This section does not prejudice the rights of a purchaser or a person deriving title under him, but applies whether the testator or intestate died before or after the commencement of this Act.

(4) The county court has jurisdiction under this section where the estate in respect of which the application is made does not exceed in amount or value the county court limit.

39   Powers of management

(1) In dealing with the real and personal estate of the deceased his personal representatives shall, for purposes of administration, or during a minority of any beneficiary or the subsistence of any life interest, or until the period of distribution arrives, have –

(i) as respects the personal estate, the same powers and discretions, including power to raise money by mortgage or charge (whether or not by deposit of documents), as a personal representative had before the commencement of this Act, with respect to personal estate vested in him; and

(ii) as respects the real estate, all the functions conferred on them by Part I of the Trusts of Land and Appointment of Trustees Act 1996; and

(iii) all the powers necessary so that every contract entered into by a personal representative shall be binding on and be enforceable against and by the personal representative for the time being of the deceased, and may be carried into effect, or be varied or rescinded by him, and, in the case of a contract entered into by a predecessor, as if it had been entered into by himself.

(1A) Subsection (1) of this section is without prejudice to the powers conferred on personal representatives by the Trustee Act 2000.

(2) Nothing in this section shall affect the right of any person to require an assent or conveyance to be made.

(3) This section applies whether the testator or intestate died before or after the commencement of this Act.

40   Powers of personal representative for raising money, etc

(1) For giving effect to beneficial interests the personal representative may limit or demise land for a term of years absolute, with or without impeachment for waste, to trustees on usual trusts for raising or securing any principal sum and the interest thereon for which the land, or any part thereof, is liable, and may limit or grant a rentcharge for giving effect to any annual or periodical sum for which the land or the income thereof or any part thereof is liable.

(2) This section applies whether the testator or intestate died before or after the commencement of this Act.

41 Powers of personal representative as to appropriation

(1) The personal representative may appropriate any part of the real or personal estate, including things in action, of the deceased in the actual condition or state of investment thereof at the time of appropriation in or towards satisfaction of any legacy bequeathed by the deceased, or of any other interest or share in his property, whether settled or not, as to the personal representative may seem just and reasonable, according to the respective rights of the persons interested in the property of the deceased:

Provided that –

(i) an appropriation shall not be made under this section so as to affect prejudicially any specific devise or bequest;

(ii) an appropriation of property, whether or not being an investment authorised by law or by the will, if any, of the deceased for the investment of money subject to the trust, shall not (save as hereinafter mentioned) be made under this section except with the following consents –

(a) when made for the benefit of a person absolutely and beneficially entitled in possession, the consent of that person;

(b) when made in respect of any settled legacy share or interest, the consent of either the trustee thereof, if any (not being also the personal representative), or the person who may for the time being be entitled to the income:

If the person whose consent is so required as aforesaid is an infant or is incapable, by reason of mental disorder within the meaning of the Mental Health Act 1983, of managing and administering his property and affairs, the consent shall be given on his behalf by his parents or parent, testamentary or other guardian or receiver, or if, in the case of an infant, there is no such parent or guardian, by the court on the application of his next friend;

(iii) no consent (save of such trustee as aforesaid) shall be required on behalf of a person who may come into existence after the time of appropriation, or who cannot be found or ascertained at that time;

(iv) if no receiver is acting for a person suffering from mental disorder, then, if the appropriation is of an investment authorised by law or by the will, if any, of the deceased for the investment of money subject to the trust, no consent shall be required on behalf of the said person;

(v) if, independently of the personal representative, there is no trustee of a settled legacy share or interest, and no person of full age and capacity entitled to the income thereof, no consent shall be required to an appropriation in respect of such legacy share or interest, provided that the appropriation is of an investment authorised as aforesaid.

(1A) The county court has jurisdiction under provision (ii) to subsection (1) of this section where the estate in respect of which the application is made does not exceed in amount or value the county court limit.

(2) Any property duly appropriated under the powers conferred by this section shall thereafter be treated as an authorised investment, and may be retained or dealt with accordingly.

(3) For the purposes of such appropriation, the personal representative may ascertain and fix the value of the respective parts of the real and personal estate and the liabilities of the deceased as he may think fit, and shall for that purpose employ a duly qualified valuer in any case where any such employment may be necessary; and may make any conveyance (including an assent) which may be requisite for giving effect to the appropriation.

(4) An appropriation made pursuant to this section shall bind all persons interested in the property of the deceased whose consent is not hereby made requisite.

(5) The personal representative shall, in making the appropriation, have regard to the rights of any person who may thereafter come into existence, or who cannot be found or ascertained at the time of appropriation, and of any other person whose consent is not required by this section.

(6) This section does not prejudice any other power of appropriation conferred by law or by the will (if any) of the deceased, and takes effect with any extended powers conferred by the will (if any) of the deceased, and where an appropriation is made under this section, in respect of a settled legacy, share or interest, the property appropriated shall remain subject to all trusts and powers of leasing, disposition, and management or varying investments which would have been applicable thereto or to the legacy, share or interest in respect of which the appropriation is made, if no such appropriation had been made.

(7) If after any real estate has been appropriated in purported exercise of the powers conferred by this section, the person to whom it was conveyed disposes of it or any interest therein, then, in favour of a purchaser, the appropriation shall be deemed to have been made in accordance with the requirements of this section and after all requisite consents, if any, had been given.

(8) In this section, a settled legacy, share or interest includes any legacy, share or interest to which a person is not absolutely entitled in possession at the date of the appropriation, also an annuity, and 'purchaser' means a purchaser for money or money's worth.

(9) This section applies whether the deceased died intestate or not, and whether before or after the commencement of this Act, and extends to property over which a testator exercises a general power of appointment, including the statutory power to dispose of entailed interests, and authorises the setting apart of a fund to answer an annuity by means of the income of that fund or otherwise.

42   Power to appoint trustees of infants' property

(1) Where an infant is absolutely entitled under the will or on the intestacy of a person dying before or after the commencement of this Act (in this subsection called 'the deceased') to a devise or legacy, or to the residue of the estate of the deceased, or any share therein, and such devise, legacy, residue or share is not under the will, if any, of the deceased, devised or bequeathed to trustees for the infant, the personal representatives of the deceased may appoint a trust corporation or two or more individuals not exceeding four (whether or not including the personal representatives or one or more of the personal representatives), to be the trustee or trustees of such devise, legacy, residue or share for the infant, and to be trustees of any land devised or any land being or forming part of such residue or share for the purposes of the Settled Land Act 1925, and of the statutory provisions relating to the management of land during a minority and may execute or do any assurance or thing requisite for vesting such devise, legacy, residue or share in the trustee or trustees so appointed.

On such appointment the personal representatives, as such, shall be discharged from all further liability in respect of such devise, legacy, residue, or share, and the same may be retained in its existing condition or state of investment, or may be converted into money, and such money may be invested in any authorised investment.

(2) Where a personal representative has before the commencement of this Act retained or sold any such devise, legacy, residue or share, and invested the same or the proceeds thereof in any investments in which he was authorised to invest money subject to the trust, then, subject to any order of the court made before such commencement, he shall not be deemed to have incurred any liability on that account, or by reason of not having paid or transferred the money or property into court.

43 Obligations of personal representative as to giving possession of land and powers of the court

(1) A personal representative, before giving an assent or making a conveyance in favour of any person entitled, may permit that person to take possession of the land, and such possession shall not prejudicially affect the right of the personal representative to take or resume possession nor his power to convey the land as if he were in possession thereof, but subject to the interest of any lessee, tenant or occupier in possession or in actual occupation of the land.

(2) Any person who as against the personal representative claims possession of real estate, or the appointment of a receiver thereof, or a conveyance thereof, or an assent to the vesting thereof, or to be registered as proprietor thereof under the Land Registration Act 1925, may apply to the court for directions with reference thereto, and the court may make such vesting or other order as may be deemed proper, and the provisions of the Trustee Act 1925, relating to vesting orders and to the appointment of a person to convey, shall apply.

(3) This section applies whether the testator or intestate died before or after the commencement of this Act.

(4) The county court has jurisdiction under this section where the estate in respect of which the application is made does not exceed in amount or value the county court limit.

44 Power to postpone distribution

Subject to the foregoing provisions of this Act, a personal representative is not bound to distribute the estate of the deceased before the expiration of one year from the death.

PART IV

DISTRIBUTION OF RESIDUARY ESTATE

45 Abolition of descent to heir, curtesy, dower and escheat

(1) With regard to the real estate and personal inheritance of every person dying after the commencement of this Act, there shall be abolished –

(a) all existing modes rules and canons of descent, and of devolution by special occupancy or otherwise, of real estate, or of a personal inheritance, whether operating by the general law or by the custom of gavelkind or borough english or by any other custom of any county, locality, or manor, or otherwise howsoever; and

(b) tenancy by the curtesy and every other estate and interest of a husband in real estate as to which his wife dies intestate, whether arising under the general law or by custom or otherwise; and

(c) dower and freebench and every other estate and interest of a wife in real estate as to which her husband dies intestate, whether arising under the general law or by custom or otherwise: Provided that where a right (if any) to freebench or other like right has attached before the commencement of this Act which cannot be barred by a testamentary or other disposition made by the husband, such right shall, unless released, remain in force as an equitable interest; and

(d) escheat to the Crown or the Duchy of Lancaster or the Duke of Cornwall or to a mesne lord for want of heirs.

(2) Nothing in this section affects the descent or devolution of an entailed interest.

46   Succession to real and personal estate on intestacy

(1) The residuary estate of an intestate shall be distributed in the manner or be held on the trusts mentioned in this section, namely –

(i) If the intestate leaves a husband or wife, then in accordance with the following Table:

TABLE

If the intestate –

(1) leaves –	the residuary estate shall be held in trust for the surviving husband or wife absolutely.
(a) no issue, and	
(b) no parent, or brother or sister of the whole blood, or issue of a brother or sister of the whole blood	
(2) leaves issue (whether or not persons mentioned in sub-paragraph (b) above also survive)	the surviving husband or wife shall take the personal chattels absolutely and, in addition, the residuary estate of the intestate (other than the personal chattels) shall stand charged with the payment of a fixed net sum, free of death duties and costs, to the

surviving husband or wife with interest thereon from the date of the death at such rate as the Lord Chancellor may specify by order until paid or appropriated, and, subject to providing for that sum and the interest thereon, the residuary estate (other than the personal chattels) shall be held –

(a) as to one half upon trust for the surviving husband or wife during his or her life, and, subject to such life interest, on the statutory trusts for the issue of the intestate, and

(b) as to the other half, on the statutory trusts for the issue of the intestate.

(3) leaves one or more of the following, that is to say, a parent, a brother or sister of the whole blood, or issue of a brother or sister of the whole blood, but leaves no issue

the surviving husband or wife shall take the personal chattels absolutely and, in addition, the residuary estate of the intestate (other than the personal chattels) shall stand charged with the payment of a fixed net sum, free of death duties and costs, to the surviving husband or wife with interest thereon from the date of the death at such rate as the Lord Chancellor may specify by order until paid or appropriated, and, subject to providing for that sum and the interest thereon, the residuary estate (other than the personal chattels) shall be held –

(a) as to one half in trust for the surviving husband or wife absolutely, and

(b) as to the other half –

(i) where the intestate leaves one parent or both parents

(whether or not brothers or sisters of the intestate or their issue also survive) in trust for the parent absolutely or, as the case may be, for the two parents in equal shares absolutely,

(ii) where the intestate leaves no parent, on the statutory trusts for the brothers and sisters of the whole blood of the intestate.

The fixed net sums referred to in paragraphs (2) and (3) of this Table shall be of the amounts provided by or under section 1 of the Family Provision Act 1966.

(ii) If the intestate leaves issue but no husband or wife the residuary estate of the intestate shall be held on the statutory trusts for the issue of the intestate;

(iii) If the intestate leaves no husband or wife and no issue but both parents, then the residuary estate of the intestate shall be held in trust for the father and mother in equal shares absolutely;

(iv) If the intestate leaves no husband or wife and no issue but one parent, then the residuary estate of the intestate shall be held in trust for the surviving father or mother absolutely;

(v) If the intestate leaves no husband or wife and no issue and no parent, then the residuary estate of the intestate shall be held in trust for the following persons living at the death of the intestate, and in the following order and manner, namely –

First, on the statutory trusts for the brothers and sisters of the whole blood of the intestate; but if no person takes an absolutely vested interest under such trusts; then

Secondly, on the statutory trusts for the brothers and sisters of the half blood of the intestate; but if no person takes an absolutely vested interested under such trusts; then

Thirdly, for the grandparents of the intestate and, if more than one survive the intestate, in equal shares; but if there is no member of this class; then

Fourthly, on the statutory trusts for the uncles and aunts of the intestate (being brothers or sisters of the whole blood of a parent of the intestate); but if no person takes an absolutely vested interest under such trusts; then

Fifthly, on the statutory trusts for the uncles and aunts of the intestate (being brothers or sisters of the half blood of a parent of the intestate).

(vi) In default of any person taking an absolute interest under the foregoing provisions, the residuary estate of the intestate shall belong to the Crown or to the Duchy of Lancaster or to the Duke of Cornwall for the time being, as the case may be, as bona vacantia, and in lieu of any right to escheat.

The Crown or the said Duchy or the said Duke may (without prejudice to the powers reserved by section 9 of the Civil List Act 1910, or any other powers), out of the whole or any part of the property devolving on them respectively, provide, in accordance with the existing practice, for dependants, whether kindred or not, of the intestate, and other persons for whom the intestate might reasonably have been expected to make provision.

(1A) The power to make orders under subsection (1) above shall be exercisable by statutory instrument subject to annulment in pursuance of a resolution of either House of Parliament; and any such order may be varied or revoked by a subsequent order made under the power.

(2) A husband and wife shall for all purposes of distribution or division under the foregoing provisions of this section be treated as two persons.

(2A) Where the intestate's husband or wife survived the intestate but died before the end of the period of 28 days beginning with the day on which the intestate died, this section shall have effect as respects the intestate as if the husband or wife had not survived the intestate.

(3) Where the intestate and the intestate's husband or wife have died in circumstances rendering it uncertain which of them survived the other and the intestate's husband or wife is by virtue of section 184 of the Law of Property Act 1925 deemed to have survived the intestate, this section shall, nevertheless, have effect as respects the intestate as if the husband or wife had not survived the intestate.

(4) The interest payable on the fixed net sum payable to a surviving husband or wife shall be primarily payable out of income.

47   Statutory trusts in favour of issue and other classes of relatives of intestate

(1) Where under this Part of this Act the residuary estate of an intestate, or any part thereof, is directed to be held on the statutory trusts for the issue of the intestate, the same shall be held upon the following trusts, namely –

(i) In trust, in equal shares if more than one, for all or any of the children or child of the intestate, living at the death of the intestate, who attain the age of eighteen years or marry under that age, and for all or any of the issue living at the death of the intestate who attain the age of eighteen years or marry under that age of any child of the intestate who predeceases the intestate, such issue to take through all degrees, according to their stocks, in equal shares if more than one, the share which their parent would have taken if living at the death of the intestate, and so that no issue shall take whose parent is living at the death of the intestate and so capable of taking;

(ii) The statutory power of advancement, and the statutory provisions which relate to maintenance and accumulation of surplus income, shall apply, but when an infant marries such infant shall be entitled to give valid receipts for the income of the infant's share or interest;

(iv) The personal representatives may permit any infant contingently interested to have the use and enjoyment of any personal chattels in such manner and subject to such conditions (if any) as the personal representatives may consider reasonable, and without being liable to account for any consequential loss.

(2) If the trusts in favour of the issue of the intestate fail by reason of no child or other issue attaining an absolutely vested interest –

(a) the residuary estate of the intestate and the income thereof and all statutory accumulations, if any, of the income thereof, or so much thereof as may not have been paid or applied under any power affecting the same, shall go, devolve and be held under the provisions of this Part of this Act as if the intestate had died without leaving issue living at the death of the intestate;

(b) references in this Part of this Act to the intestate 'leaving no issue' shall be construed as 'leaving no issue who attain an absolutely vested interest';

(c) references in this Part of this Act to the intestate 'leaving issue' or 'leaving a child or other issue' shall be construed as 'leaving issue who attain an absolutely vested interest'.

(3) Where under this Part of this Act the residuary estate of an intestate or any part thereof is directed to be held on the statutory trusts for any class of relatives of the intestate, other than issue of the intestate, the same shall be held on trusts corresponding to the statutory trusts for the issue of the intestate (other than the provision for bringing any money or property into account) as if such trusts (other than as aforesaid) were repeated with the substitution of references to the members or member of that class for references to the children or child of the intestate.

(4) References in paragraph (i) of subsection (1) of the last foregoing section to the intestate leaving, or not leaving, a member of the class consisting of brothers or sisters of the whole blood of the intestate and issue of brothers or sisters of the whole blood of the intestate shall be construed as references to the intestate leaving, or not leaving, a member of that class who attains an absolutely vested interest.

47A Right of surviving spouse to have his own life interest redeemed

(1) Where a surviving husband or wife is entitled to a life interest in part of the residuary estate, and so elects, the personal representative shall purchase or redeem the life interest by paying the capital value thereof to the tenant for life, or the persons deriving title under the tenant for life, and the costs of the transaction; and thereupon the residuary estate of the intestate may be dealt with and distributed free from the life interest.

(3) An election under this section shall only be exercisable if at the time of the election the whole of the said part of the residuary estate consists of property in possession, but, for the purposes of this section, a life interest in property partly in possession and partly not in possession may be treated as consisting of two separate life interests in those respective parts of the property.

(3A) The capital value shall be reckoned in such manner as the Lord Chancellor may by order direct, and an order under this subsection may include transitional provisions.

(3B) The power to make orders under subsection (3A) above shall be exercisable by statutory instrument subject to annulment in pursuance of a resolution of either House of Parliament; and any such order may be varied or revoked by a subsequent order made under the power.

(5) An election under this section shall be exercisable only within the period of twelve months from the date on which representation with respect to the estate of the intestate is first taken out:

Provided that if the surviving husband or wife satisfies the court that the limitation to the said period of twelve months will operate unfairly –

   (a) in consequence of the representation first taken out being probate of a will subsequently revoked on the ground that the will was invalid or,

   (b) in consequence of a question whether a person had an interest in the estate, or as to the nature of an interest in the estate, not having been determined at the time when representation was first taken out, or

(c) in consequence of some other circumstances affecting the administration or distribution of the estate,

the court may extend the said period.

(6) An election under this section shall be exercisable, except where the tenant for life is the sole personal representative, by notifying the personal representative (or, where there are two or more personal representatives of whom one is the tenant for life, all of them except the tenant for life) in writing; and a notification in writing under this subsection shall not be revocable except with the consent of the personal representative.

(7) Where the tenant for life is the sole personal representative an election under this section shall not be effective unless written notice thereof is given to the Senior Registrar of the Family Division of the High Court within the period within which it must be made; and provision may be made by probate rules for keeping a record of such notices and making that record available to the public.

In this subsection the expression 'probate rules' means rules of court made under section 127 of the Supreme Court Act 1981.

(8) An election under this section by a tenant for life who is an infant shall be as valid and binding as it would be if the tenant for life were of age; but the personal representative shall, instead of paying the capital value of the life interest to the tenant for life, deal with it in the same manner as with any other part of the residuary estate to which the tenant for life is absolutely entitled.

(9) In considering for the purposes of the foregoing provisions of this section the question when representation was first taken out, a grant limited to settled land or to trust property shall be left out of account and a grant limited to real estate or to personal estate shall be left out of account unless a grant limited to the remainder of the estate has previously been made or is made at the same time.

48 Powers of personal representative in respect of interests of surviving spouse

(2) The personal representatives may raise –

(a) the fixed net sum or any part thereof and the interest thereon payable to the surviving husband or wife of the intestate on the security of the whole or any part of the residuary estate of the intestate (other than the personal chattels), so far as that estate may be sufficient for the purpose or the said sum and interest may not have been satisfied by an appropriation under the statutory power available in that behalf; and

(b) in like manner the capital sum, if any, required for the purchase or redemption of the life interest of the surviving husband or wife of the intestate, or any part thereof not satisfied by the application for that purpose of any part of the residuary estate of the intestate;

and in either case the amount, if any, properly required for the payment of the costs of the transaction.

49   Application to cases of partial intestacy

(1) Where any person dies leaving a will effectively disposing of part of his property, this Part of this Act shall have effect as respects the part of his property not so disposed of subject to the provisions contained in the will and subject to the following modifications –

(b) the personal representative shall, subject to his rights and powers for the purposes of administration, be a trustee for the persons entitled under this Part of this Act in respect of the part of the estate not expressly disposed of unless it appears by the will that the personal representative is intended to take such part beneficially.

(4) The references in subsection (3) of section 47A of this Act to property are references to property comprised in the residuary estate and, accordingly, where a will of the deceased creates a life interest in property in possession, and the remaining interest in that property forms part of the residuary estate, the said references are references to that remaining interest (which, until the life interest determines, is property not in possession).

50   Construction of documents

(1) References to any Statutes of Distribution in an instrument inter vivos made or in a will coming into operation after the commencement of this Act, shall be construed as references to this Part of this Act; and references in such an instrument or will to statutory next of kin shall be construed, unless the context otherwise requires, as referring to the persons who would take beneficially on an intestacy under the foregoing provisions of this Part of this Act.

(2) Trusts declared in an instrument inter vivos made, or in a will coming into operation, before the commencement of this Act by reference to the Statutes of Distribution, shall, unless the contrary thereby appears, be construed as referring to the enactments (other than the Intestates' Estates

Act 1890) relating to the distribution of effects of intestates which were in force immediately before the commencement of this Act.

(3) In subsection (1) of this section the reference to this Part of this Act, or the foregoing provisions of this Part of this Act, shall in relation to an instrument inter vivos made, or a will or codicil coming into operation, after the coming into force of section 18 of the Family Law Reform Act 1987 (but not in relation to instruments inter vivos made or wills or codicils coming into operation earlier) be construed as including references to that section.

51 Savings ...

(3) Where an infant dies after the commencement of this Act without having been married and without issue, and independently of this subsection he would, at his death, have been equitably entitled under a trust or settlement (including a will) to a vested estate in fee simple or absolute interest in freehold land, or in any property to devolve therewith or as freehold land, such infant shall be deemed to have had a life interest, and the trust or settlement shall be construed accordingly.

52 Interpretation of Part IV

In this Part of this Act 'real and personal estate' means every beneficial interest (including rights of entry and reverter) of the intestate in real and personal estate which (otherwise than in right of a power of appointment or of the testamentary power conferred by statute to dispose of entailed interests) he could, if of full age and capacity, have disposed of by his will and references (however expressed) to any relationship between two persons shall be construed in accordance with s1 of the Family Law Reform Act 1987.

PART V

SUPPLEMENTAL

55 Definitions

In this Act, unless the context otherwise requires, the following expressions have the meanings hereby assigned to them respectively, that is to say –

(1) (i) 'Administration' means, with reference to the real and personal estate of a deceased person, letters of administration, whether general or limited, or with the will annexed or otherwise;

(ii) 'Administrator' means a person to whom administration is granted; ...

(v) 'Income' includes rents and profits;

(vi) 'Intestate' includes a person who leaves a will but dies intestate as to some beneficial interest in his real or personal estate;

(via) 'Land' has the same meaning as in the Law of Property Act 1925; ...

(ix) 'Pecuniary legacy' includes an annuity, a general legacy, a demonstrative legacy so far as it is not discharged out of the designated property, and any other general direction by a testator for the payment of money, including all death duties free from which any devise, bequest, or payment is made to take effect;

(x) 'Personal chattels' mean carriages, horses, stable furniture and effects (not used for business purposes), motor cars and accessories (not used for business purposes), garden effects, domestic animals, plate, plated articles, linen, china, glass, books, pictures, prints, furniture, jewellery, articles of household or personal use or ornament, musical and scientific instruments and apparatus, wines, liquors and consumable stores, but do not include any chattels used at the death of the intestate for business purposes nor money or securities for money.

(xi) 'Personal representative' means the executor, original or by representation, or administrator for the time being of a deceased person, and as regards any liability for the payment of death duties includes any person who takes possession of or intermeddles with the property of a deceased person without the authority of the personal representatives or the court, and 'executor' includes a person deemed to be appointed executor as respects settled land; ...

(xiv) 'Probate' means the probate of a will;

(xviii) 'Purchaser' means a lessee, mortgagee or other person who in good faith acquires an interest in property for valuable consideration, also an intending purchaser and 'valuable consideration' includes marriage, but does not include a nominal consideration in money;

(xix) 'Real estate' save as provided in Part IV of this Act means real estate, including chattels real, which by virtue of Part I of this Act devolves on the personal representative of a deceased person;

(xx) 'Representation' means the probate of a will and administration, and the expression 'taking out representation' refers to the obtaining of the probate of a will or of the grant of administration; ...

(xxiii) 'Securities' includes stocks, funds, or shares; ...

(xxviii) 'Will' includes codicil.

(2) References to a child or issue living at the death of any person include a child or issue en ventre sa mere at the death.

(3) References to the estate of a deceased person include property over which

the deceased exercises a general power of appointment (including the statutory power to dispose of entailed interests) by his will.

FIRST SCHEDULE

PART II

ORDER OF APPLICATION OF ASSETS WHERE THE ESTATE IS SOLVENT

1. Property of the deceased undisposed of by will, subject to the retention thereout of a fund sufficient to meet any pecuniary legacies.

2. Property of the deceased not specifically devised or bequeathed but included (either by a specific or general description) in a residuary gift, subject to the retention out of such property of a fund sufficient to meet any pecuniary legacies, so far as not provided for as aforesaid.

3. Property of the deceased specifically appropriated or devised or bequeathed (either by a specific or general description) for the payment of debts.

4. Property of the deceased charged with, or devised or bequeathed (either by a specific or general description) subject to a charge for the payment of debts.

5. The fund, if any, retained to meet pecuniary legacies.

6. Property specifically devised or bequeathed, rateably according to value.

7. Property appointed by will under a general power, including the statutory power to dispose of entailed interests, rateably according to value.

8. The following provisions shall also apply –

    (a) The order of application may be varied by the will of the deceased.

As amended by the Intestates Estates Act 1952, ss1, 2, 3; Mental Health Act 1959, s149(1), Schedule 7, Pt I; Family Provision Act 1966, s1; Family Law Reform Act 1969, s3(2); Administration of Justice Act 1970, s1(6), Schedule 2, paras 3, 5; Administration of Estates Act 1971, s9; Administration of Justice Act 1977, ss28(1), (2), (3), 32(4), Schedule 5, Pt VI; Limitation Amendment Act 1980, s10; Supreme Court Act 1981, s152(1), Schedule 5; Mental Health Act 1983, s148, Schedule 4, para 7; County Courts Act 1984, s148(1), Schedule 2, Pt III, paras 11, 12, 13, 14; Family Law Reform Act 1987, s33(1), Schedule 2, paras 3, 4; Law of Property (Miscellaneous Provisions) Act 1994, ss14(1), 16(1), 21(2), Schedule 2; Law Reform (Succession) Act 1995, ss1(1), (2)(a), (b), (3), 5, Schedule; Trusts of Land and Appointment of Trustees Act 1996, ss5(1), 25(1), (2), Schedule 2, para 5, Schedule 3, para 6(1)–(5), Schedule 4; Trustee Act 2000, s40, Schedule 2, paras 27, 28.

INTESTATES' ESTATES ACT 1952
(15 & 16 Geo 6 & 1 Eliz 2 c 64)

5   Rights of surviving spouse as respects the matrimonial home

The Second Schedule to this Act shall have effect for enabling the surviving husband or wife of a person dying intestate after the commencement of this Act to acquire the matrimonial home.

6   Interpretation and construction

(1) In this Part of this Act the expression 'intestate' has the meaning assigned to it by section 55 of the principal Act [ie the Administration of Estates Act 1925].

(2) The references in subsection (1) of section 50 of the principal Act (which relates to the construction of documents) to Part IV of that Act, or to the foregoing provisions of that Part, shall in relation to an instrument inter vivos made or a will coming into operation after the commencement of this Act, but not in relation to instruments inter vivos made or wills coming into operation earlier, be construed as including references to this Part of this Act and the Schedules to be read therewith.

SECOND SCHEDULE

RIGHTS OF SURVIVING SPOUSE AS RESPECTS
THE MATRIMONIAL HOME

1. (1) Subject to the provisions of this Schedule, where the residuary estate of the intestate comprises an interest in a dwelling-house in which the surviving husband or wife was resident at the time of the intestate's death, the surviving husband or wife may require the personal representative, in exercise of the power conferred by section 41 of the principal Act (and with due regard to the requirements of that section as to valuation), to appropriate the said interest in the dwelling-house in or towards satisfaction of any absolute interest of the surviving husband or wife in the real and personal estate of the intestate.

(2) The right conferred by this paragraph shall not be exercisable where the interest is –

(a) a tenancy which at the date of the death of the intestate was a tenancy which would determine within the period of two years from that date; or

(b) a tenancy which the landlord by notice given after that date could determine within the remainder of that period.

(3) Nothing in subsection (5) of section 41 of the principal Act (which requires the personal representative, in making an appropriation to any person under that section, to have regard to the rights of others) shall prevent the personal representative from giving effect to the right conferred by this paragraph.

(4) The reference in this paragraph to an absolute interest in the real and personal estate of the intestate includes a reference to the capital value of a life interest which the surviving husband or wife has under this Act elected to have redeemed.

(5) Where part of a building was, at the date of the death of the intestate, occupied as a separate dwelling, that dwelling shall for the purposes of this Schedule be treated as a dwelling-house.

2. Where –

(a) the dwelling-house forms part of a building and an interest in the whole of the building is comprised in the residuary estate; or

(b) the dwelling-house is held with agricultural land and an interest in the agricultural land is comprised in the residuary estate; or

(c) the whole or a part of the dwelling-house was at the time of the intestate's death used as a hotel or lodging house; or

(d) a part of the dwelling-house was at the time of the intestate's death used for purposes other than domestic purposes,

the right conferred by paragraph 1 of this Schedule shall not be exercisable unless the court, on being satisfied that the exercise of that right is not likely to diminish the value of assets in the residuary estate (other than the said interest in the dwelling-house) or make them more difficult to dispose of, so orders.

3. (1) The right conferred by paragraph 1 of this Schedule –

(a) shall not be exercisable after the expiration of twelve months from the first taking out of representation with respect to the intestate's estate;

(b) shall not be exercisable after the death of the surviving husband or wife;

(c) shall be exercisable, except where the surviving husband or wife is the sole personal representative, by notifying the personal representative (or, where there are two or more personal representatives of whom one is the surviving husband or wife, all of them except the surviving husband or wife) in writing.

(2) A notification in writing under paragraph (c) of the foregoing sub-paragraph shall not be revocable except with the consent of the personal representative; but the surviving husband or wife may require the personal representative to have the said interest in the dwelling-house valued in accordance with section 41 of the principal Act and to inform him or her of the result of that valuation before he or she decides whether to exercise the right.

(3) Subsection (9) of the section 47A added to the principal Act by section 2 of this Act shall apply for the purposes of the construction of the reference in this paragraph to the first taking out of representation, and the proviso to subsection (5) of that section shall apply for the purpose of enabling the surviving husband or wife to apply for an extension of the period of twelve months mentioned in this paragraph.

4. (1) During the period of twelve months mentioned in paragraph 3 of this Schedule the personal representative shall not without the written consent of the surviving husband or wife sell or otherwise dispose of the said interest in the dwelling-house except in the course of administration owing to want of other assets.

(2) An application to the court under paragraph 2 of this Schedule may be made by the personal representative as well as by the surviving husband or wife, and if, on an application under that paragraph, the court does not order that the right conferred by paragraph 1 of this Schedule shall be exercisable by the surviving husband or wife, the court may authorise the personal representative to dispose of the said interest in the dwelling-house within the said period of twelve months.

(3) Where the court under sub-paragraph (3) of paragraph 3 of this Schedule extends the said period of twelve months, the court may direct that this paragraph shall apply in relation to the extended period as it applied in relation to the original period of twelve months.

(4) This paragraph shall not apply where the surviving husband or wife is the sole personal representative or one of two or more personal representatives.

(5) Nothing in this paragraph shall confer any right on the surviving husband or wife as against a purchaser from the personal representative.

5. (1) Where the surviving husband or wife is one of two or more personal representatives, the rule that a trustee may not be a purchaser of trust property shall not prevent the surviving husband or wife from purchasing out of the estate of the intestate an interest in a dwelling-house in which the surviving husband or wife was resident at the time of the intestate's death.

(2) The power of appropriation under section 41 of the principal Act shall include power to appropriate an interest in a dwelling-house in which the surviving husband or wife was resident at the time of the intestate's death partly in satisfaction of an interest of the surviving husband or wife in the real and personal estate of the intestate and partly in return for a payment of money by the surviving husband or wife to the personal representative.

6. (1) Where the surviving husband or wife is a person of unsound mind or a defective, a requirement or consent under this Schedule may be made or given on his or her behalf by the committee or receiver, if any, or, where there is no committee or receiver, by the court.

(2) A requirement or consent made or given under this Schedule by a surviving husband or wife who is an infant shall be as valid and binding as it would be if he or she were of age; and, as respects an appropriation in pursuance of paragraph 1 of this Schedule, the provisions of section 41 of the principal Act as to obtaining the consent of the infant's parent or guardian, or of the court on behalf of the infant, shall not apply.

7. (1) Except where the context otherwise requires, references in this Schedule to a dwelling-house include references to any garden or portion of ground attached to and usually occupied with the dwelling-house or otherwise required for the amenity or convenience of the dwelling-house.

(2) This Schedule shall be construed as one with Part IV of the principal Act.

HUMAN TISSUE ACT 1961
(9 & 10 Eliz 2 c 54)

1   Removal of parts of bodies for medical purposes

(1) If any person, either in writing at any time or orally in the presence of two or more witnesses during his last illness, has expressed a request that his body or any specified part of his body be used after his death for therapeutic purposes or for purposes of medical education or research, the person lawfully in possession of his body after his death may, unless he has reason to believe that the request was subsequently withdrawn, authorise the removal from the body of any part or, as the case may be, the specified part, for use in accordance with the request.

(2) Without prejudice to the foregoing subsection, the person lawfully in possession of the body of a deceased person may authorise the removal of any part from the body for use for the said purposes if, having made such reasonable enquiry as may be practicable, he has no reason to believe –

    (a) that the deceased had expressed an objection to his body being so dealt with after his death, and had not withdrawn it; or

    (b) that the surviving spouse or any surviving relative of the deceased objects to the body being so dealt with ...

(5) Where a person has reason to believe that an inquest may be required to be held on any body or that a post-mortem examination of any body may be required by the coroner, he shall not, except with the consent of the coroner, –

    (a) give an authority under this section in respect of the body; or

    (b) act on such an authority given by any other person.

(6) No authority shall be given under this section in respect of any body by a person entrusted with the body for the purpose only of its interment or cremation.

(7) In the case of a body lying in a hospital, nursing home or other institution, any authority under this section may be given on behalf of the

person having the control and management thereof by any officer or person designated for that purpose by the first-mentioned person.

(8) Nothing in this section shall be construed as rendering unlawful any dealing with, or with any part of, the body of a deceased person which is lawful apart from this Act ...

WILLS ACT 1963
(1963 c 44)

1   General rule as to formal validity

A will shall be treated as properly executed if its execution conformed to the internal law in force in the territory where it was executed, or in the territory where, at the time of its execution or of the testator's death, he was domiciled or had his habitual residence, or in a state of which, at either of those times, he was a national.

2   Additional rules

(1) Without prejudice to the preceding section, the following shall be treated as properly executed –

(a) a will executed on board a vessel or aircraft of any description, if the execution of the will conformed to the internal law in force in the territory with which, having regard to its registration (if any) and other relevant circumstances, the vessel or aircraft may be taken to have been most closely connected;

(b) a will so far as it disposes of immovable property, if its execution conformed to the internal law in force in the territory where the property was situated;

(c) a will so far as it revokes a will which under this Act would be treated as properly executed or revokes a provision which under this Act would be treated as comprised in a properly executed will, if the execution of the later will conformed to any law by reference to which the revoked will or provision would be so treated;

(d) a will so far as it exercises a power of appointment, if the execution of the will conformed to the law governing the essential validity of the power.

(2) A will so far as it exercises a power of appointment shall not be treated as improperly executed by reason only that its execution was not in accordance with any formal requirements contained in the instrument creating the power.

3   Certain requirements to be treated as formal

Where (whether in pursuance of this Act or not) a law in force outside the United Kingdom falls to be applied in relation to a will, any requirement of that law whereby special formalities are to be observed by testators answering a particular description, or witnesses to the execution of a will are to possess certain qualifications, shall be treated, notwithstanding any rule of that law to the contrary, as a formal requirement only.

4   Construction of wills

The construction of a will shall not be altered by reason of any change in the testator's domicile after the execution of the will.

6   Interpretation

(1) In this Act –

'internal law' in relation to any territory or state means the law which would apply in a case where no question of the law in force in any other territory or state arose;

'state' means a territory or group of territories having its own law of nationality;

'will' includes any testamentary instrument or act, and 'testator' shall be construed accordingly.

(2) Where under this Act the internal law in force in any territory or state is to be applied in the case of a will, but there are in force in that territory or state two or more systems of internal law relating to the formal validity of wills, the system to be applied shall be ascertained as follows –

(a) if there is in force throughout the territory or state a rule indicating which of those systems can properly be applied in the case in question, that rule shall be followed; or

(b) if there is no such rule, the system shall be that with which the testator was most closely connected at the relevant time, and for this purpose the relevant time is the time of the testator's death where the matter is to be determined by reference to circumstances prevailing at his death, and the time of execution of the will in any other case.

(3) In determining for the purposes of this Act whether or not the execution of a will conformed to a particular law, regard shall be had to the formal requirements of that law at the time of execution, but this shall not prevent

account being taken of an alteration of law affecting wills executed at that time if the alteration enables the will to be treated as properly executed.

7 Short title, commencement, repeal and extent

(2) This Act shall come into operation on 1 January 1964.

(4) This Act shall not apply to a will of a testator who died before the time of the commencement of this Act and shall apply to a will of a testator who dies after that time whether the will was executed before or after that time ...

ADMINISTRATION OF ESTATES (SMALL PAYMENTS) ACT 1965
(1965 c 32)

1 Increase in amounts disposable on death without representation

(1) In the enactments and instruments listed in Schedule 1 to this Act, of which –

(a) those listed in Part I are enactments authorising the disposal of property on death, without the necessity for probate or other proof of title, to persons appearing to be beneficially entitled thereto, to relatives or dependants of the deceased or to other persons described in the enactments, but subject to a limit which is in most cases £100 and which does not in any case exceed £100;

(b) those listed in Part II are enactments giving power to make rules or regulations containing corresponding provisions subject to a limit of £100; and

(c) those listed in Part III are such rules and regulations as aforesaid and instruments containing corresponding provisions made under other enactments and containing a limit which does not in any case exceed £200;

the said limit shall, subject to the provisions of that Schedule, in each case be £5,000 instead of the limit specified in the enactment or instrument; and for references to the said limits in those enactments and instruments there shall accordingly be substituted references to £5,000.

2 Increase in amounts disposable on death by nomination

(1) In the enactments and instrument listed in Schedule 2 to this Act (which enable a person by nomination to dispose of property on his death up to a limit of £100 or, in some cases, £200) the said limit shall, subject to the provisions of that Schedule, in each case be £5,000 instead of the limit specified in the enactments or instrument; and for references to the said

limits in the said enactments and instrument there shall accordingly be substituted references to £5,000.

(2) This section shall apply in relation to any nomination delivered at or sent to the appropriate office, or made in the appropriate book, after the expiration of a period of one month beginning with the date on which this Act is passed.

3   Extension of certain enactments relating to intestacies to cases where deceased leaves a will

(1) The enactments mentioned in Schedule 3 to this Act (all of which are listed in Part I of Schedule 1 to this Act) shall have effect subject to the amendments in that Schedule, which are amendments extending the operation of those enactments to cases where the deceased leaves a will. ...

6   Power to provide for further increases

(1) The Treasury may from time to time by order direct that –

(a) sections 1 and 2 of this Act, so far as they relate to any enactment; and

(b) section 68 of the Friendly Societies Act 1974 (which contains provisions similar to the enactments to which section 1 of this Act relates but subject to a limit of £500); and

(e) sections 66 and 67 of the said Act of 1974 (which contain provisions similar to the enactments to which section 2 of this Act relates but subject to a limit of £500);

shall have effect as if for references to £500 there were substituted references to such higher amount as may be specified in the order. ...

SCHEDULE 1

STATUTORY PROVISIONS AUTHORISING DISPOSAL OF PROPERTY ON DEATH WITHOUT REPRESENTATION

PART I

ENACTMENTS

[In addition to a number of public and private Acts of limited importance, the following Acts are amended –

The Navy and Marines (Property of Deceased) Act 1865

The Regimental Debts Act 1893

The Superannuation (Ecclesiastical Commissioners and Queen Anne's Bounty) Act 1914

The Government Annuities Act 1929

The Superannuation (Various Services) Act 1938

The Local Government Superannuation Act 1953

The Industrial and Provident Societies Act 1965]

PART II

ENABLING ENACTMENTS

The Pensions and Yeomanry Pay Act 1884

The Elementary School Teachers (Superannuation) Act 1898

PART III

INSTRUMENTS

[Certain statutory instruments are amended]

SCHEDULE 2

STATUTORY PROVISIONS AUTHORISING DISPOSAL OF PROPERTY ON DEATH BY NOMINATION

[Certain local and other Acts are amended]

SCHEDULE 3

EXTENSION OF ENACTMENTS RELATING TO INTESTACIES

[Certain private Acts and other Acts are extended]

As amended by the National Debt Act 1972, s6(3); Friendly Societies Act 1974, s116(1), Schedule 9, para 20; Administration of Estates (Small Payments) (Increase of Limit) Order 1984; Statute Law (Repeals) Act 1993, s1(1), Schedule 1, Pt IX; Merchant Shipping Act 1995, s314(1), Schedule 12; National Savings Stock Register (Closure of Register to Gilts) Order 1998.

FAMILY PROVISION ACT 1966
(1966 c 35)

1 Increase of net sum payable to surviving husband or wife on intestacy

(1) In the case of a person dying after the coming into force of this section, section 46(1) of the Administration of Estates Act 1925, as amended by section 1 of the Intestates' Estates Act 1952 and set out in Schedule 1 to that Act, shall apply as if the net sums charged by paragraph (i) on the residuary estate in favour of a surviving husband or wife were as follows, that is to say –

(a) under paragraph (2) of the Table (which charges a net sum ... where the intestate leaves issue) a sum of £125,000 or of such larger amount as may from time to time be fixed by order of the Lord Chancellor; and

(b) under paragraph (3) of the Table (which charges a net sum ... where the intestate leaves certain close relatives but no issue) a sum of £200,000 or of such larger amount as may from time to time be so fixed.

As amended by the Family Provision (Intestate Succession) Order 1993 as respects persons dying after 1 December 1993.

WILLS ACT 1968
(1968 c 28)

1   Restriction of operation of Wills Act 1837, s15

(1) For the purposes of section 15 of the Wills Act 1837 (avoidance of gifts to attesting witnesses and their spouses) the attestation of a will by a person to whom or to whose spouse there is given or made any such disposition as is described in that section shall be disregarded if the will is duly executed without his attestation and without that of any other such person.

(2) This section applies to the will of any person dying after the passing of this Act, whether executed before or after the passing of this Act.

FAMILY LAW REFORM ACT 1969
(1969 c 46)

3   Provisions relating to wills and intestacy

(3) Any will which –

    (a) has been made, whether before or after the coming into force of this section, by a person under the age of eighteen; and

    (b) is valid by virtue of the provisions of section 11 of the [Wills Act] 1837 and the [Wills (Soldiers and Sailors) Act] 1918,

may be revoked by that person notwithstanding that he is still under that age whether or not the circumstances are then such that he would be entitled to make a valid will under those provisions.

(4) In this section 'will' has the same meaning as in the said Act of 1837 and 'intestate' has the same meaning as in the [Administration of Estates Act] 1925.

TAXES MANAGEMENT ACT 1970
(1970 c 9)

PART VII

PERSONS CHARGEABLE IN A REPRESENTATIVE CAPACITY, ETC

74 Personal representatives

(1) If a person chargeable to income tax dies, the executor or administrator of the person deceased shall be liable for the tax chargeable on such deceased person, and may deduct any payments made under this section out of the assets and effects of the person deceased.

(2) On neglect or refusal of payment, any person liable under this section may be proceeded against in like manner as any other defaulter.

77 Application of Part VII to capital gains tax

(1) This part of this Act (except section 76 above [protection for certain trustees, agents and receivers]) shall apply in relation to capital gains tax as it applies in relation to income tax, and subject to any necessary modifications.

(2) This part of this Act as applied by this section shall not affect the question of who is the person to whom chargeable gains accrue, or who is chargeable to capital gains tax, so far as that question is relevant for the purposes of any exemption, or of any provision determining the rate at which capital gains tax is chargeable.

As amended by the Finance Act 1971, ss37(2), 38, 69(7), Schedule 14, Pt II.

ADMINISTRATION OF ESTATES ACT 1971
(1971 c 25)

10 Retainer, preference and the payment of debts by personal representatives

(1) The right of retainer of a personal representative and his right to prefer creditors are hereby abolished.

(2) Nevertheless a personal representative –

(a) other than one mentioned in paragraph (b) below, who, in good faith and at a time when he has no reason to believe that the deceased's estate is insolvent, pays the debt of any person (including himself) who is a creditor of the estate; or

(b) to whom letters of administration had been granted solely by reason of his being a creditor and who, in good faith and at such a time pays the debt of another person who is a creditor of the estate;

shall not, if it subsequently appears that the estate is insolvent, be liable to account to a creditor of the same degree as the paid creditor for the sum so paid.

INHERITANCE (PROVISION FOR FAMILY AND DEPENDANTS) ACT 1975

(1975 c 63)

1   Application for financial provision from deceased's estate

(1) Where after the commencement of this Act a person dies domiciled in England and Wales and is survived by any of the following persons –

(a) the wife or husband of the deceased;

(b) a former wife or former husband of the deceased who has not remarried;

(ba) any person (not being a person included in paragraph (a) or (b) above) to whom subsection (1A) below applies;

(c) a child of the deceased;

(d) any person (not being a child of the deceased) who, in the case of any marriage to which the deceased was at any time a party, was treated by the deceased as a child of the family in relation to that marriage;

(e) any person (not being a person included in the foregoing paragraphs of this subsection) who immediately before the death of the deceased was being maintained, either wholly or partly, by the deceased;

that person may apply to the court for an order under section 2 of this Act on the ground that the disposition of the deceased's estate effected by his will or the law relating to intestacy, or the combination of his will and that law, is not such as to make reasonable financial provision for the applicant.

(1A) This subsection applies to a person if the deceased died on or after 1st January 1996 and, during the whole of the period of two years ending immediately before the date when the deceased died, the person was living –

(a) in the same household as the deceased, and

(b) as the husband or wife of the deceased.

(2) In this Act 'reasonable financial provision' –

(a) in the case of an application made by virtue of subsection (1)(a) above by the husband or wife of the deceased (except where the marriage with the deceased was the subject of a decree of judicial separation and at the date of death the decree was in force and the separation was continuing), means such financial provision as it would be reasonable in all the circumstances of the case for a husband or wife to receive, whether or not that provision is required for his or her maintenance;

(b) in the case of any other application made by virtue of subsection (1) above, means such financial provision as it would be reasonable in all the circumstances of the case for the applicant to receive for his maintenance.

(3) For the purposes of subsection (1)(e) above, a person shall be treated as being maintained by the deceased, either wholly or partly, as the case may be, if the deceased, otherwise than for full valuable consideration, was making a substantial contribution in money or money's worth towards the reasonable needs of that person.

2   Powers of court to make orders

(1) Subject to the provisions of this Act, where an application is made for an order under this section, the court may, if it is satisfied that the disposition of the deceased's estate effected by his will or the law relating to intestacy, or the combination of his will and that law, is not such as to make reasonable financial provision for the applicant, make any one or more of the following orders –

(a) an order for the making to the applicant out of the net estate of the deceased of such periodical payments and for such term as may be specified in the order;

(b) an order for the payment to the applicant out of that estate of a lump sum of such amount as may be so specified;

(c) an order for the transfer to the applicant of such property comprised in that estate as may be so specified;

(d) an order for the settlement for the benefit of the applicant of such property comprised in that estate as may be so specified;

(e) an order for the acquisition out of property comprised in that estate of such property as may be so specified and for the transfer of the property so acquired to the applicant or for the settlement thereof for his benefit;

(f) an order varying any ante-nuptial or post-nuptial settlement (including such a settlement made by will) made on the parties to a marriage to which the deceased was one of the parties, the variation being for the benefit of the surviving party to that marriage, or any child of that marriage, or any person who was treated by the deceased as a child of the family in relation to that marriage.

(2) An order under subsection (1)(a) above providing for the making out of the net estate of the deceased of periodical payments may provide for –

(a) payments of such amount as may be specified in the order,

(b) payments equal to the whole of the income of the net estate or of such portion thereof as may be so specified,

(c) payments equal to the whole of the income of such part of the net estate as the court may direct to be set aside or appropriated for the making out of the income thereof of payments under this section,

or may provide for the amount of the payments or any of them to be determined in any other way the court thinks fit.

(3) Where an order under subsection (1)(a) above provides for the making of payments of an amount specified in the order, the order may direct that such part of the net estate as may be so specified shall be set aside or appropriated for the making out of the income thereof of those payments; but no larger part of the net estate shall be so set aside or appropriated than is sufficient, at the date of the order, to produce by the income thereof the amount required for the making of those payments.

(4) An order under this section may contain such consequential and supplemental provisions as the court thinks necessary or expedient for the purpose of giving effect to the order or for the purpose of securing that the order operates fairly as between one beneficiary of the estate of the deceased and another and may, in particular, but without prejudice to the generality of this subsection –

(a) order any person who holds any property which forms part of the net estate of the deceased to make such payment or transfer such property as may be specified in the order;

(b) vary the disposition of the deceased's estate effected by the will or the law relating to intestacy, or by both the will and the law relating to intestacy, in such manner as the court thinks fair and reasonable having regard to the provisions of the order and all the circumstances of the case;

(c) confer on the trustees of any property which is the subject of an order under this section such powers as appear to the court to be necessary or expedient.

3 Matters to which court is to have regard in exercising powers under s2

(1) Where an application is made for an order under section 2 of this Act, the court shall, in determining whether disposition of the deceased's estate effected by his will or the law relating to intestacy, or the combination of his will and that law, is such as to make reasonable financial provision for the applicant and, if the court considers that reasonable financial provision has not been made, in determining whether and in what manner it shall exercise its powers under that section, have regard to the following matters, that is to say –

(a) the financial resources and financial needs which the applicant has or is likely to have in the foreseeable future;

(b) the financial resources and financial needs which any other applicant for an order under section 2 of this Act has or is likely to have in the foreseeable future;

(c) the financial resources and financial needs which any beneficiary of the estate of the deceased has or is likely to have in the foreseeable future;

(d) any obligations and responsibilities which the deceased had towards any applicant for an order under the said section 2 or towards any beneficiary of the estate of the deceased;

(e) the size and nature of the net estate of the deceased;

(f) any physical or mental disability of any applicant for an order under the said section 2 or any beneficiary of the estate of the deceased;

(g) any other matter, including the conduct of the applicant or any other person, which in the circumstances of the case the court may consider relevant.

(2) Without prejudice to the generality of paragraph (g) of subsection (1) above, where an application for an order under section 2 of this Act is made by virtue of section 1(1)(a) or 1(1)(b) of this Act, the court shall, in addition to the matters specifically mentioned in paragraphs (a) to (f) of that subsection, have regard to –

(a) the age of the applicant and the duration of the marriage;

(b) the contribution made by the applicant to the welfare of the family of the deceased, including any contribution made by looking after the home or caring for the family;

and, in the case of an application by the wife or husband of the deceased, the court shall also, unless at the date of death a decree of judicial separation was in force and the separation was continuing, have regard to the provision which the applicant might reasonably have expected to receive if on the day on which the deceased died the marriage, instead of being terminated by death, had been terminated by a decree of divorce.

(2A) Without prejudice to the generality of paragraph (g) of subsection (1) above, where an application for an order under section 2 of this Act is made by virtue of section 1(1)(ba) of this Act, the court shall, in addition to the matters specifically mentioned in paragraphs (a) to (f) of that subsection, have regard to –

(a) the age of the applicant and the length of the period during which the applicant lived as the husband or wife of the deceased and in the same household as the deceased;

(b) the contribution made by the applicant to the welfare of the family of the deceased, including any contribution made by looking after the home or caring for the family.

(3) Without prejudice to the generality of paragraph (g) of subsection (1) above, where an application for an order under section 2 of this Act is made by virtue of section 1(1)(c) or 1(1)(d) of this Act, the court shall, in addition to the matters specifically mentioned in paragraphs (a) to (f) of that subsection, have regard to the manner in which the applicant was being or in which he might expect to be educated or trained, and where the application is made by virtue of section 1(1)(d) the court shall also have regard –

(a) to whether the deceased had assumed any responsibility for the applicant's maintenance and, if so, to the extent to which and the basis upon which the deceased assumed that responsibility and to the length of time for which the deceased discharged that responsibility;

(b) to whether in assuming and discharging that responsibility the deceased did so knowing that the applicant was not his own child;

(c) to the liability of any other person to maintain the applicant.

(4) Without prejudice to the generality of paragraph (g) of subsection (1) above, where an application for an order under section 2 of this Act is made by virtue of section 1(1)(e) of this Act, the court shall, in addition to the matters specifically mentioned in paragraphs (a) to (f) of that subsection, have regard to the extent to which and the basis upon which the deceased assumed responsibility for the maintenance of the applicant, and to the length of time for which the deceased discharged that responsibility.

(5) In considering the matters to which the court is required to have regard under this section, the court shall take into account the facts as known to the court at the date of the hearing.

(6) In considering the financial resources of any person for the purposes of this section the court shall take into account his earning capacity and in considering the financial needs of any person for the purposes of this section the court shall take into account his financial obligations and responsibilities.

4   Time-limit for applications

An application for an order under section 2 of this Act shall not, except with the permission of the court, be made after the end of the period of six months from the date on which representation with respect to the estate of the deceased is first taken out.

5   Interim orders

(1) Where on an application for an order under section 2 of this Act it appears to the court –

(a) that the applicant is in immediate need of financial assistance, but it is not yet possible to determine what order (if any) should be made under that section; and

(b) that property forming part of the net estate of the deceased is or can be made available to meet the need of the applicant;

the court may order that, subject to such conditions or restrictions, if any, as the court may impose and to any further order of the court, there shall be paid to the applicant out of the net estate of the deceased such sum or sums and (if more than one) at such intervals as the court thinks reasonable; and the court may order that, subject to the provisions of this Act, such payments are to be made until such date as the court may specify, not being later than the date on which the court either makes an order under the said section 2 or decides not to exercise its powers under that section.

(2) Subsections (2), (3) and (4) of section 2 of this Act shall apply in relation to an order under this section as they apply in relation to an order under that section.

(3) In determining what order, if any, should be made under this section the court shall, so far as the urgency of the case admits, have regard to the same matters as those to which the court is required to have regard under section 3 of this Act.

(4) An order made under section 2 of this Act may provide that any sum paid to the applicant by virtue of this section shall be treated to such an extent

and in such manner as may be provided by that order as having been paid on account of any payment provided for by that order.

6 Variation, discharge, etc of orders for periodical payments

(1) Subject to the provisions of this Act, where the court has made an order under section 2(1)(a) of this Act (in this section referred to as 'the original order') for the making of periodical payments to any person (in this section referred to as 'the original recipient'), the court, on an application under this section, shall have power by order to vary or discharge the original order or to suspend any provision of it temporarily and to revive the operation of any provision so suspended.

(2) Without prejudice to the generality of subsection (1) above, an order made on an application for the variation of the original order may –

(a) provide for the making out of any relevant property of such periodical payments and for such term as may be specified in the order to any person who has applied, or would but for section 4 of this Act be entitled to apply, for an order under section 2 of this Act (whether or not, in the case of any application, an order was made in favour of the applicant);

(b) provide for the payment out of any relevant property of a lump sum of such amount as may be so specified to the original recipient or to any such person as is mentioned in paragraph (a) above;

(c) provide for the transfer of the relevant property, or such part thereof as may be so specified, to the original recipient or to any such person as is so mentioned.

(3) Where the original order provides that any periodical payments payable thereunder to the original recipient are to cease on the occurrence of an event specified in the order (other than the remarriage of a former wife or former husband) or on the expiration of a period so specified, then, if, before the end of the period of six months from the date of the occurrence of that event or of the expiration of that period, an application is made for an order under this section, the court shall have power to make any order which it would have had power to make if the application had been made before the date (whether in favour of the original recipient or any such person as is mentioned in subsection (2)(a) above and whether having effect from that date or from such later date as the court may specify).

(4) Any reference in this section to the original order shall include a reference to an order made under this section and any reference in this section to the original recipient shall include a reference to any person to whom periodical payments are required to be made by virtue of an order under this section.

(5) An application under this section may be made by any of the following persons, that is to say –

(a) any person who by virtue of section 1(1) of this Act has applied, or would but for section 4 of this Act be entitled to apply, for an order under section 2 of this Act,

(b) the personal representatives of the deceased,

(c) the trustees of any relevant property, and

(d) any beneficiary of the estate of the deceased.

(6) An order under this section may only affect –

(a) property the income of which is at the date of the order applicable wholly or in part for the making of the periodical payments to any person who has applied for an order under this Act, or

(b) in the case of an application under subsection (3) above in respect of payments which have ceased to be payable on the occurrence of an event or the expiration of a period, property the income of which was so applicable immediately before the occurrence of that event or the expiration of that period, as the case may be,

and any such property as is mentioned in paragraph (a) or (b) above is in subsections (2) and (5) above referred to as 'relevant property'.

(7) In exercising the powers conferred by this section the court shall have regard to all the circumstances of the case, including any change in any of the matters to which the court was required to have regard when making the order to which the application relates.

(8) Where the court makes an order under this section, it may give such consequential directions as it thinks necessary or expedient having regard to the provisions of the order.

(9) No such order as is mentioned in section 2(1)(d), (e) or (f), 9, 10 or 11 of this Act shall be made on an application under this section.

(10) For the avoidance of doubt it is hereby declared that, in relation to an order which provides for the making of periodical payments which are to cease on the occurrence of an event specified in the order (other than the remarriage of a former wife or former husband) or on the expiration of a period so specified, the power to vary an order includes power to provide for the making of periodical payments after the expiration of that period or the occurrence of that event.

7   Payment of lump sums by instalments

(1) An order under section 2(1)(b) or 6(2)(b) of this Act for the payment of a lump sum may provide for the payment of that sum by instalments of such amount as may be specified in the order.

(2) Where an order is made by virtue of subsection (1) above, the court shall have power, on an application made by the person to whom the lump sum is payable, by the personal representatives of the deceased or by the trustees of the property out of which the lump sum is payable, to vary that order by varying the number of instalments payable, the amount of any instalment and the date on which any instalment becomes payable.

8   Property treated as part of 'net estate'

(1) Where a deceased person has in accordance with the provisions of any enactment nominated any person to receive any sum of money or other property on his death and that nomination is in force at the time of his death, that sum of money, after deducting therefrom any inheritance tax payable in respect thereof, or that other property, to the extent of the value thereof at the date of the death of the deceased after deducting therefrom any inheritance tax so payable, shall be treated for the purposes of this Act as part of the net estate of the deceased; but this subsection shall not render any person liable for having paid that sum or transferred that other property to the person named in the nomination in accordance with the directions given in the nomination.

(2) Where any sum of money or other property is received by any person as a donatio mortis causa made by a deceased person, that sum of money, after deducting therefrom any inheritance tax payable thereon, or that other property, to the extent of the value thereof at the date of the death of the deceased after deducting therefrom any inheritance tax so payable, shall be treated for the purposes of this Act as part of the net estate of the deceased; but this subsection shall not render any person liable for having paid that sum or transferred that other property in order to give effect to that donatio mortis causa.

(3) The amount of inheritance tax to be deducted for the purposes of this section shall not exceed the amount of that tax which has been borne by the person nominated by the deceased or, as the case may be, the person who has received a sum of money or other property as a donatio mortis causa.

9   Property held on a joint tenancy

(1) Where a deceased person was immediately before his death beneficially entitled to a joint tenancy of any property, then, if, before the end of the period of six months from the date on which representation with respect to the estate of the deceased was first taken out, an application is made for an order under section 2 of this Act, the court for the purpose of facilitating the making of financial provision for the applicant under this Act may order that the deceased's severable share of that property, at the value thereof immediately before his death, shall, to such extent as appears to the court to be just in all the circumstances of the case, be treated for the purposes of this Act as part of the net estate of the deceased.

(2) In determining the extent to which any severable share is to be treated as part of the net estate of the deceased by virtue of an order under subsection (1) above, the court shall have regard to any inheritance tax payable in respect of that severable share.

(3) Where an order is made under subsection (1) above, the provisions of this section shall not render any person liable for anything done by him before the order was made.

(4) For the avoidance of doubt it is hereby declared that for the purposes of this section there may be a joint tenancy of a chose in action.

10   Dispositions intended to defeat applications for financial provision

(1) Where an application is made to the court for an order under section 2 of this Act the applicant may, in the proceedings on that application, apply to the court for an order under subsection (2) below.

(2) Where on an application under subsection (1) above the court is satisfied –

(a) that, less than six years before the date of the death of the deceased, the deceased with the intention of defeating an application for financial provision under this Act made a disposition, and

(b) that full valuable consideration for that disposition was not given by the person to whom or for the benefit of whom the disposition was made (in this section referred to as 'the donee') or by any other person, and

(c) that the exercise of the powers conferred by this section would facilitate the making of financial provision for the applicant under this Act,

then, subject to the provisions of this section and of sections 12 and 13 of this

Act, the court may order the donee (whether or not at the date of the order he holds any interest in the property disposed of to him or for his benefit by the deceased) to provide, for the purpose of the making of that financial provision, such sum of money or other property as may be specified in the order.

(3) Where an order is made under subsection (2) above as respects any disposition made by the deceased which consisted of the payment of money to or for the benefit of the donee, the amount of any sum of money or the value of any property ordered to be provided under that subsection shall not exceed the amount of the payment made by the deceased after deducting therefrom any inheritance tax borne by the donee in respect of that payment.

(4) Where an order is made under subsection (2) above as respects any disposition made by the deceased which consisted of the transfer of property (other than a sum of money) to or for the benefit of the donee, the amount of any sum of money or the value of any property ordered to be provided under that subsection shall not exceed the value at the date of the death of the deceased of the property disposed of by him to or for the benefit of the donee (or if that property has been disposed of by the person to whom it was transferred by the deceased, the value at the date of that disposal thereof) after deducting therefrom any inheritance tax borne by the donee in respect of the transfer of that property by the deceased.

(5) Where an application (in this subsection referred to as 'the original application') is made for an order under subsection (2) above in relation to any disposition, then, if on an application under this subsection by the donee or by any applicant for an order under section 2 of this Act the court is satisfied –

> (a) that, less than six years before the date of the death of the deceased, the deceased with the intention of defeating an application for financial provision under this Act made a disposition other than the disposition which is the subject of the original application, and
> (b) that full valuable consideration for that other disposition was not given by the person to whom or for the benefit of whom that other disposition was made or by any other person,

the court may exercise in relation to the person to whom or for the benefit of whom that other disposition was made the powers which the court would have had under subsection (2) above if the original application had been made in respect of that other disposition and the court had been satisfied as to the matters set out in paragraphs (a), (b) and (c) of that subsection; and where any application is made under this subsection, any reference in this section (except in subsection (2)(b)) to the donee shall include a reference to the person to whom or for the benefit of whom that other disposition was made.

(6) In determining whether and in what manner to exercise its powers under this section, the court shall have regard to the circumstances in which any disposition was made and any valuable consideration which was given therefor, the relationship, if any, of the donee to the deceased, the conduct and financial resources of the donee and all the other circumstances of the case.

(7) In this section 'disposition' does not include –

(a) any provision in a will, any such nomination as is mentioned in section 8(1) of this Act or any donatio mortis causa, or

(b) any appointment of property made, otherwise than by will, in the exercise of a special power of appointment,

but, subject to these exceptions, includes any payment of money (including the payment of a premium under a policy of assurance) and any conveyance, assurance, appointment or gift of property of any description, whether made by an instrument or otherwise.

(8) The provisions of this section do not apply to any disposition made before the commencement of this Act.

11   Contracts to leave property by will

(1) Where an application is made to a court for an order under section 2 of this Act, the applicant may, in the proceedings on that application, apply to the court for an order under this section.

(2) Where on an application under subsection (1) above the court is satisfied –

(a) that the deceased made a contract by which he agreed to leave by his will a sum of money or other property to any person or by which he agreed that a sum of money or other property would be paid or transferred to any person out of his estate, and

(b) that the deceased made that contract with the intention of defeating an application for financial provision under this Act, and

(c) that when the contract was made full valuable consideration for that contract was not given or promised by the person with whom or for the benefit of whom the contract was made (in this section referred to as 'the donee') or by any other person, and

(d) that the exercise of the powers conferred by this section would facilitate the making of financial provision for the applicant under this Act,

then, subject to the provisions of this section and of sections 12 and 13 of this Act, the court may make any one or more of the following orders, that is to say –

(i) if any money has been paid or any other property has been transferred to or for the benefit of the donee in accordance with the contract, an order directing the donee to provide, for the purpose of the making of that financial provision, such sum of money or other property as may be specified in the order;

(ii) if the money or all the money has not been paid or the property or all the property has not been transferred in accordance with the contract, an order directing the personal representatives not to make any payment or transfer any property, or not to make any further payment or transfer any further property, as the case may be, in accordance therewith or directing the personal representatives only to make such payment or transfer such property as may be specified in the order.

(3) Notwithstanding anything in subsection (2) above, the court may exercise its powers thereunder in relation to any contract made by the deceased only to the extent that the court considers that the amount of any sum of money paid or to be paid or the value of any property transferred or to be transferred in accordance with the contract exceeds the value of any valuable consideration given or to be given for that contract, and for this purpose the court shall have regard to the value of property at the date of the hearing.

(4) In determining whether and in what manner to exercise its powers under this section, the court shall have regard to the circumstances in which the contract was made, the relationship, if any, of the donee to the deceased, the conduct and financial resources of the donee and all the other circumstances of the case.

(5) Where an order has been made under subsection (2) above in relation to any contract, the rights of any person to enforce that contract or to recover damages or to obtain other relief for the breach thereof shall be subject to any adjustment made by the court under section 12(3) of this Act and shall survive to such extent only as is consistent with giving effect to the terms of that order.

(6) The provisions of this section do not apply to a contract made before the commencement of this Act.

12 Provisions supplementary to ss10 and 11

(1) Where the exercise of any of the powers conferred by section 10 or 11 of this Act is conditional on the court being satisfied that a disposition or contract was made by a deceased person with the intention of defeating an application for financial provision under this Act, that condition shall be fulfilled if the court is of the opinion that, on a balance of probabilities, the intention of the deceased (though not necessarily his sole intention) in making the disposition or contract was to prevent an order for financial provision being made under this Act or to reduce the amount of the provision which might otherwise be granted by an order thereunder.

(2) Where an application is made under section 11 of this Act with respect to any contract made by the deceased and no valuable consideration was given or promised by any person for that contract then, notwithstanding anything in subsection (1) above, it shall be presumed, unless the contrary is shown, that the deceased made that contract with the intention of defeating an application for financial provision under this Act.

(3) Where the court makes an order under section 10 or 11 of this Act it may give such consequential directions as it thinks fit (including directions requiring the making of any payment or the transfer of any property) for giving effect to the order or for securing a fair adjustment of the rights of the persons affected thereby.

(4) Any power conferred on the court by the said section 10 or 11 to order the donee, in relation to any disposition or contract, to provide any sum of money or other property shall be exercisable in like manner in relation to the personal representative of the donee, and –

> (a) any reference in section 10(4) to the disposal of property by the donee shall include a reference to disposal by the personal representative of the donee, and
>
> (b) any reference in section 10(5) to an application by the donee under that subsection shall include a reference to an application by the personal representative of the donee;

but the court shall not have power under the said section 10 or 11 to make an order in respect of any property forming part of the estate of the donee which has been distributed by the personal representative; and the personal representative shall not be liable for having distributed any such property before he has notice of the making of an application under the said section 10 or 11 on the ground that he ought to have taken into account the possibility that such an application would be made.

13   Provisions as to trustees in relation to ss10 and 11

(1) Where an application is made for –

(a) an order under section 10 of this Act in respect of a disposition made by the deceased to any person as a trustee, or

(b) an order under section 11 of this Act in respect of any payment made or property transferred, in accordance with a contract made by the deceased, to any person as a trustee,

the powers of the court under the said section 10 or 11 to order that trustee to provide a sum of money or other property shall be subject to the following limitation (in addition, in a case of an application under section 10, to any provision regarding the deduction of inheritance tax) namely, that the amount of any sum of money or the value of any property ordered to be provided –

(i) in the case of an application in respect of a disposition which consisted of the payment of money or an application in respect of the payment of money in accordance with a contract, shall not exceed the aggregate of so much of that money as is at the date of the order in the hands of the trustee and the value at that date of any property which represents that money or is derived therefrom and is at that date in the hands of the trustee;

(ii) in the case of an application in respect of a disposition which consisted of the transfer of property (other than a sum of money) or an application in respect of the transfer of property (other than a sum of money) in accordance with a contract, shall not exceed the aggregate of the value at the date of the order of so much of that property as is at that date in the hands of the trustee and the value at that date of any property which represents the first mentioned property or is derived therefrom and is at that date in the hands of the trustee.

(2) Where any such application is made in respect of a disposition made to any person as a trustee or in respect of any payment made or property transferred in pursuance of a contract to any person as a trustee, the trustee shall not be liable for having distributed any money or other property on the ground that he ought to have taken into account the possibility that such an application would be made.

(3) Where any such application is made in respect of a disposition made to any person as a trustee or in respect of any payment made or property transferred in accordance with a contract to any person as a trustee, any reference in the said section 10 or 11 to the donee shall be construed as including a reference to the trustee or trustees for the time being of the trust

in question and any reference in subsection (1) or (2) above to a trustee shall be construed in the same way.

14   Provision as to cases where no financial relief was granted in divorce proceedings, etc

(1) Where, within twelve months from the date on which a decree of divorce or nullity of marriage has been made absolute or a decree of judicial separation has been granted, a party to the marriage dies and –

(a) an application for a financial provision order under section 23 of the Matrimonial Causes Act 1973 or a property adjustment order under section 24 of that Act has not been made by the other party to that marriage, or

(b) such an application has been made but the proceedings thereon have not been determined at the time of the death of the deceased,

then, if an application for an order under section 2 of this Act is made by that other party, the court shall, notwithstanding anything in section 1 or section 3 of this Act, have power, if it thinks it just to do so, to treat that party for the purposes of that application as if the decree of divorce or nullity of marriage had not been made absolute or the decree of judicial separation had not been granted, as the case may be.

(2) This section shall not apply in relation to a decree of judicial separation unless at the date of the death of the deceased the decree was in force and the separation was continuing.

15   Restriction imposed in divorce proceedings, etc on application under this Act

(1) On the grant of a decree of divorce, a decree of nullity of marriage or a decree of judicial separation or at any time thereafter the court, if it considers it just to do so, may, on the application of either party to the marriage, order that the other party to the marriage shall not on the death of the applicant be entitled to apply for an order under section 2 of this Act.

In this subsection 'the court' means the High Court or, where a county court has jurisdiction by virtue of Part V of the Matrimonial and Family Proceedings Act 1984, a county court.

(2) In the case of a decree of divorce or nullity of marriage an order may be made under subsection (1) above before or after the decree is made absolute, but if it is made before the decree is made absolute it shall not take effect unless the decree is made absolute.

(3) Where an order made under subsection (1) above on the grant of a decree of divorce or nullity of marriage has come into force with respect to a party to a marriage, then, on the death of the other party to that marriage, the court shall not entertain any application for an order under section 2 of this Act made by the first-mentioned party.

(4) Where an order made under subsection (1) above on the grant of a decree of judicial separation has come into force with respect to any party to a marriage, then, if the other party to that marriage dies while the decree is in force and the separation is continuing, the court shall not entertain any application for an order under section 2 of this Act made by the first-mentioned party.

19   Effect, duration and form of orders

(1) Where an order is made under section 2 of this Act then for all purposes, including the purposes of the enactments relating to inheritance tax, the will or the law relating to intestacy, or both the will and the law relating to intestacy, as the case may be, shall have effect and be deemed to have had effect as from the deceased's death subject to the provisions of the order.

(2) Any order made under section 2 or 5 of this Act in favour of –

(a) an applicant who was the former husband or former wife of the deceased, or

(b) an applicant who was the husband or wife of the deceased in a case where the marriage with the deceased was the subject of a decree of judicial separation and at the date of death the decree was in force and the separation was continuing,

shall, in so far as it provides for the making of periodical payments, cease to have effect on the remarriage of the applicant, except in relation to any arrears due under the order on the date of the remarriage.

(3) A copy of every order made under this Act, other than an order made under section 15(1) of this Act, shall be sent to the principal registry of the Family Division for entry and filing, and a memorandum of the order shall be endorsed on, or permanently annexed to, the probate or letters of administration under which the estate is being administered.

20   Provisions as to personal representatives

(1) The provisions of this Act shall not render the personal representative of a deceased person liable for having distributed any part of the estate of the deceased, after the end of the period of six months from the date on which

representation with respect to the estate of the deceased is first taken out, on the ground that he ought to have taken into account the possibility –

(a) that the court might permit the making of an application for an order under section 2 of this Act after the end of that period, or

(b) that, where an order has been made under the said section 2, the court might exercise in relation thereto the powers conferred on it by section 6 of this Act,

but this subsection shall not prejudice any power to recover, by reason of the making of an order under this Act, any part of the estate so distributed.

(2) Where the personal representative of a deceased person pays any sum directed by an order under section 5 of this Act to be paid out of the deceased's net estate, he shall not be under any liability by reason of that estate not being sufficient to make the payment, unless at the time of making the payment he has reasonable cause to believe that the estate is not sufficient.

(3) Where a deceased person entered into a contract by which he agreed to leave by his will any sum of money or other property to any person or by which he agreed that a sum of money or other property would be paid or transferred to any person out of his estate, then, if the personal representative of the deceased has reason to believe that the deceased entered into the contract with the intention of defeating an application for financial provision under this Act, he may, notwithstanding anything in that contract, postpone the payment of that sum of money or the transfer of that property until the expiration of the period of six months from the date on which representation with respect to the estate of the deceased is first taken out or, if during that period an application is made for an order under section 2 of this Act, until the determination of the proceedings on that application.

23 Determination of date on which representation was first taken out

In considering for the purposes of this Act when representation with respect to the estate of a deceased person was first taken out, a grant limited to settled land or to trust property shall be left out of account, and a grant limited to real estate or to personal estate shall be left out of account unless a grant limited to the remainder of the estate has previously been made or is made at the same time.

24 Effect of this Act on s46(1)(vi) of Administration of Estates Act 1925

Section 46(1)(vi) of the Administration of Estates Act 1925, in so far as it provides for the devolution of property on the Crown, the Duchy of Lancaster or the Duke of Cornwall as bona vacantia, shall have effect subject to the provisions of this Act.

25 Interpretation

(1) In this Act –

'beneficiary', in relation to the estate of a deceased person, means –

(a) a person who under the will of the deceased or under the law relating to intestacy is beneficially interested in the estate or would be so interested if an order had not been made under this Act, and

(b) a person who has received any sum of money or other property which by virtue of section 8(1) or 8(2) of this Act is treated as part of the net estate of the deceased or would have received that sum or other property if an order had not been made under this Act;

'child' includes an illegitimate child and a child en ventre sa mere at the death of the deceased;

'the court', unless the context otherwise requires, means the High Court, or where a county court has jurisdiction by virtue of section 22 of this Act, a county court;

'former wife' or 'former husband' means a person whose marriage with the deceased was during the lifetime of the deceased either –

(a) dissolved or annulled by a decree of divorce or a decree of nullity of marriage granted under the law of any part of the British Islands, or

(b) dissolved or annulled in any country or territory outside the British Islands by a divorce or annulment which is entitled to be recognised as valid by the law of England and Wales;

'net estate', in relation to a deceased person, means –

(a) all property of which the deceased had power to dispose by his will (otherwise than by virtue of a special power of appointment) less the amount of his funeral, testamentary and administration expenses, debts and liabilities, including any inheritance tax payable out of his estate on his death;

(b) any property in respect of which the deceased held a general power of appointment (not being a power exercisable by will) which has not been exercised;

(c) any sum of money or other property which is treated for the purposes of this Act as part of the net estate of the deceased by virtue of section 8(1) or (2) of this Act;

(d) any property which is treated for the purposes of this Act as part of the net estate of the deceased by virtue of an order made under section 9 of this Act;

(e) any sum of money or other property which is, by reason of a disposition or contract made by the deceased, ordered under section 10 or 11 of this Act to be provided for the purpose of the making of financial provision under this Act;

'property' includes any chose in action;

'reasonable financial provision' has the meaning assigned to it by section 1 of this Act;

'valuable consideration' does not include marriage or a promise of marriage;

'will' includes codicil.

(2) For the purposes of paragraph (a) of the definition of 'net estate' in subsection (1) above a person who is not of full age and capacity shall be treated as having power to dispose by will of all property of which he would have had power to dispose by will if he had been of full age and capacity.

(3) Any reference in this Act to provision out of the net estate of a deceased person includes a reference to provision extending to the whole of that estate.

(4) For the purposes of this Act any reference to a wife or husband shall be treated as including a reference to a person who in good faith entered into a void marriage with the deceased unless either –

(a) the marriage of the deceased and that person was dissolved or annulled during the lifetime of the deceased and the dissolution or annulment is recognised by the law of England and Wales, or

(b) that person has during the lifetime of the deceased entered into a later marriage.

(5) Any reference in this Act to remarriage or to a person who has remarried includes a reference to a marriage which is by law void or voidable or to a person who has entered into such a marriage, as the case may be, and a marriage shall be treated for the purposes of this Act as a remarriage, in

relation to any party thereto, notwithstanding that the previous marriage of that party was void or voidable.

(6) Any reference in this Act to an order or decree made under the Matrimonial Causes Act 1973 or under any section of that Act shall be construed as including a reference to an order or decree which is deemed to have been made under that Act or under that section thereof, as the case may be.

(7) Any reference in this Act to any enactment is a reference to that enactment as amended by or under any subsequent enactment.

As amended by the Administration of Justice Act 1982, s52; Matrimonial and Family Proceedings Act 1984, ss8, 25(2); Law Reform (Succession) Act 1995, s2(1)–(4).

LEGITIMACY ACT 1976
(1976 c 31)

1 Legitimacy of children in certain void marriages

(1) The child of a void marriage, whenever born, shall, subject to subsection (2) below and Schedule 1 to this Act, be treated as the legitimate child of his parents if at the time of the insemination resulting in the birth or, where there was no such insemination, the child's conception (or at the time of the celebration of the marriage if later) both or either of the parties reasonably believed that the marriage was valid.

(2) This section only applies where the father of the child was domiciled in England and Wales at the time of the birth or, if he died before the birth, was so domiciled immediately before his death.

(3) It is hereby declared for the avoidance of doubt that subsection (1) above applies notwithstanding that the belief that the marriage was valid was due to a mistake as to law …

2 Legitimation by subsequent marriage of parents

Subject to the following provisions of this Act, where the parents of an illegitimate person marry one another, the marriage shall, if the father of the illegitimate person is at the date of marriage domiciled in England and Wales, render that person, if living, legitimate from the date of the marriage.

3 Legitimation by extraneous law

Subject to the following provisions of this Act, where the parents of an illegitimate person marry one another and the father of the illegitimate person is not at the time of the marriage domiciled in England and Wales but is domiciled in a country by the law of which the illegitimate person became legitimated by virtue of such subsequent marriage, that person, if living, shall in England and Wales be recognised as having been so legitimated from the date of the marriage notwithstanding that, at the time of his birth, his father was domiciled in a country the law of which did not permit legitimation by subsequent marriage.

4   Legitimation of adopted child

(1) Section 39 of the Adoption Act 1976 does not prevent an adopted child being legitimated under section 2 or 3 above if either natural parent is the sole adoptive parent.

(2) Where an adopted child (with a sole adoptive parent) is legitimated –

(a) subsection (2) of the said section 39 shall not apply after the legitimation to the natural relationship with the other natural parent, and

(b) revocation of the adoption order in consequence of the legitimation shall not affect section 39, 41 or 42 of the Adoption Act 1976 as it applies to any instrument made before the date of legitimation.

5   Rights of legitimated persons and others to take interests in property

(1) Subject to any contrary indication, the rules of construction contained in this section apply to any instrument other than an existing instrument, so far as the instrument contains a disposition of property.

(2) For the purposes of this section, provisions of the law of intestate succession applicable to the estate of a deceased person shall be treated as if contained in an instrument executed by him (while of full capacity) immediately before his death.

(3) A legitimated person, and any other person, shall be entitled to take any interest as if the legitimated person had been born legitimate.

(4) A disposition which depends on the date of birth of a child or children of the parent or parents shall be construed as if –

(a) a legitimated child had been born on the date of legitimation,

(b) two or more legitimated children legitimated on the same date had been born on that date in the order of their actual births,

but this does not affect any reference to the age of a child.

(5) Examples of phrases in wills on which subsection (4) above can operate are –

1. Children of A 'living at my death or born afterwards'.

2. Children of A 'living at my death or born afterwards before any one of such children for the time being in existence attains a vested interest, and who attain the age of 21 years'.

3. As in example 1 or 2, but referring to grandchildren of A, instead of children of A.

4. A for life 'until he has a child' and then to his child or children.

Note. Subsection (4) above will not affect the reference to the age of 21 years in example 2.

(6) If an illegitimate person or a person adopted by one of his natural parents dies, or has died before the commencement of this Act, and –

(a) after his death his parents marry or have married; and

(b) the deceased would, if living at the time of the marriage, have become a legitimated person,

this section shall apply for the construction of the instrument so far as it relates to the taking of interests by, or in succession to, his spouse, children and remoter issue as if he had been legitimated by virtue of the marriage.

(7) In this section 'instrument' includes a private Act settling property, but not any other enactment.

6   Dispositions depending on date of birth

(1) Where a disposition depends on the date of birth of a child who was born illegitimate and who is legitimated (or, if deceased, is treated as legitimated), section 5(4) above does not affect entitlement under Part II of the Family Law Reform Act 1969 (illegitimate children).

(2) Where a disposition depends on the date of birth of an adopted child who is legitimated (or, if deceased, is treated as legitimated) section 5(4) above does not affect entitlement by virtue of section 42(2) of the Adoption Act 1976.

(3) This section applies for example where –

(a) a testator dies in 1976 bequeathing a legacy to his eldest grandchild living at a specified time,

(b) a daughter has an illegitimate child in 1977 who is the first grandchild,

(c) his married son has a child in 1978,

(d) subsequently the illegitimate child is legitimated,

and in all those cases the daughter's child remains the eldest grandchild of the testator throughout.

7 Protection of trustees and personal representatives

(1) A trustee or personal representative is not under a duty, by virtue of the law relating to trusts or the administration of estates, to enquire, before conveying or distributing any property, whether any person is illegitimate or has been adopted by one of his natural parents, and could be legitimated (or if deceased be treated as legitimated), if that fact could affect entitlement to the property.

(2) A trustee or personal representative shall not be liable to any person by reason of a conveyance or distribution of the property made without regard to any such fact if he has not received notice of the fact before the conveyance or distribution.

(3) This section does not prejudice the right of a person to follow the property, or any property representing it, into the hands of another person, other than a purchaser, who has received it.

10 Interpretation

(1) In this Act, except where the context otherwise requires, –

'disposition' includes the conferring of a power of appointment and any other disposition of an interest in or right over property;

'existing', in relation to an instrument, means one made before 1 January 1976;

'legitimated person' means a person legitimated or recognised as legitimated –

(a) under section 2 or 3 above; or

(b) under section 1 or 8 of the Legitimacy Act 1926; or

(c) except in section 8, by a legitimation (whether or not by virtue of the subsequent marriage of his parents) recognised by the law of England and Wales and effected under the law of any other country;

and cognate expressions shall be construed accordingly;

'power of appointment' includes any discretionary power to transfer a beneficial interest in property without the furnishing of valuable consideration;

'void marriage' means a marriage, not being voidable only, in respect of which the High Court has or had jurisdiction to grant a decree of nullity, or would have or would have had such jurisdiction if the parties were domiciled in England and Wales ...

(3) For the purpose of this Act, except where the context otherwise requires, –

(a) the death of the testator is the date at which a will or codicil is to be regarded as made;

(b) an oral disposition of property shall be deemed to be contained in an instrument made when the disposition was made.

As amended by the Adoption Act 1976, s73(2), Schedule 3, paras 23, 24; Family Law Reform Act 1987, s28; Trusts of Land and Appointment of Trustees Act 1996, s25(2), (4), (5), Schedule 4.

ADOPTION ACT 1976
(1976 c 36)

39   Status conferred by adoption

(1) An adopted child shall be treated in law –

(a) where the adopters are a married couple, as if he had been born as a child of the marriage (whether or not he was in fact born after the marriage was solemnised);

(b) in any other case, as if he had been born to the adopter in wedlock (but not as a child of any actual marriage of the adopter).

(2) An adopted child shall, subject to subsections (3) and (3A), be treated in law as if he were not the child of any person other than the adopters or adopter.

(3) In the case of a child adopted by one of its natural parents as sole adoptive parent, subsection (2) has no effect as respects entitlement to property depending on relationship to that parent, or as respects anything else depending on that relationship.

(3A) Where, in the case of a Convention adoption, the High Court is satisfied, on an application under this subsection –

(a) that under the law of the country in which the adoption was effected the adoption is not a full adoption;

(b) that the consents referred to in Article 4(c) and (d) of the Convention have not been given for a full adoption, or that the United Kingdom is not the receiving State (within the meaning of Article 2 of the Convention); and

(c) that it would be more favourable to the adopted child for a direction to be given under this subsection,

the Court may direct that subsection (2) shall not apply, or shall not apply to such extent as may be specified in the direction. In this subsection 'full adoption' means an adoption by virtue of which the adopted child falls to be treated in law as if he were not the child of any person other than the adopters or adopter.

(3B) The following provisions of the Family Law Act 1986 –

(a) section 59 (provisions relating to the Attorney General); and

(b) section 60 (supplementary provision as to declarations),

shall apply in relation to, and to an application for, a direction under subsection (3A) as they apply in relation to, and to an application for, a declaration under Part III of that Act.

(4) It is hereby declared that this section prevents an adopted child from being illegitimate.

(5) This section has effect –

(a) in the case of an adoption before 1 January 1976, from that date, and

(b) in the case of any other adoption, from the date of the adoption.

(6) Subject to the provisions of this Part, this section –

(a) applies for the construction of enactments or instruments passed or made before the adoption or later, and so applies subject to any contrary indication; and

(b) has effect as respects things done, or events occurring, after the adoption, or after 31 December 1975, whichever is the later.

41   Adoptive relatives

(1) A relationship existing by virtue of section 39 may be referred to as an adoptive relationship, and –

(a) a male adopter may be referred to as the adoptive father;

(b) a female adopter may be referred to as the adoptive mother;

(c) any other relative of any degree under an adoptive relationship may be referred to as an adoptive relative of that degree,

but this section does not prevent the term 'parent', or any other term not qualified by the word 'adoptive', being treated as including an adoptive relative.

42   Rules of construction for instruments concerning property

(1) Subject to any contrary indication, the rules of construction contained in this section apply to any instrument, other than an existing instrument, so far as it contains a disposition of property.

(2) In applying section 39(1) to a disposition which depends on the date of birth of a child or children of the adoptive parent or parents, the disposition shall be construed as if –

(a) the adopted child had been born on the date of adoption,

(b) two or more children adopted on the same date had been born on that date in the order of their actual births,

but this does not affect any reference to the age of a child.

(3) Examples of phrases in wills on which subsection (2) can operate are –

1. Children of A 'living at my death or born afterwards'.

2. Children of A 'living at my death or born afterwards before any one of such children for the time being in existence attains a vested interest and who attain the age of 21 years'.

3. As in example 1 or 2, but referring to grandchildren of A instead of children of A.

4. A for life 'until he has a child', and then to his child or children.

Note. Subsection (2) will not affect the reference to the age of 21 years in example 2.

(4) Section 39(2) does not prejudice any interest vested in possession in the adopted child before the adoption, or any interest expectant (whether immediately or not) upon an interest so vested.

(5) Where it is necessary to determine for the purposes of a disposition of property effected by an instrument whether a woman can have a child, it shall be presumed that once a woman has attained the age of 55 years she will not adopt a child after execution of the instrument, and, notwithstanding section 39, if she does so that child shall not be treated as her child or as the child of her spouse (if any) for the purposes of the instrument.

(6) In this section, 'instrument' includes a private Act settling property, but not any other enactment.

45   Protection of trustees and personal representatives

(1) A trustee or personal representative is not under a duty, by virtue of the law relating to trusts or the administration of estates, to enquire, before conveying or distributing any property, whether any adoption has been effected or revoked if that fact could affect entitlement to the property.

(2) A trustee or personal representative shall not be liable to any person by

reason of a conveyance or distribution of the property made without regard to any such fact if he has not received notice of the fact before the conveyance or distribution.

(3) This section does not prejudice the right of a person to follow the property, or any property representing it, into the hands of another person, other than a purchaser, who has received it.

46   Meaning of 'disposition'

(1) In this Part, unless the context otherwise requires, –

'disposition' includes the conferring of a power of appointment and any other disposition of an interest in or right over property;

'power of appointment' includes any discretionary power to transfer a beneficial interest in property without the furnishing of valuable consideration.

(2) This Part applies to an oral disposition as if contained in an instrument made when the disposition was made.

(3) For the purposes of this Part, the death of the testator is the date at which a will or codicil is to be regarded as made.

(4) For the purposes of this Part, provisions of the law of intestate succession applicable to the estate of a deceased person shall be treated as if contained in an instrument executed by him (while of full capacity) immediately before his death.

NB The convention mentioned in s39(3A), above, is the Convention on Protection of Children and Co-operation in respect of Intercountry Adoption, concluded at the Hague on 29 May 1993.

As amended by the Trusts of Land and Appointment of Trustees Act 1996, s25(2), (4), (5), Schedule 4; Adoption (Intercountry Aspects) Act 1999, s4(2), (3).

INTERPRETATION ACT 1978
(1978 c 30)

5 Definitions

In any Act, unless the contrary intention appears, words and expressions listed in Schedule 1 to this Act are to be construed according to that Schedule.

6 Gender and number

In any Act, unless the contrary intention appears, –

(a) words importing the masculine gender include the feminine;

(b) words importing the feminine gender include the masculine;

(c) words in the singular include the plural and words in the plural include the singular.

SCHEDULE 1

WORDS AND EXPRESSIONS DEFINED ...

In relation to England and Wales –

(a) references (however expressed) to any relationship between two persons;

(b) references to a person whose father and mother were or were not married to each other at the time of his birth; and

(c) references cognate with references falling within paragraph (b) above,

shall be construed in accordance with section 1 of the Family Law Reform Act 1987.

As amended by the Family Law Reform Act 1987, s33(1), Schedule 2, para 73.

LIMITATION ACT 1980
(1980 c 58)

15   Time limit for actions to recover land

(1) No action shall be brought by any person to recover any land after the expiration of twelve years from the date on which the right of action accrued to him or, if it first accrued to some person through whom he claims, to that person ...

(6) Part I of Schedule 1 to this Act contains provisions for determining the date of accrual of rights of action to recover land in the cases there mentioned ...

21   Time limit for actions in respect of trust property

(1) No period of limitation prescribed by this Act shall apply to an action by a beneficiary under a trust, being an action –

  (a) in respect of any fraud or fraudulent breach of trust to which the trustee was a party or privy; or

  (b) to recover from the trustee trust property or the proceeds of trust property in the possession of the trustee, or previously received by the trustee and converted to his use.

(2) Where a trustee who is also a beneficiary under the trust received or retains trust property or its proceeds as his share on a distribution of trust property under the trust, his liability in any action brought by virtue of subsection (1)(b) above to recover that property or its proceeds after the expiration of the period of limitation prescribed by this Act for bringing an action to recover trust property shall be limited to the excess over his proper share.

This subsection only applies if the trustee acted honestly and reasonably in making the distribution.

(3) Subject to the preceding provisions of this section, an action by a beneficiary to recover trust property or in respect of any breach of trust, not being an action for which a period of limitation is prescribed by any

other provision of this Act, shall not be brought after the expiration of six years from the date on which the right of action accrued.

For the purposes of this subsection, the right of action shall not be treated as having accrued to any beneficiary entitled to a future interest in the trust property until the interest fell into possession.

(4) No beneficiary as against whom there would be a good defence under this Act shall derive any greater or other benefit from a judgment or order obtained by any other beneficiary than he could have obtained if he had brought the action and this Act had been pleaded in defence.

22   Time limit for actions claiming personal estate of a deceased person

Subject to section 21(1) and (2) of this Act –

(a) no action in respect of any claim to the personal estate of a deceased person or to any share or interest in any such estate (whether under a will or on intestacy) shall be brought after the expiration of twelve years from the date on which the right to receive the share or interest accrued; and

(b) no action to recover arrears of interest in respect of any legacy, or damages in respect of such arrears, shall be brought after the expiration of six years from the date on which the interest became due.

26   Administration to date back to death

For the purposes of the provisions of this Act relating to actions for the recovery of land and advowsons an administrator of the estate of a deceased person shall be treated as claiming as if there had been no interval of time between the death of the deceased person and the grant of the letters of administration.

SCHEDULE 1

PROVISIONS WITH RESPECT TO ACTIONS TO RECOVER LAND

PART I

ACCRUAL OF RIGHTS OF ACTION TO RECOVER LAND ...

2. Where any person brings an action to recover any land of a deceased person (whether under a will or on intestacy) and the deceased person –

(a) was on the date of his death in possession of the land or, in the case of a rentcharge created by will or taking effect upon his death, in possession of the land charged; and

(b) was the last person entitled to the land to be in possession of it;

the right of action shall be treated as having accrued on the date of his death. ...

SUPREME COURT ACT 1981
(1981 c 54)

61 Distribution of business among Divisions

(1) Subject to any provision made by or under this or any other Act (and in particular to any rules of court made in pursuance of subsection (2) and any order under subsection (3)), business in the High Court of any description mentioned in Schedule 1, as for the time being in force, shall be distributed among the Divisions in accordance with that Schedule. ...

PART V

PROBATE CAUSES AND MATTERS

105 Applications

Applications for grants of probate or administration and for the revocation of grants may be made to –

(a) the Principal Registry of the Family Division (in this Part referred to as 'the Principal Registry'); or

(b) a district probate registry.

106 Grants by district probate registrars

(1) Any grant made by a district probate registrar shall be made in the name of the High Court under the seal used in the registry.

107 No grant where conflicting applications

Subject to probate rules, no grant in respect of the estate, or part of the estate, of a deceased person shall be made out of the Principal Registry or any district probate registry on any application if, at any time before the making of a grant, it appears to the registrar concerned that some other application has been made in respect of that estate or, as the case may be, that part of it and has not been either refused or withdrawn.

108 Caveats

(1) A caveat against a grant of probate or administration may be entered in the Principal Registry or in any district probate registry.

(2) On a caveat being entered in a district probate registry, the district probate registrar shall immediately send a copy of it to the Principal Registry to be entered among the caveats in that Registry.

109 Refusal of grant where capital transfer tax unpaid

(1) Subject to subsections (2) and (3), no grant shall be made, and no grant made outside the United Kingdom shall be resealed, except on the production of an account prepared in pursuance of the Inheritance Tax Act 1984 showing by means of such receipt or certification as may be prescribed by the Commissioners of Inland Revenue (in this and the following section referred to as 'the Commissioners') either –

(a) that the inheritance tax payable on the delivery of the account has been paid; or

(b) that no such tax is so payable.

(2) Arrangements may be made between the President of the Family Division and the Commissioners providing for the purposes of this section in such cases as may be specified in the arrangements that the receipt or certification of an account may be dispensed with or that some other document may be substituted for the account required by the Inheritance Tax Act 1984.

(3) Nothing in subsection (1) applies in relation to a case where the delivery of the account required by that Part of that Act has for the time being been dispensed with by any regulations under section 256(1)(a) of the Inheritance Tax Act 1984.

111 Records of grants

(1) There shall continue to be kept records of all grants which are made in the Principal Registry or in any district probate registry.

(2) Those records shall be in such form, and shall contain such particulars, as the President of the Family Division may direct.

112 Summons to executor to prove or renounce

The High Court may summon any person named as executor in a will to prove, or renounce probate of, the will, and to do such other things concerning the will as the court had power to order such a person to do immediately before the commencement of this Act.

113 Power of court to sever grant

(1) Subject to subsection (2), the High Court may grant probate or administration in respect of any part of the estate of a deceased person, limited in any way the court thinks fit.

(2) Where the estate of a deceased person is known to be insolvent, the grant of representation to it shall not be severed under subsection (1) except as regards a trust estate in which he had no beneficial interest.

114 Number of personal representatives

(1) Probate or administration shall not be granted by the High Court to more than four persons in respect of the same part of the estate of a deceased person.

(2) Where under a will or intestacy any beneficiary is a minor or a life interest arises, any grant of administration by the High Court shall be made either to a trust corporation (with or without an individual) or to not less than two individuals, unless it appears to the court to be expedient in all the circumstances to appoint an individual as sole administrator.

(3) For the purpose of determining whether a minority or life interest arises in any particular case, the court may act on such evidence as may be prescribed.

(4) If at any time during the minority of a beneficiary or the subsistence of a life interest under a will or intestacy there is only one personal representative (not being a trust corporation), the High Court may, on the application of any person interested or the guardian or receiver of any such person, and in accordance with probate rules, appoint one or more additional personal represent-atives to act while the minority or life interest subsists and until the estate is fully administered.

(5) An appointment of an additional personal representative under subsection (4) to act with an executor shall not have the effect of including him in any chain of representation.

115 Grants to trust corporations

(1) The High Court may –

(a) where a trust corporation is named in a will as executor, grant probate to the corporation either solely or jointly with any other person named in the will as executor, as the case may require; or

(b) grant administration to a trust corporation, either solely or jointly with another person;

and the corporation may act accordingly as executor or administrator, as the case may be.

(2) Probate or administration shall not be granted to any person as nominee of a trust corporation.

(3) Any officer authorised for the purpose by a trust corporation or its directors or governing body may, on behalf of the corporation, swear affidavits, give security and do any other act which the court may require with a view to the grant to the corporation of probate or administration; and the acts of an officer so authorised shall be binding on the corporation.

116 Power of court to pass over prior claims to grant

(1) If by reason of any special circumstances it appears to the High Court to be necessary or expedient to appoint as administrator some person other than the person who, but for this section, would in accordance with probate rules have been entitled to the grant, the court may in its discretion appoint as administrator such person as it thinks expedient.

(2) Any grant of administration under this section may be limited in any way the court thinks fit.

117 Administration pending suit

(1) Where any legal proceedings concerning the validity of the will of a deceased person, or for obtaining, recalling or revoking any grant, are pending, the High Court may grant administration of the estate of the deceased person in question to an administrator pending suit, who shall, subject to subsection (2), have all the rights, duties and powers of a general administrator.

(2) An administrator pending suit shall be subject to the immediate control of the court and act under its direction; and, except in such circumstances as may be prescribed, no distribution of the estate, or any part of the estate, of the deceased person in question shall be made by such an administrator without the leave of the court.

(3) The court may, out of the estate of the deceased, assign an administrator pending suit such reasonable remuneration as it thinks fit.

118 Effect of appointment of minor as executor

Where a testator by his will appoints a minor to be an executor, the appointment shall not operate to vest in the minor the estate, or any part of the estate, of the testator, or to constitute him a personal representative for any purpose, unless and until probate is granted to him in accordance with probate rules.

119 Administration with will annexed

(1) Administration with the will annexed shall be granted, subject to and in accordance with probate rules, in every class of case in which the High Court had power to make such a grant immediately before the commencement of this Act.

(2) Where administration with the will annexed is granted, the will of the deceased shall be performed and observed in the same manner as if probate of it had been granted to an executor.

120 Power to require administrators to produce sureties

(1) As a condition of granting administration to any person the High Court may, subject to the following provisions of this section and subject to and in accordance with probate rules, require one or more sureties to guarantee that they will make good, within any limit imposed by the court on the total liability of the surety or sureties, any loss which any person interested in the administration of the estate of the deceased may suffer in consequence of a breach by the administrator of his duties as such.

(2) A guarantee given in pursuance of any such requirement shall enure for the benefit of every person interested in the administration of the estate of the deceased as if contained in a contract under seal made by the surety or sureties with every such person and, where there are two or more sureties, as if they had bound themselves jointly and severally.

(3) No action shall be brought on any such guarantee without the leave of the High Court.

(4) Stamp duty shall not be chargeable on any such guarantee.

(5) This section does not apply where administration is granted to the Treasury Solicitor, the Official Solicitor, the Public Trustee, the Solicitor for the affairs of the Duchy of Lancaster or the Duchy of Cornwall or the Crown Solicitor for Northern Ireland, or to the consular officer of a foreign state to which section 1 of the Consular Conventions Act 1949 applies, or in such other cases as may be prescribed.

121 Revocation of grants and cancellation of resealing at instance of court

(1) Where it appears to the High Court that a grant either ought not to have been made or contains an error, the court may call in the grant and, if satisfied that it would be revoked at the instance of a party interested, may revoke it.

(2) A grant may be revoked under subsection (1) without being called in, if it cannot be called in.

(3) Where it appears to the High Court that a grant resealed under the Colonial Probates Acts 1892 and 1927 ought not to have been resealed, the court may call in the relevant document and, if satisfied that the resealing would be cancelled at the instance of a party interested, may cancel the resealing.

In this and the following subsection 'the relevant document' means the original grant or, where some other document was sealed by the court under those Acts, the document.

(4) A resealing may be cancelled under subsection (3) without the relevant document being called in, if it cannot be called in.

122 Examination of person with knowledge of testamentary document

(1) Where it appears that there are reasonable grounds for believing that any person has knowledge of any document which is or purports to be a testamentary document, the High Court may, whether or not any legal proceedings are pending, order him to attend for the purpose of being examined in open court.

(2) The court may –

(a) require any person who is before it in compliance with an order under subsection (1) to answer any question relating to the document concerned; and

(b) if appropriate, order him to bring in the document in such manner as the court may direct.

(3) Any person who, having been required by the court to do so under this section, fails to attend for examination, answer any question or bring in any document shall be guilty of contempt of court.

123 Subpoena to bring in testamentary document

Where it appears that any person has in his possession, custody or power any document which is or purports to be a testamentary document, the High Court may, whether or not any legal proceedings are pending, issue a subpoena requiring him to bring in the document in such manner as the court may in the subpoena direct.

124 Place for deposit of original wills and other documents

All original wills and other documents which are under the control of the High Court in the Principal Registry or in any district probate registry shall be deposited and preserved in such places as the Lord Chancellor may direct; and any wills or other documents so deposited shall, subject to the control of the High Court and to probate rules, be open to inspection.

128 Interpretation of Part V and other probate provisions

In this Part, and in the other provisions of this Act relating to probate causes and matters, unless the context otherwise requires –

'administration' includes all letters of administration of the effects of deceased persons, whether with or without a will annexed, and whether granted for general, special or limited purposes;

'estate' means real and personal estate, and 'real estate' includes –

(a) chattels real and land in possession, remainder or reversion and every interest in or over land to which the deceased person was entitled at the time of his death, and

(b) real estate held on trust or by way of mortgage or security, but not money secured or charged on land;

'grant' means a grant of probate or administration;

'non-contentious or common form probate business' means the business of obtaining probate and administration where there is no contention as to the right thereto, including –

(a) the passing of probates and administration through the High Court in contentious cases where the contest has been terminated,

(b) all business of a non-contentious nature in matters of testacy and intestacy not being proceedings in any action, and

(c) the business of lodging caveats against the grant of probate or administration;

'Principal Registry' means the Principal Registry of the Family Division;

'probate rules' means rules of court made under section 127;

'trust corporation' means the Public Trustee or a corporation either appointed by the court in any particular case to be a trustee or authorised by rules made under section 4(3) of the Public Trustee Act 1906 to act as a custodian trustee;

'will' includes a nuncupative will and any testamentary document of which probate may be granted.

SCHEDULE 1

DISTRIBUTION OF BUSINESS IN HIGH COURT

1. To the Chancery Division are assigned all causes and matters relating to – ...

(d) the administration of the estates of deceased persons; ...

(h) probate business, other than non-contentious or common form business; ...

3. To the Family Division are assigned – ...

(b) all causes and matters (whether at first instance or on appeal) relating to –

(i) legitimacy; ...

(iv) non-contentious or common form probate business; ...

(g) all proceedings for the purpose of enforcing an order made in any proceedings of a type described in this paragraph. ...

As amended by the Inheritance Tax Act 1984, s276, Schedule 8, para 20; Courts and Legal Services Act 1990, s54(2); High Court (Distribution of Business) Order 1991; Trusts of Land and Appointment of Trustees Act 1996, s25(2), Schedule 4.

FORFEITURE ACT 1982
(1982 c 34)

1 The 'forfeiture rule'

(1) In this Act, the 'forfeiture rule' means the rule of public policy which in certain circumstances precludes a person who has unlawfully killed another from acquiring a benefit in consequence of the killing.

(2) References in this Act to a person who has unlawfully killed another include a reference to a person who has unlawfully aided, abetted, counselled or procured the death of that other and references in this Act to unlawful killing shall be interpreted accordingly.

2 Power to modify the rule

(1) Where a court determines that the forfeiture rule has precluded a person (in this section referred to as 'the offender') who has unlawfully killed another from acquiring any interest in property mentioned in subsection (4) below, the court may make an order under this section modifying the effect of that rule.

(2) The court shall not make an order under this section modifying the effect of the forfeiture rule in any case unless it is satisfied that, having regard to the conduct of the offender and of the deceased and to such other circumstances as appear to the court to be material, the justice of the case requires the effect of the rule to be so modified in that case.

(3) In any case where a person stands convicted of an offence of which unlawful killing is an element, the court shall not make an order under this section modifying the effect of the forfeiture rule in that case unless proceedings for the purpose are brought before the expiry of the period of three months beginning with his conviction.

(4) The interests in property referred to in subsection (1) above are –

   (a) any beneficial interest in property which (apart from the forfeiture rule) the offender would have acquired –

(i) under the deceased's will (including, as respects Scotland, any writing having testamentary effect) or the law relating to intestacy or by way of ius relicti, ius relictae or legitim;

(ii) on the nomination of the deceased in accordance with the provisions of any enactment;

(iii) as a donatio mortis causa made by the deceased; or

(iv) under a special destination (whether relating to heritable or moveable property); or

(b) any beneficial interest in property which (apart from the forfeiture rule) the offender would have acquired in consequence of the death of the deceased, being property which, before the death, was held on trust for any person.

(5) An order under this section may modify the effect of the forfeiture rule in respect of any interest in property to which the determination referred to in subsection (1) above relates and may do so in either or both of the following ways, that is –

(a) where there is more than one such interest, by excluding the application of the rule in respect of any (but not all) of those interests; and

(b) in the case of any such interest in property, by excluding the application of the rule in respect of part of the property.

(6) On the making of an order under this section, the forfeiture rule shall have effect for all purposes (including purposes relating to anything done before the order is made) subject to the modifications made by the order.

(7) The court shall not make an order under this section modifying the effect of the forfeiture rule in respect of any interest in property which, in consequence of the rule, has been acquired before the coming into force of this section by a person other than the offender or a person claiming through him.

(8) In this section –

'property' includes any chose in action or incorporeal moveable property; and

'will' includes codicil.

3   Application for financial provision not affected by the rule

(1) The forfeiture rule shall not be taken to preclude any person from making any application under a provision mentioned in subsection (2) below or the making of any order on the application.

(2) The provisions referred to in subsection (1) above are –

(a) any provision of the Inheritance (Provision for Family and Dependants) Act 1975 ...

5 Exclusion of murderers

Nothing in this Act or in any order made under section 2 or referred to in section 3(1) of this Act ... shall affect the application of the forfeiture rule in the case of a person who stands convicted of murder.

ADMINISTRATION OF JUSTICE ACT 1982
(1982 c 53)

20 Rectification

(1) If a court is satisfied that a will is so expressed that it fails to carry out the testator's intentions, in consequence –

(a) of a clerical error; or

(b) of a failure to understand his instructions,

it may order that the will shall be rectified so as to carry out his intentions.

(2) An application for an order under this section shall not, except with the permission of the court, be made after the end of the period of six months from the date on which representation with respect to the estate of the deceased is first taken out.

(3) The provisions of this section shall not render the personal representatives of a deceased person liable for having distributed any part of the estate of the deceased, after the end of the period of six months from the date on which representation with respect to the estate of the deceased is first taken out, on the ground that they ought to have taken into account the possibility that the court might permit the making of an application for an order under this section after the end of that period; but this subsection shall not prejudice any power to recover, by reason of the making of an order under this section, any part of the estate so distributed.

(4) In considering for the purposes of this section when representation with respect to the estate of a deceased person was first taken out, a grant limited to settled land or to trust property shall be left out of account, and a grant limited to real estate or to personal estate shall be left out of account unless a grant limited to the remainder of the estate has previously been made or is made at the same time.

21 Interpretation of wills – general rules as to evidence

(1) This section applies to a will –

(a) in so far as any part of it is meaningless;

(b) in so far as the language used in any part of it is ambiguous on the face of it;

(c) in so far as evidence, other than evidence of the testator's intention, shows that the language used in any part of it is ambiguous in the light of surrounding circumstances.

(2) In so far as this section applies to a will extrinsic evidence, including evidence of the testator's intention, may be admitted to assist in its interpretation.

22   Presumption as to effect of gifts to spouses

Except where a contrary intention is shown it shall be presumed that if a testator devises or bequeaths property to his spouse in terms which in themselves would give an absolute interest to the spouse, but by the same instrument purports to give his issue an interest in the same property, the gift to the spouse is absolute notwithstanding the purported gift to the issue.

23   Deposit and registration of wills of living persons

(1) The following, namely –

(a) the Principal Registry of the Family Division of the High Court of Justice; ...

shall be registering authorities for the purposes of this section.

(2) Each registering authority shall provide and maintain safe and convenient depositories for the custody of the wills of living persons.

(3) Any person may deposit his will in such a depository in accordance with regulations under section 25 below and on payment of the prescribed fee.

(4) It shall be the duty of a registering authority to register in accordance with regulations under section 25 below –

(a) any will deposited in a depository maintained by the authority; and

(b) any other will whose regulation is requested under Article 6 of the Registration Convention. ...

(6) In this section 'prescribed' means –

(a) in the application of this section to England and Wales, prescribed by an order under section 130 of the Supreme Court Act 1981; ...

NB 'the Registration Convention' means the Convention on the Establishment of a Scheme of Registration of Wills concluded at Basle on 16 May 1972.

MENTAL HEALTH ACT 1983
(1983 c 20)

94   Exercise of the judge's functions: 'the patient'

(1) Subject to subsection (1A) below, the functions expressed to be conferred by this Part of this Act on the judge shall be exercisable by the Lord Chancellor or by any nominated judge, and shall also be exercisable by the Master of the Court of Protection, by the Public Trustee or by any nominated officer, but –

(a) in the case of the Master, the Public Trustee or any nominated officer, subject to any express provision to the contrary in this Part of this Act or any rules made under this Part of this Act,

(aa) in the case of the Public Trustee, subject to any directions of the Master and so far only as may be provided by any rules made under this Part of this Act or (subject to any such rules) by directions of the Master,

(b) in the case of any nominated officer, subject to any directions of the Master and so far only as may be provided by the instrument by which he is nominated;

and references in this Part of this Act to the judge shall be construed accordingly.

(1A) In such cases or circumstances as may be prescribed by any rules under this Part of this Act or (subject to any such rules) by directions of the Master, the functions of the judge under this Part of this Act shall be exercised by the Public Trustee (but subject to any directions of the Master as to their exercise).

(2) The functions of the judge under this Part of this Act shall be exercisable where, after considering medical evidence, he is satisfied that a person is incapable, by reason of mental disorder, of managing and administering his property and affairs; and a person as to whom the judge is so satisfied is referred to in this Part of this Act as a patient.

95 General functions of the judge with respect to property and affairs of patient

(1) The judge may, with respect to the property and affairs of a patient, do or secure the doing of all such things as appear necessary or expedient –

(a) for the maintenance or other benefit of the patient,

(b) for the maintenance or other benefit of members of the patient's family,

(c) for making provision for other persons or purposes for whom or which the patient might be expected to provide if he were not mentally disordered, or

(d) otherwise for administering the patient's affairs.

(2) In the exercise of the powers conferred by this section regard shall be had first of all to the requirements of the patient, and the rules of law which restricted the enforcement by a creditor of rights against property under the control of the judge in lunacy shall apply to property under the control of the judge; but, subject to the foregoing provisions of this subsection, the judge shall, in administering a patient's affairs, have regard to the interests of creditors and also to the desirability of making provision for obligations of the patient notwithstanding that they may not be legally enforceable.

96 Powers of the judge as to patient's property and affairs

(1) Without prejudice to the generality of section 95 above, the judge shall have power to make such orders and give such directions and authorities as he thinks fit for the purposes of that section and in particular may for those purposes make orders or give directions or authorities for –

(e) the execution for the patient of a will making any provision (whether by way of disposing of property or exercising a power or otherwise) which could be made by a will executed by the patient if he were not mentally disordered; ...

(4) The power of the judge to make or give an order, direction or authority for the execution of a will for a patient –

(a) shall not be exercisable at any time when the patient is a minor, and

(b) shall not be exercised unless the judge has reason to believe that the patient is incapable of making a valid will for himself. ...

97 Supplementary provisions as to wills executed under s96

(1) Where under section 96(1) above the judge makes or gives an order,

direction or authority requiring or authorising a person (in this section referred to as 'the authorised person') to execute a will for a patient, any will executed in pursuance of that order, direction or authority shall be expressed to be signed by the patient acting by the authorised person, and shall be –

(a) signed by the authorised person with the name of the patient, and with his own name, in the presence of two or more witnesses present at the same time, and

(b) attested and subscribed by those witnesses in the presence of the authorised person, and

(c) sealed with the official seal of the Court of Protection.

(2) The Wills Act 1837 shall have effect in relation to any such will as if it were signed by the patient by his own hand, except that in relation to any such will –

(a) section 9 of that Act (which makes provision as to the signing and attestation of wills) shall not apply, and

(b) in the subsequent provisions of that Act any reference to execution in the manner required by the previous provisions of that Act shall be construed as a reference to execution in the manner required by subsection (1) above.

(3) Subject to the following provisions of this section, any such will executed in accordance with subsection (1) above shall have the same effect for all purposes as if the patient were capable of making a valid will and the will had been executed by him in the manner required by the Wills Act 1837.

(4) So much of subsection (3) above as provides for such a will to have effect as if the patient were capable of making a valid will –

(a) shall not have effect in relation to such a will in so far as it disposes of any immovable property, other than immovable property in England and Wales, and

(b) where at the time when such a will is executed the patient is domiciled in Scotland or Northern Ireland or in a country or territory outside the United Kingdom, shall not have effect in relation to that will in so far as it relates to any other property or matter, except any property or matter in respect of which, under the law of his domicile, any question of his testamentary capacity would fall to be determined in accordance with the law of England and Wales.

98   Judge's powers in cases of emergency

Where it is represented to the judge, and he has reason to believe, that a person may be incapable, by reason of mental disorder, of managing and administering his property and affairs, and the judge is of the opinion that it is necessary to make immediate provision for any of the matters referred to in section 95 above, then pending the determination of the question whether that person is so incapable the judge may exercise in relation to the property and affairs of that person any of the powers conferred on him in relation to the property and affairs of a patient by this Part of this Act so far as is requisite for enabling that provision to be made.

As amended by the Public Trustee and Administration of Funds Act 1986, s2(1), (2).

COUNTY COURTS ACT 1984
(1984 c 28)

23   Equity jurisdiction

A county court shall have all the jurisdiction of the High Court to hear and determine –

(a) proceedings for the administration of the estate of a deceased person, where the estate does not exceed in amount or value the county court limit;

(b) proceedings –

(i) for the execution of any trust, or

(ii) for a declaration that a trust subsists, or

(iii) under section 1 of the Variation of Trusts Act 1958,

where the estate or fund subject, or alleged to be subject, to the trust does not exceed in amount or value the county court limit; ...

(g) proceedings for relief against fraud or mistake, where the damage sustained or the estate or fund in respect of which relief is sought does not exceed in amount or value the county court limit.

24   Jurisdiction by agreement in certain equity proceedings

(1) If, as respects any proceedings to which this section applies, the parties agree, by a memorandum signed by them or by their respective legal representatives or agents, that a county court specified in the memorandum shall have jurisdiction in the proceedings, that court shall, notwithstanding anything in any enactment, have jurisdiction to hear and determine the proceedings accordingly.

(2) Subject to subsection (3), this section applies to any proceedings in which a county court would have jurisdiction by virtue of – ...

(d) sections 17(2), 38(4), 41(1A), and 43(4) of the Administration of Estates Act 1925, ...

(g) sections 23 and 25 of this Act,

but for the limits of the jurisdiction of the court provided in those enactments.

(3) This section does not apply to proceedings under section 1 of the Variation of Trusts Acts 1958.

25   Jurisdiction under Inheritance (Provision for Family and Dependants) Act 1975

A county court shall have jurisdiction to hear and determine any application for an order under section 2 of the Inheritance (Provision for Family and Dependants) Act 1975 (including any application for permission to apply for such an order and any application made, in the proceedings on an application for such an order, for an order under any other provision of that Act).

32   Contentious probate jurisdiction

(1) Where –

(a) an application for the grant or revocation of probate or administration has been made through the principal registry of the Family Division or district probate registry under section 105 of the Supreme Court Act 1981; and

(b) it is shown to the satisfaction of a county court that the value at the date of the death of the deceased of his net estate does not exceed the county court limit,

the county court shall have the jurisdiction of the High Court in respect of any contentious matter arising with the grant or revocation.

(2) In subsection (1) 'net estate', in relation to a deceased person, means the estate of that person exclusive of any property he was possessed of or entitled to as a trustee and not beneficially, and after making allowances for funeral expenses and for debts and liabilities.

Note. By virtue of the County Court Jurisdiction Order 1981, for the purposes of s23, above, the county court limit is £30,000.

As amended by the Administration of Justice Act 1985, s51(1); Courts and Legal Services Act 1990, s125(3), Schedule 18, para 49(3).

INHERITANCE TAX ACT 1984
(1984 c51)

PART I

GENERAL

1 Charge on transfers

Inheritance tax shall be charged on the value transferred by a chargeable transfer.

2 Chargeable transfers and exempt transfers

(1) A chargeable transfer is a transfer of value which is made by an individual but is not (by virtue of Part II of this Act or any other enactment) an exempt transfer.

(2) A transfer of value made by an individual and exempt only to a limited extent –

(a) is, if all the value transferred by it is within the limit, an exempt transfer, and

(b) is, if that value is partly within and partly outside the limit, a chargeable transfer of so much of that value as is outside the limit as well as an exempt transfer of so much of that value as is within the limit.

(3) Except where the context otherwise requires, references in this Act to chargeable transfers, to their making or to the values transferred by them shall be construed as including references to occasions on which tax is chargeable under Chapter III of Part III of this Act (apart from section 79), to their occurrence or to the amounts on which tax is then chargeable.

3 Transfers of value

(1) Subject to the following provisions of this Part of this Act, a transfer of value is a disposition made by a person (the transferor) as a result of which

the value of his estate immediately after the disposition is less than it would be but for the disposition; and the amount by which it is less is the value transferred by the transfer.

(2) For the purposes of subsection (1) above no account shall be taken of the value of excluded property which ceases to form part of a person's estate as a result of a disposition.

(3) Where the value of a person's estate is diminished and that of another person's estate, or of settled property in which no interest in possession subsists, is increased by the first-mentioned person's omission to exercise a right, he shall be treated for the purposes of this section as having made a disposition at the time (or latest time) when he could have exercised the right, unless it is shown that the omission was not deliberate.

(4) Except as otherwise provided, references in this Act to a transfer of value made, or made by any person, include references to events on the happening of which tax is chargeable as if a transfer of value had been made, or, as the case may be, had been made by that person; and 'transferor' shall be construed accordingly.

3A Potentially exempt transfers

(1) Any reference in this Act to a potentially exempt transfer is a reference to a transfer of value –

(a) which is made by an individual on or after 18th March 1986; and

(b) which, apart from this section, would be a chargeable transfer (or to the extent to which, apart from this section, it would be such a transfer); and

(c) to the extent that it constitutes either a gift to another individual or a gift into an accumulation and maintenance trust or a disabled trust;

but this subsection has effect subject to any provision of this Act which provides that a disposition (or transfer of value) of a particular description is not a potentially exempt transfer.

(2) Subject to subsection (6) below, a transfer of value falls within subsection (1)(c) above, as a gift to another individual, –

(a) to the extent that the value transferred is attributable to property which, by virtue of the transfer, becomes comprised in the estate of that other individual, or

(b) so far as that value is not attributable to property which becomes comprised in the estate of another person, to the extent that, by virtue of the transfer, the estate of that other individual is increased.

(3) Subject to subsection (6) below, a transfer of value falls within subsection (1)(c) above, as a gift into an accumulation and maintenance trust or a disabled trust, to the extent that the value transferred is attributable to property which, by virtue of the transfer, becomes settled property to which section 71 or 89 of this Act applies.

(4) A potentially exempt transfer which is made seven years or more before the death of the transferor is an exempt transfer and any other potentially exempt transfer is a chargeable transfer.

(5) During the period beginning on the date of a potentially exempt transfer and ending immediately before –

(a) the seventh anniversary of that date, or

(b) if it is earlier, the death of the transferor,

it shall be assumed for the purposes of this Act that the transfer will prove to be an exempt transfer.

(6) Where, under any provision of this Act other than section 52, tax is in any circumstances to be charged as if a transfer of value has been made, that transfer shall be taken to be a transfer which is not a potentially exempt transfer.

(7) In the application of this section to an event on the happening of which tax is chargeable under section 52 below, the reference in subsection (1)(a) above to the individual by whom the transfer of value is made is a reference to the person who, by virtue of section 3(4) above, is treated as the transferor.

4   Transfers on death

(1) On the death of any person tax shall be charged as if, immediately before his death, he had made a transfer of value and the value transferred by it had been equal to the value of his estate immediately before his death.

(2) For the purposes of this section, where it cannot be known which of two or more persons who have died survived the other or others they shall be assumed to have died at the same instant.

5   Meaning of estate

(1) For the purposes of this Act a person's estate is the aggregate of all the property to which he is beneficially entitled, except that the estate of a person immediately before his death does not include excluded property.

(2) A person who has a general power which enables him, or would if he were sui juris enable him, to dispose of any property other than settled property, or to charge money on any property other than settled property, shall be treated as beneficially entitled to the property or money; and for this purpose 'general power' means a power or authority enabling the person by whom it is exercisable to appoint or dispose of property as he thinks fit.

(3) In determining the value of a person's estate at any time his liabilities at that time shall be taken into account, except as otherwise provided by this Act.

(4) The liabilities to be taken into account in determining the value of a transferor's estate immediately after a transfer of value include his liability for inheritance tax on the value transferred but not his liability (if any) for any other tax or duty resulting from the transfer.

(5) Except in the case of a liability imposed by law, a liability incurred by a transferor shall be taken into account only to the extent that it was incurred for a consideration in money or money's worth.

6   Excluded property

(1) Property situated outside the United Kingdom is excluded property if the person beneficially entitled to it is individually domiciled outside the United Kingdom.

(1A) A holding in an authorised unit trust and a share in an open-ended investment company is excluded property if the person beneficially entitled to it is an individual domiciled outside the United Kingdom.

(2) Where securities have been issued by the Treasury subject to a condition authorised by section 22 of the Finance (No 2) Act 1931 (or section 47 of the Finance (No 2) Act 1915) for exemption from taxation so long as the securities are in the beneficial ownership of persons of a description specified in the condition, the securities are excluded property if they are in the beneficial ownership of such a person.

(3) Where the person beneficially entitled to the rights conferred by any of the following, namely –

   (a) war savings certificates;
   (b) national savings certificates (including Ulster savings certificates);
   (c) premium savings bonds;
   (d) deposits with the National Savings Bank or with a trustee savings bank;

(e) a certified contractual savings scheme within the meaning of section 326 of the Taxes Act 1988;

is domiciled in the Channel Islands or the Isle of Man, the rights are excluded property.

(4) Property to which this subsection applies by virtue of section 155(1) [superannuation schemes] below is excluded property.

7   Rates

(1) Subject to subsections (2), (4) and (5) below, the tax charged on the value transferred by a chargeable transfer made by any transferor shall be charged at the following rate or rates, that is to say –

(a) if the transfer is the first chargeable transfer made by that transferor in the period of seven years ending with the date of the transfer, at the rate or rates applicable to that value under the Table in Schedule 1 to this Act;

(b) in any other case, at the rate or rates applicable under that Table to such part of the aggregate of –

(i) that value, and

(ii) the values transferred by previous chargeable transfers made by him in that period,

as is the highest part of that aggregate and is equal to that value.

(2) Except as provided by subsection (4) below, the tax charged on the value transferred by a chargeable transfer made before the death of the transferor shall be charged at one half of the rate or rates referred to in subsection (1) above.

(3) In the Table in Schedule 1 to this Act any rate shown in the third column is that applicable to such portion of the value concerned as exceeds the lower limit shown in the first column but does not exceed the upper limit (if any) shown in the second column.

(4) Subject to subsection (5) below, subsection (2) above does not apply in the case of a chargeable transfer made at any time within the period of seven years ending with the death of the transferor but, in the case of a chargeable transfer made within that period but more than three years before the death, the tax charged on the value transferred shall be charged at the following percentage of the rate or rates referred to in subsection (1) above –

(a) where the transfer is made more than three but not more than four years before the death, 80 per cent;

(b) where the transfer is made more than four but not more than five years before the death, 60 per cent;

(c) where the transfer is made more than five but not more than six years before the death, 40 per cent; and

(d) where the transfer is made more than six but not more than seven years before the death, 20 per cent.

(5) If, in the case of a chargeable transfer made before the death of the transferor, the tax which would fall to be charged in accordance with subsection (4) above is less than the tax which would have been chargeable (in accordance with subsection (2) above) if the transferor had not died within the period of seven years beginning with the date of the transfer, subsection (4) above shall not apply in the case of that transfer.

8   Indexation of rate bands

(1) If the retail prices index for the month of September in 1993 or any later year is higher than it was for the previous September, then, unless Parliament otherwise determines, section 7 above and Schedule 1 to this Act shall apply to chargeable transfers made on or after 6th April in the following year with the substitution of a new Table for the Table applying (whether by virtue of this section or otherwise) to earlier chargeable transfers.

(2) The new Table shall differ from the Table it replaces in that for each of the a mounts specified in the first and second columns there shall be substituted amounts arrived at by increasing the previous amounts by the same percentage as the percentage increase in the retail prices index and, if the result is not a multiple of £1,000, rounding it up to the nearest amount which is such a multiple.

(3) The references in this section to the retail prices index are references to the general index of retail prices (for all items) published by the Office for National Statistics; and if that index is not published for a month of September those references shall be construed as references to any substituted index or index figures published by that Office.

(4) The Treasury shall before 6th April 1994 and each subsequent 6th April make an order specifying the amounts which by virtue of this section will be treated, in relation to chargeable transfers on or after that date, as specified in the Table in Schedule 1 to this Act; and any such order shall be made by statutory instrument.

10   Dispositions not intended to confer gratuitous benefit

(1) A disposition is not a transfer of value if it is shown that it was not intended, and was not made in a transaction intended, to confer any gratuitous benefit on any person and either –

(a) that it was made in a transaction at arm's length between persons not connected with each other, or

(b) that it was such as might be expected to be made in a transaction at arm's length between persons not connected with each other.

(2) Subsection (1) above shall not apply to a sale of unquoted shares or unquoted debentures unless it is shown that the sale was at a price freely negotiated at the time of the sale or at a price such as might be expected to have been freely negotiated at the time of the sale.

(3) In this section –

'disposition' includes anything treated as a disposition by virtue of section 3(3) above;

'transaction' includes a series of transactions and any associated operations.

11   Dispositions for maintenance of family

(1) A disposition is not a transfer of value if it is made by one party to a marriage in favour of the other party or of a child of either party and is –

(a) for the maintenance of the other party, or

(b) for the maintenance, education or training of the child for a period ending not later than the year in which he attains the age of eighteen or, after attaining that age, ceases to undergo full-time education or training.

(2) A disposition is not a transfer of value if it is made in favour of a child who is not in the care of a parent of his and is for his maintenance, education or training for a period ending not later than the year in which –

(a) he attains the age of eighteen, or

(b) after attaining that age he ceases to undergo full-time education or training;

but paragraph (b) above applies only if before attaining that age the child has for substantial periods been in the care of the person making the disposition.

(3) A disposition is not a transfer of value if it is made in favour of a dependent relative of the person making the disposition and is a reasonable provision for his care or maintenance.

(4) A disposition is not a transfer of value if it is made in favour of an illegitimate child of the person making the disposition and is for the maintenance, education or training of the child for a period ending not later than the year in which he attains the age of eighteen or, after attaining that age, ceases to undergo full-time education or training.

(5) Where a disposition satisfies the conditions of the preceding provisions of this section to a limited extent only, so much of it as satisfies them and so much of it as does not satisfy them shall be treated as separate dispositions.

(6) In this section –

'child' includes a step-child and an adopted child and 'parent' shall be construed accordingly;

'dependent relative' means in relation to any person –

(a) relative of his, or of his spouse, who is incapacitated by old age or infirmity from maintaining himself, or

(b) his mother or his spouse's mother, if she is widowed, or living apart from her husband, or a single woman in consequence of dissolution or annulment of marriage;

'marriage', in relation to a disposition made on the occasion of the dissolution or annulment of a marriage, and in relation to a disposition varying a disposition so made, includes a former marriage;

'year' means period of twelve months ending with 5th April.

12 Dispositions allowable for income tax or conferring retirement benefits

(1) A disposition made by any person is not a transfer of value if it is allowable in computing that person's profits or gains for the purposes of income tax or corporation tax or would be so allowable if those profits or gains were sufficient and fell to be so computed. ...

17 Changes in distribution of deceased's estate, etc

None of the following is a transfer of value –

(a) a variation or disclaimer to which section 142(1) below applies;
(b) a transfer to which section 143 below applies;

(c) an election by a surviving spouse under section 47A of the Administration of Estates Act 1925; ...

PART II

EXEMPT TRANSFERS

CHAPTER I

GENERAL

18 Transfers between spouses

(1) A transfer of value is an exempt transfer to the extent that the value transferred is attributable to property which becomes comprised in the estate of the transferor's spouse or, so far as the value transferred is not so attributable, to the extent that that estate is increased.

(2) If, immediately before the transfer, the transferor but not the transferor's spouse is domiciled in the United Kingdom the value in respect of which the transfer is exempt (calculated as a value on which no tax is chargeable) shall not exceed £55,000 less any amount previously taken into account for the purposes of the exemption conferred by this section.

(3) Subsection (1) above shall not apply in relation to property if the testamentary or other disposition by which it is given –

(a) takes effect on the termination after the transfer of value of any interest or period, or
(b) depends on a condition which is not satisfied within twelve months after the transfer;

but paragraph (a) above shall not have effect by reason only that the property is given to a spouse only if he survives the other spouse for a specified period.

(4) For the purposes of this section, property is given to a person if it becomes his property or is held on trust for him.

19 Annual exemption

(1) Transfers of value made by a transferor in any one year are exempt to the extent that the values transferred by them (calculated as values on which no tax is chargeable) do not exceed £3,000.

(2) Where those values fall short of £3,000, the amount by which they fall short shall, in relation to the next following year, be added to the £3,000 mentioned in subsection (1) above.

(3) Where those values exceed £3,000, the excess –

(a) shall, as between transfers made on different days, be attributed so far as possible to a later rather than an earlier transfer, and

(b) shall, as between transfers made on the same day, be attributed to them in proportion to the values transferred by them.

(3A) A transfer of value which is a potentially exempt transfer –

(a) shall in the first instance be left out of account for the purposes of subsections (1) to (3) above; and

(b) if it proves to be a chargeable transfer, shall for the purposes of those subsections be taken into account as if, in the year in which it was made, it was made later than any transfer of value which was not a potentially exempt transfer.

(4) In this section 'year' means period of twelve months ending with 5th April.

(5) Section 3(4) above shall not apply for the purposes of this section (but without prejudice to sections 57 and 94(5) below).

20   Small gifts

(1) Transfers of value made by a transferor in any one year by outright gifts to any one person are exempt if the values transferred by them (calculated as values on which no tax is chargeable) do not exceed £250.

(2) In this section 'year' means period of twelve months ending with 5th April.

(3) Section 3(4) above shall not apply for the purposes of this section.

21   Normal expenditure out of income

(1) A transfer of value is an exempt transfer if, or to the extent that, it is shown –

(a) that it was made as part of the normal expenditure of the transferor, and

(b) that (taking one year with another) it was made out of his income, and

(c) that, after allowing for all transfers of value forming part of his normal expenditure, the transferor was left with sufficient income to maintain his usual standard of living.

(2) A payment of a premium on a policy of insurance on the transferor's life, or a gift of money or money's worth applied, directly or indirectly, in payment of such a premium, shall not for the purposes of this section be regarded as part of his normal expenditure if, when the insurance was made or at any earlier or later time, an annuity was purchased on his life, unless it is shown that –

(a) the purchase of the annuity, and

(b) the making or any variation of the insurance or of any prior insurance for which the first-mentioned insurance was directly or indirectly substituted,

were not associated operations.

(3) So much of a purchased life annuity (within the meaning of section 657 of the Taxes Act 1988) as is, for the purposes of the provisions of the Tax Acts relating to income tax on annuities and other annual payments, treated as the capital element contained in the annuity, shall not be regarded as part of the transferor's income for the purposes of this section.

(4) Subsection (3) above shall not apply to annuities purchased before 13th November 1974.

(5) Section 3(4) above shall not apply for the purposes of this section.

22   Gifts in consideration of marriage

(1) Transfers of value made by gifts in consideration of marriage are exempt to the extent that the values transferred by such transfers made by any one transferor in respect of any one marriage (calculated as value son which no tax is chargeable) do not exceed –

(a) in the case of gifts within subsection (2) below by a parent of a party to the marriage, £5,000,

(b) in the case of other gifts within subsection (2) below, £2,500, and

(c) in any other case £1,000;

any excess being attributed to the transfers in proportion to the values transferred.

(2) A gift is within this subsection if –

(a) it is an outright gift to a child or remoter descendant of the transferor or

(b) the transferor is a parent or remoter ancestor of either party to the marriage, and either the gift is an outright gift to the other party to the marriage or the property comprised in the gift is settled by the gift, or

(c) the transferor is a party to the marriage, and either the gift is an outright gift to the other party to the marriage or the property comprised in the gift is settled by the gift;

and in this section 'child' includes an illegitimate child, an adopted child and a step-child and 'parent', 'descendant' and 'ancestor' shall be construed accordingly.

(3) A disposition which is an outright gift shall not be treated for the purposes of this section as a gift made in consideration of marriage if, or in so far as, it is a gift to a person other than a party to the marriage.

(4) A disposition which is not an outright gift shall not be treated for the purposes of this section as a gift made in consideration of marriage if the persons who are or may become entitled to any benefit under the disposition include any person other than –

(a) the parties to the marriage, issue of the marriage, or a wife or husband of any such issue;

(b) persons becoming entitled on the failure of trusts for any such issue under which trust property would (subject only to any power of appointment to a person falling within paragraph (a) or (c) of this subsection) vest indefeasibly on the attainment of a specified age or either on the attainment of such an age or on some earlier event, or persons becoming entitled (subject as aforesaid) on the failure of any limitation in tail;

(c) a subsequent wife or husband of a party to the marriage, or any issue, or the wife or husband of any issue, of a subsequent marriage of either party;

(d) persons becoming entitled under such trusts, subsisting under the law of England and Wales ..., as are specified in section 33(1) of the Trustee Act 1925 ... (protective trusts), the principal beneficiary being a person falling within paragraph (a) or (c) of this subsection, or under such trusts, modified by the enlargement, as respects any period during which there is no such issue as aforesaid in existence, of the class of potential beneficiaries specified in paragraph (ii) of the said section 33(1) ...

(f) as respects a reasonable amount of remuneration, the trustees of the settlement.

(5) References in subsection (4) above to issue shall apply as if any person legitimated by a marriage, or adopted by the husband and wife jointly, were included among the issue of that marriage.

(6) Section 3(4) above shall not apply for the purposes of this section (but without prejudice to section 57 below).

23 Gifts to charities

(1) Transfers of value are exempt to the extent that the values transferred by them are attributable to property which is given to charities.

(2) Subsection (1) above shall not apply in relation to property if the testamentary or other disposition by which it is given –

> (a) takes effect on the termination after the transfer of value of any interest or period, or
>
> (b) depends on a condition which is not satisfied within twelve months after the transfer, or
>
> (c) is defeasible;

and for this purpose any disposition which has not been defeated at a time twelve months after the transfer of value and is not defeasible after that time shall be treated as not being defeasible (whether or not it was capable of being defeated before that time).

(3) Subsection (1) above shall not apply in relation to property which is an interest in other property if –

> (a) that interest is less than the donor's, or
>
> (b) the property is given for a limited period;

and for this purpose any question whether an interest is less than the donor's shall be decided as at a time twelve months after the transfer of value.

(4) Subsection (1) above shall not apply in relation to any property if –

> (a) the property is land or a building and is given subject to an interest reserved or created by the donor which entitles him, his spouse or a person connected with him to possession of, or to occupy, the whole or any part of the land or building rent-free or at a rent less than might be expected to be obtained in a transaction at arm's length between persons not connected with each other, or
>
> (b) the property is not land or a building and is given subject to an interest reserved or created by the donor other than –

(i) an interest created by him for full consideration in money or money's worth, or

(ii) an interest which does not substantially affect the enjoyment of the property by the person or body to whom it is given;

and for this purpose any question whether property is given subject to an interest shall be decided as at a time twelve months after the transfer of value.

(5) Subsection (1) above shall not apply in relation to property if it or any part of it may become applicable for purposes other than charitable purposes or those of a body mentioned in section 24 or 25 below or, where it is land, of a body mentioned in section 24A below.

(6) For the purposes of this section property is given to charities if it becomes the property of charities or is held on trust for charitable purposes only, and 'donor' shall be construed accordingly.

24   Gifts to political parties

(1) Transfers of value are exempt to the extent that the values transferred by them –

(a) are attributable to property which becomes the property of a political party qualifying for exemption under this section.

(2) A political party qualifies for exemption under this section if, at the last general election preceding the transfer of value, –

(a) two members of that party were elected to the House of Commons, or

(b) one member of that party was elected to the House of Commons and not less than 150,000 votes were given to candidates who were members of that party.

(3) Subsections (2) to (5) of section 23 above shall apply in relation to subsection (1) above as they apply in relation to section 23(1).

(4) For the purposes of section 23(2) to (5) as they apply by virtue of subsection (3) above property is given to any person or body if it becomes the property of or is held on trust for that person or body, and 'donor' shall be construed accordingly.

24A Gifts to housing associations

(1) A transfer of value is exempt to the extent that the value transferred by

it is attributable to land in the United Kingdom given to a body falling within subsection (2) below.

(2) A body falls within this subsection if it is –

(a) registered social landlord within the meaning of Part I of the Housing Act 1996;

(b) a registered housing association within the meaning of the Housing Associations Act 1985; ...

(3) Subsections (2) to (5) of section 23 and subsection (4) of section 24 above shall apply in relation to subsection (1) above as they apply in relation to section 24(1).

25   Gifts for national purposes, etc

(1) A transfer of value is an exempt transfer to the extent that the value transferred by it is attributable to property which becomes the property of a body within Schedule 3 to this Act.

(2) Subsections (2) to (5) of section 23 and subsection (4) of section 24 above shall apply in relation to subsection (1) above as they apply in relation to section 24(1), except that section 23(3) shall not prevent subsection (1) above from applying in relation to property consisting of the benefit of an agreement restricting the use of land.

26A Potentially exempt transfer of property subsequently held for national purposes, etc

A potentially exempt transfer which would (apart from this section) have proved to be a chargeable transfer shall be an exempt transfer to the extent that the value transferred by it is attributable to property which has been or could be designated under section 31(1) below and which, during the period beginning with the date of the transfer and ending with the death of the transferor, –

(a) has been disposed of by sale by private treaty to a body mentioned in Schedule 3 to this Act or has been disposed of to such a body otherwise than by sale, or

(b) has been disposed of in pursuance of section 230 below.

27   Maintenance funds for historic buildings, etc

(1) Subject to subsection (1A) below, a transfer of value is an exempt transfer

to the extent that the value transferred by it is attributable to property which by virtue of the transfer becomes comprised in a settlement and in respect of which –

(a) a direction under paragraph 1 of Schedule 4 to this Act has effect at the time of the transfer, or

(b) such a direction is given after the time of the transfer.

(1A) Subsection (1) above does not apply in the case of a direction given after the time of the transfer unless the claim for the direction (if it is not made before that time) is made no more than two years after the date of that transfer, or within such longer period as the Board may allow.

(2) Subsections (2) and (3) of section 23 and subsection (4) of section 24 above shall apply in relation to subsection (1) above as they apply in relation to section 24(1).

CHAPTER II

CONDITIONAL EXEMPTION

30 Conditionally exempt transfers

(1) A transfer of value is an exempt transfer to the extent that the value transferred by it is attributable to property –

(a) which, on a claim made for the purpose, is designated by the Treasury under section 31 below, and

(b) with respect to which the requisite undertaking described in that section is given by such person as the Treasury think appropriate in the circumstances of the case or (where the property is an area of land within subsection (1)(d) of that section) with respect to which the requisite undertakings described in that section are given by such person or persons as the Treasury think appropriate in the circumstances of the case.

(2) A transfer of value exempt with respect to any property under this section or under section 76 of the Finance Act 1976 [repealed] is referred to in this Act as a conditionally exempt transfer of that property.

(3) Subsection (1) above shall not apply to a transfer of value other than one which under section 4 above a person makes on his death unless –

(a) the transferor or his spouse, or the transferor and his spouse between them, have been beneficially entitled to the property throughout the six years ending with the transfer, or

(b) the transferor acquired the property on a death on the occasion of which there was a transfer of value under section 4 above which was itself a conditionally exempt transfer of the property.

(3A) The provisions of this section shall be disregarded in determining under section 3A above whether a transfer of value is a potentially exempt transfer.

(3B) No claim may be made under subsection (1) above with respect to a potentially exempt transfer until the transferor has died.

(3BA) A claim under subsection (1) above must be made no more than two years after the date of the transfer of value to which it relates or, in the case of a claim with respect to a potentially exempt transfer, the date of the death, or (in either case) within such longer period as the Board may allow.

(3C) Subsection (1) above shall not apply to a potentially exempt transfer to the extent that the value transferred by it is attributable to property which has been disposed of by sale during the period beginning with the date of the transfer and ending with the death of the transferor.

(4) Subsection (1) above does not apply to the transfer of value to the extent to which it is an exempt transfer under section 18 or 23 above.

31 Designation and undertakings

(1) The Treasury may designate under this section –

(a) any relevant object which appears to the Board to be pre-eminent for its national, scientific, historic or artistic interest;

(aa) any collection or group of relevant objects which, taken as a whole, appears to the Board to be pre-eminent for its national, scientific, historic or artistic interest;

(b) any land which in the opinion of the Treasury is of outstanding scenic or historic or scientific interest;

(c) any building for the preservation of which special steps should in the opinion of the Treasury be taken by reason of its outstanding historic or architectural interest;

(d) any area of land which in the opinion of the Treasury is essential for the protection of the character and amenities of such a building as is mentioned in paragraph (c) above;

(e) any object which in the opinion of the Treasury is historically associated with such a building as is mentioned in paragraph (c) above.

(1A) Where the transfer of value in relation to which the claim for designation is made is a potentially exempt transfer which (apart from section 30 above) has proved to be a chargeable transfer, the question whether any property is appropriate for designation under this section shall be determined by reference to circumstances existing after the death of the transferor.

(2) In the case of property within subsection (1)(a) or (aa) above, the requisite understanding is that, until the person beneficially entitled to the property dies or the property is disposed of, whether by sale or gift or otherwise –

(a) the property will be kept permanently in the United Kingdom and will not leave it temporarily except for a purpose and a period approved by the Treasury and

(b) such steps as are agreed between the Treasury and the person giving the undertaking, and are set out in it, will be taken for the preservation of the property and for securing reasonable access to the public.

(3) If it appears to the Treasury, on a claim made for the purpose, that any documents which are designated or to be designated under subsection (1)(a) or (aa) above contain information which for personal or other reasons ought to be treated as confidential, they may exclude those documents, either altogether or to such extent as they think fit, from so much of an undertaking given or to be given under subsection (2)(b) above as relates to public access.

(4) In the case of other property within subsection (1) above, the requisite undertaking is that, until the person beneficially entitled to the property dies or the property is disposed of, whether by sale or gift or otherwise, such steps as are agreed between the Treasury and the person giving the undertaking, and are set out in it, will be taken –

(a) in the case of land falling within subsection (1)(b) above, for the maintenance of the land and the preservation of its character, and

(b) in the case of any other property, for the maintenance, repair and preservation of the property and, if it is an object falling within subsection (1)(e) above, for keeping it associated with the building concerned;

and for securing reasonable access to the public.

(4A) In the case of an area of land within subsection (1)(d) above (relevant land) there is an additional requisite undertaking, which is that, until the person beneficially entitled to property falling within subsection (4C) below dies, or it is disposed of, whether by sale or gift or otherwise, specified steps will be taken for its maintenance, repair and preservation and for securing reasonable access to the public; and 'specified steps' means such steps as are agreed between the Treasury and the person giving the undertaking, and are set out in it.

(4B) Where different persons are entitled (either beneficially or otherwise) to different properties falling within subsection (4C) below, subsection (4A) above shall have effect to require separate undertakings as to the maintenance, repair, preservation and access of each of the properties to be given by such persons as the Treasury think appropriate in the circumstances of the case.

(4C) The following property falls within this subsection –

(a) the building for the protection of whose character and amenities the relevant land is in the opinion of the Treasury essential;

(b) any other area (or areas) of land which, in relation to the building, falls (or fall) within subsection (1)(d) above and which either lies (or lie) between the relevant land and the building or is (or are) in the opinion of the Treasury physically closely connected with the relevant land or the building.

(4D) Where subsection (4A) above requires an undertaking for the maintenance, repair, preservation and access of property, such an undertaking is required notwithstanding that some other undertaking for its maintenance, repair, preservation and access is effective.

(4E) Any undertaking given in pursuance of subsection (4A) above is for the purposes of this Act given with respect to the relevant land.

(4F) It is for the person seeking the designation of relevant land to secure that any undertaking required under subsection (4A) above is given.

(4FA) For the purposes of this section, the steps agreed for securing reasonable access to the public must ensure that the access that is secured is not confined to access only where a prior appointment has been made.

(4FB) Subject to subsection (3) above, where the steps that may be set out in any undertaking include steps for securing reasonable access to the public to any property, the steps that may be agreed and set out in that undertaking may also include steps involving the publication of –

(a) the terms of any undertaking given or to be given for any of the purposes of this Act with respect to the property; or

(b) any other information relating to the property which (apart from this subsection) would fall to be treated as confidential;

and references in this Act to an undertaking for access to any property shall be construed as including references to so much of any undertaking as provides for the taking of steps involving any such publication.

(4G) In a case where –

(a) the transfer of value in question is a potentially exempt transfer which (apart from section 30 above) has proved to be a chargeable transfer, and

(b) at the time of the transferor's death an undertaking by such a person as is mentioned in section 30(1)(b) above given under paragraph 3(3) of Schedule 4 to this Act or under section 258 of the 1992 Act is in force with respect to any property to which the value transferred by the transfer is attributable,

that undertaking shall be treated for the purposes of this Chapter as an undertaking given under section 30 above.

(5) In this section –

'national interest' includes interest within any part of the United Kingdom; and 'relevant object' means –

(a) a picture, print, book, manuscript, work of art of scientific object, or

(b) anything not falling within paragraph (a) above that does not yield income;

and in determining under subsection (1)(a) or (aa) above whether an object or a collection or group of objects is pre-eminent, regard shall be had to any significant association of the object, collection or group with a particular place.

32   Chargeable events

(1) Where there has been a conditionally exempt transfer of any property, tax shall be charged under this section on the first occurrence after the transfer (or, if the transfer was a potentially exempt transfer, after the death of the transferor) of an event which under this section is a chargeable event with respect to the property.

(2) If the Treasury are satisfied that at any time an undertaking given with respect to the property under section 30 above or subsection (5AA) below has not been observed in a material respect, the failure to observe the undertaking is a chargeable event with respect to the property.

(3) If –

(a) the person beneficially entitled to the property dies, or

(b) the property is disposed of, whether by sale or gift or otherwise,

the death or disposal is, subject to subsections (4) and (5) below, a chargeable event with respect to the property.

(4) A death or disposal is not a chargeable event with respect to any property if the personal representatives of the deceased (or, in the case of settled property, the trustees or the person next entitled) within three years of the death make or, as the case may be, the disposal is –

(a) a disposal of the property by sale by private treaty to a body mentioned in Schedule 3 to this Act, or a disposal of it to such a body otherwise than by sale, or

(b) a disposal in pursuance of section 230 below,

and a death or disposal of the property after such a disposal as is mentioned in paragraph (a) or (b) above is not a chargeable event with respect to the property unless there has again been a conditionally exempt transfer of it after that disposal.

(5) A death or disposal otherwise than by sale is not a chargeable event with respect to any property if –

(a) the transfer of value made on the death or the disposal of itself a conditionally exempt transfer of the property, or

(b) the condition specified in subsection (5AA) below is satisfied with respect to the property.

(5AA) The condition referred to in subsection (5)(b) above is satisfied if –

(a) the requisite undertaking described in section 31 above is given with respect to the property by such person as the Board think appropriate in the circumstances of the case, or

(b) (where the property is an area of land within section 31(1)(d) above) the requisite undertakings described in that section are given with respect to the property by such person or persons as the Board think appropriate in the circumstances of the case.

(5A) This section does not apply where section 32A below applies.

32A Associated properties

(1) For the purposes of this section the following properties are associated with each other, namely, a building falling within section 31(1)(c) above and (to the extent that any of the following exists) an area or areas of land falling within section 31(1)(d) above in relation to the building and an object

or objects falling within section 31(1)(e) above in relation to the building; and this section applies where there are such properties, which are referred to as associated properties.

(2) Where there has been a conditionally exempt transfer of any property (or part), tax shall be charged under this section in respect of that property (or part) on the first occurrence after the transfer (or, if the transfer was a potentially exempt transfer, after the death of the transferor) of an event which under this section is a chargeable event with respect to that property (or part).

(3) If the Treasury are satisfied that at any time an undertaking given under section 30 above or this section for the maintenance, repair, preservation, access or keeping of any of the associated properties has not been observed in a material respect, then (subject to subsection (10) below) the failure to observe the undertaking is a chargeable event with respect to the whole of each of the associated properties of which there has been a conditionally exempt transfer.

(4) If –

(a) the person beneficially entitled to property dies, or

(b) property (or part of it) is disposed of, whether by sale or gift or otherwise,

then, if the property is one of the associated properties and an undertaking for its maintenance, repair, preservation, access or keeping has been given under section 30 above or this section, the death or disposal is (subject to subsections (5) to (10) below) a chargeable event with respect to the whole of each of the associated properties of which there has been a conditionally exempt transfer.

(5) Subject to subsection (6) below, the death of a person beneficially entitled to property, or the disposal of property (or part), is not a chargeable event if the personal representatives of the deceased (or, in the case of settled property, the trustees or the person next entitled) within three years of the death make or, as the case may be, the disposal is –

(a) a disposal of the property (or part) concerned by sale by private treaty to a body mentioned in Schedule 3 to this Act, or to such a body otherwise than by sale, or

(b) a disposal of the property (or part) concerned in pursuance of section 230 below.

(6) Where a disposal mentioned in subsection (5)(a) or (b) above is a part disposal, that subsection does not make the event non-chargeable with respect to property other than that disposed of unless –

(a) the requisite undertaking described in section 31 above is given with respect to the property (or part) not disposed of by such person as the Board think appropriate in the circumstances of the case, or

(b) (where any of the property or part not disposed of is an area of land within section 31(1)(d) above) the requisite undertakings described in that section are given with respect to that property (or that part) by such person or persons as the Board think appropriate in the circumstances of the case;

and in this subsection 'part disposal' means a disposal of property which does not consist of or include the whole of each property which is one of the associated properties and of which there has been a conditionally exempt transfer.

(7) Where, after a relevant disposal (that is, a disposal mentioned in subsection (5)(a) or (b) above made in circumstances where that subsection applies), a person beneficially entitled to the property (or part) concerned dies or the property (or part) concerned is disposed of, the death or disposal is not a chargeable event with respect to the property (or part) concerned unless there has again been a conditionally exempt transfer of the property (or part) concerned after the relevant disposal.

(8) The death of a person beneficially entitled to property, or the disposal of property (or part) otherwise than by sale, is not a chargeable event if –

(a) the transfer of value made on the death or the disposal is itself a conditionally exempt transfer of the property (or part) concerned, or

(b) the condition specified in subsection (8A) below is satisfied with respect to the property (or part) concerned.

(8A) The condition referred to in subsection (8)(b) above is satisfied if –

(a) the requisite undertaking described in section 31 above is given with respect to the property (or part) by such person as the Board think appropriate in the circumstances of the case, or

(b) (where any of the property or part is an area of land within section 31(1)(d) above) the requisite undertakings described in that section are given with respect to the property (or part) by such person or persons as the Board think appropriate in the circumstances of the case.

(9) If the whole or part of any property is disposed of by sale and –

(a) the requisite undertaking described in section 31 above is given with respect to the property (or part) by such person as the Board think appropriate in the circumstances of the case, or

(b) (where any property or part is an area of land within section 31(1)(d) above) the requisite undertakings described in that section are given with respect to the property (or part) by such person or persons as the Board think appropriate in the circumstances of the case,

the disposal is a chargeable event only with respect to the whole or part actually disposed of (if it is a chargeable event with respect to such whole or part apart from this subsection).

(10) If –

(a) the Treasury are satisfied that there has been a failure to observe, as to one of the associated properties or part of it, an undertaking for the property's maintenance, repair, preser-vation, access or keeping, or

(b) there is a disposal of one of the associated properties or part of it,

and it appears to the Treasury that the entity consisting of the associated properties has not been materially affected by the failure or disposal, they may direct that it shall be a chargeable event only with respect to the property or part as to which there has been a failure or disposal (if it is a chargeable event with respect to that property or part apart from this subsection).

35A Variation of undertakings

(1) An undertaking given under section 30, 32 or 32A above or paragraph 5 of Schedule 5 to this Act may be varied from time to time by agreement between the Board and the person bound by the undertaking.

(2) Where a Special Commissioner is satisfied that –

(a) the Board have made a proposal for the variation of such an undertaking to the person bound by the undertaking,

(b) that person has failed to agree to the proposed variation within six months after the date on which the proposal was made, and

(c) it is just and reasonable, in all the circumstances, to require the proposed variation to be made,

the Commissioner may direct that the undertaking is to have effect from a date specified by him as if the proposed variation had been agreed to by the person bound by the undertaking. ...

CHAPTER III

ALLOCATION OF EXEMPTIONS

36 Preliminary

Where any one or more of sections 18, 23 to 27 and 30 above apply in relation to a transfer of value but the transfer is not wholly exempt –

(a) any question as to the extent to which it is exempt or, where it is exempt up to a limit, how an excess over the limit is to be attributed to the gifts concerned shall be determined in accordance with sections 37 to 40 below; and

(b) section 41 below shall have effect as respects the burden of tax.

37 Abatement of gifts

(1) Where a gift would be abated owing to an insufficiency of assets and without regard to any tax chargeable, the gift shall be treated for the purposes of the following provisions of this Chapter as so abated.

(2) Where the value attributable, in accordance with section 38 below, to specific gifts exceeds the value transferred the gifts shall be treated as reduced to the extent necessary to reduce their value to that of the value transferred; and the reduction shall be made in the order in which, under the terms of the relevant disposition or any rule of law, it would fall to be made on a distribution of assets.

38 Attribution of value to specific gifts

(1) Such part of the value transferred shall be attributable to specific gifts as corresponds to the value of the gifts; but if or to the extent that the gifts –

(a) are not gifts with respect to which the transfer is exempt or are outside the limit up to which the transfer is exempt, and

(b) do not bear their own tax,

the amount corresponding to the value of the gifts shall be taken to be the amount arrived at in accordance with subsections (3) to (5) below.

(2) Where any question arises as to which of two or more specific gifts are outside the limit up to which a transfer is exempt or as to the extent to which a specific gift is outside that limit –

(a) the excess shall be attributed to gifts not bearing their own tax before being attributed to gifts bearing their own tax; and

(b) subject to paragraph (a) above, the excess shall be attributed to gifts in proportion to their values.

(3) Where the only gifts with respect to which the transfer is or might be chargeable are specific gifts which do not bear their own tax, the amount referred to in subsection (1) above is the aggregate of –

(a) the sum of the value of those gifts; and

(b) the amount of tax which would be chargeable if the value transferred equalled that aggregate.

(4) Where the specific gifts not bearing their own tax are not the only gifts with respect to which the transfer is or might be chargeable, the amount referred to in subsection (1) above is such amount as, after deduction of tax at the assumed rate specified in subsection (5) below, would be equal to the sum of the value of those gifts.

(5) For the purposes of subsection (4) above –

(a) the assumed rate is the rate found by dividing the assumed amount of tax by that part of the value transferred with respect to which the transfer would be chargeable on the hypothesis that –

(i) the amount corresponding to the value of specific gifts not bearing their own tax is equal to the aggregate referred to in subsection (3) above, and

(ii) the parts of the value transferred attributable to specific gifts and to gifts of residue or shares in residue are determined accordingly; and

(b) the assumed amount of tax is the amount that would be charged on the value transferred on the hypothesis mentioned in paragraph (a) above.

(6) For the purposes of this section, any liability of the transferor which is not to be taken into account under section 5(5) above or by virtue of section 103 of the Finance Act 1986 shall be treated as a specific gift and, to the extent that any liability of the transferor is abated under the said section 103, that liability shall be treated as a specific gift.

39 Attribution of value to residuary gifts

Such part only of the value transferred shall be attributed to gifts of residue or shares in residue as is not attributed under section 38 above to specific gifts.

39A Operation of sections 38 and 39 in cases of business or agricultural relief

(1) Where any part of the value transferred by a transfer of value is attributable to –

(a) the value of relevant business property, or

(b) the agricultural value of agricultural property,

then, for the purpose of attributing the value transferred (as reduced in accordance with section 104 or 116 below), to specific gifts and gifts of residue or shares of residue, sections 38 and 39 above shall have effect subject to the following provisions of this section.

(2) The value of any specific gifts of relevant business property or agricultural property shall be taken to be their value as reduced in accordance with section 104 or 116 below.

(3) The value of any specific gifts not falling within subsection (2) above shall be taken to be the appropriate fraction of their value.

(4) In subsection (3) above 'the appropriate fraction' means a fraction of which –

(a) the numerator is the difference between the value transferred and the value, reduced as mentioned in subsection (2) above, of any gifts falling within that subsection, and

(b) the denominator is the difference between the unreduced value transferred and the value, before the reduction mentioned in subsection (2) above, of any gifts falling within that subsection;

and in paragraph (b) above 'the unreduced value transferred' means the amount which would be the value transferred by the transfer but for the reduction required by sections 104 and 116 below.

(5) If or to the extent that specific gifts fall within paragraphs (a) and (b) of subsection (1) of section 38 above, the amount corresponding to the value of the gifts shall be arrived at in accordance with subsections (3) to (5) of that section by reference to their value reduced as mentioned in subsection (2) or, as the case may be, subsection (3) of this section.

(6) For the purposes of this section the value of a specific gift of relevant business property or agricultural property does not include the value of any other gift payable out of that property; and that other gift shall not itself be treated as a specific gift of relevant business property or agricultural property.

(7) In this section –

'agricultural property' and 'the agricultural value of agricultural property' have the same meaning as in Chapter II of Part V of this Act; and

'relevant business property' has the same meaning as in Chapter I of that Part.

40   Gifts made separately out of different funds

Where gifts taking effect on a transfer of value take effect separately out of different funds the preceding provisions of this Chapter shall be applied separately to the gifts taking effect out of each of those funds, with the necessary adjustments of values and amounts referred to in those provisions.

41   Burden of tax

Notwithstanding the terms of any disposition –

(a) none of the tax on the value transferred shall fall on any specific gift if or to the extent that the transfer is exempt with respect to the gift, and

(b) none of the tax attributable to the value of the property comprised in residue shall fall on any gift of a share of residue if or to the extent that the transfer is exempt with respect to the gift.

42   Supplementary

(1) In this Chapter –

'gift', in relation to any transfer of value, means the benefit of any disposition or rule of law by which, on the making of the transfer, any property becomes (or would but for any abatement become) the property of any person or applicable for any purpose;

'given' shall be construed accordingly;

'specific gift' means any gift other than a gift of residue or of a share in residue.

(2) For the purposes of this Chapter a gift bears its own tax if the tax attributable to it falls on the person who becomes entitled to the property given or (as the case may be) is payable out of property applicable for the purposes for which the property given becomes applicable.

(3) Where –

(a) the whole or part of the value transferred by a transfer of value is attributable to property which is the subject of two or more gifts, and

(b) the aggregate of the values of the property given by each of those gifts is less than the value transferred or, as the case may be, that part of it,

then for the purposes of this Chapter (and notwithstanding the definition of a gift in subsection (1) above) the value of each gift shall be taken to be the relevant proportion of the value transferred or, as the case may be, that part of it; and the relevant proportion in relation to any gift is the proportion which the value of the property given by it bears to the said aggregate. ...

PART III

SETTLED PROPERTY

CHAPTER I

PRELIMINARY

43 Settlement and related expressions

(1) The following provisions of this section apply for determining what is to be taken for the purposes of this Act to be a settlement, and what property is, accordingly, referred to as property comprised in a settlement or as settled property.

(2) 'Settlement' means any disposition or dispositions of property, whether effected by instrument, by parol or by operation of law, or partly in one way and partly in another whereby the property is for the time being –

(a) held in trust for persons in succession or for any person subject to a contingency, or

(b) held by trustees on trust to accumulate the whole or part of any income of the property or with power to make payments out of that income at the discretion of the trustees or some other person, with or without power to accumulate surplus income, or

(c) charged or burdened (otherwise than for full consideration in money or money's worth paid for his own use or benefit to the person making the disposition) with the payment of any annuity or other periodical payment payable for a life or any other limited or terminable period,

or would be so held or charged or burdened if the disposition or dispositions were regulated by the law of any part of the United Kingdom; or whereby, under the law of any other country, the administration of the property is for the time being governed by the provisions equivalent in effect to those which would apply if the property were so held, charged or burdened.

(3) A lease of property which is for life or lives, or for a period ascertainable only by reference to a death, or which is terminable on, or at a date ascertainable only by reference to, a death, shall be treated as a settlement and the property as settled property, unless the lease was granted for full consideration in money or money's worth; and where a lease not granted as a lease at a rack rent is at any time to become a lease at an increased rent it shall be treated as terminable at that time. ...

44   Settlor

(1) In this Act 'settlor', in relation to a settlement, includes any person by whom the settlement was made directly or indirectly, and in particular (but without prejudice to the generality of the preceding words) includes any person who has provided funds directly or indirectly for the purpose of or in connection with the settlement or has made with any other person a reciprocal arrangement for that other person to make the settlement.

(2) Where more than one person is a settlor in relation to a settlement and the circumstances so require, this Part of this Act (except section 48(4) to (6)) shall have effect in relation to it as if the settled property were comprised in separate settlements.

45   Trustee

In this Act 'trustee', in relation to a settlement in relation to which there would be no trustee apart from this section means any person in whom the settled property or its management is for the time being vested.

47   Reversionary interest

In this Act 'reversionary interest' means a future interest under a settlement, whether it is vested or contingent (including an interest expectant on the termination of an interest in possession which, by virtue of section 50 below, is treated as subsisting in part of any property) and in relation to Scotland includes an interest in the fee of property subject to a proper liferent.

47A Settlement power

In this Act 'settlement power' means any power over, or exercisable (whether directly or indirectly) in relation to, settled property or a settlement.

48   Excluded property

(1) A reversionary interest is excluded property unless –

(a) it has at any time been acquired (whether by the person entitled to it or by a person previously entitled to it) for a consideration in money or money's worth, or

(b) it is one to which either the settlor or his spouse is or has been beneficially entitled, or

(c) it is the interest expectant on the determination of a lease treated as a settlement by virtue of section 43(3) above.

(2) In relation to a reversionary interest under a settlement made before 16th April 1976, subsection (1) above shall have effect with the omission of paragraph (b); and, if the person entitled to a reversionary interest under a settlement made on or after 16th April 1976 acquired the interest before 10th March 1981, that subsection shall have effect with the omission of the words 'or has been' in paragraph (b).

(3) Where property comprised in a settlement is situated outside the United Kingdom –

(a) the property (but not a reversionary interest in the property) is excluded property unless the settlor was domicile din the United Kingdom at the time the settlement was made, and

(b) section 6(1) above applies to a reversionary interest in the property but does not otherwise apply in relation to the property.

(3A) Where property comprised in a settlement is a holding in an authorised unit trust or a share in an open-ended investment company –

(a) the property (but not a reversionary interest in the property) is excluded property unless the settlor was domiciled in the United Kingdom at the time the settlement was made, and

(b) section 6(1A) above applies to a reversionary interest in the property but does not otherwise apply in relation to the property.

(4) Where securities issued by the Treasury subject to a condition of the kind mentioned in subsection (2) of section 6 above are comprised in a settlement, that subsection shall not apply to them; but the securities are excluded property if –

(a) a person of a description specified in the condition in question is entitled to a qualifying interest in possession in them, or

(b) no qualifying interest in possession subsists in them but it is shown that all known persons for whose benefit the settled property or income from it has been or might be applied, or who are or might become beneficially entitled to an interest in possession in it, are persons of a description specified in the condition in question.

(5) Where –

(a) property ceased to be comprised in one settlement before 10th December 1981 and after 19th April 1978 and, by the same disposition, became comprised in another settlement, or

(b) property ceased to be comprised in one settlement after 9th December 1981 and became comprised in another without any person having in the meantime become beneficially entitled to the property (and not merely to an interest in possession in the property),

subsection (4)(b) above shall, in its application to the second settlement, be construed as requiring the matters there stated to be shown both in relation to the property comprised in that settlement and in relation to the property that was comprised in the first settlement.

(6) Subsection (5) above shall not apply where a reversionary interest in the property expectant on the termination of a qualifying interest in possession subsisting under the first settlement was settled on the trusts of the second settlement before 10th December 1981.

(7) In this section 'qualifying interest in possession' has the same meaning as in Chapter III of this Part of this Act.

CHAPTER II

INTERESTS IN POSSESSION, REVERSIONARY INTERESTS AND SETTLEMENT POWERS

49 Treatment of interests in possession

(1) A person beneficially entitled to an interest in possession in settled property shall be treated for the purposes of this Act as beneficially entitled to the property in which the interest subsists.

(2) Where a person becomes entitled to an interest in possession in settled property as a result of a disposition for a consideration in money or money's worth, any question whether and to what extent the giving of the

consideration is a transfer of value or chargeable transfer shall be determined without regard to subsection (1) above.

50 Interests in part, etc

(1) Where the person referred to in section 49(1) above is entitled to part only of the income (if any) of the property, the interest shall be taken to subsist in such part only of the property as bears to the whole the same proportion as the part of the income to which he is entitled bears to the whole of the income.

(2) Where the part of the income of any property to which a person is entitled is a specified amount (or the whole less a specified amount) in any period, his interest in the property shall be taken, subject to subsection (3) below, to subsist in such part (or in the whole less such part) of the property as produces that amount in that period.

(3) The Treasury may from time to time by order prescribe a higher and a lower rate for the purposes of this section; and where tax is chargeable in accordance with subsection (2) above by reference to the value of the part of a property which produces a specified amount or by reference to the value of the remainder (but not where chargeable transfers are made simultaneously and tax is chargeable by reference to the value of that part as well as by reference to he value of the remainder) the value of the part producing that specified amount –

> (a) shall, if tax is chargeable by reference to the value of that part, be taken to be not less than it would be if the property produced income at the higher rate so prescribed, and
> (b) shall, if tax is chargeable by reference to the value of the remainder, be taken to be not more than it would be if the property produced income at the lower rate so prescribed;

but the value to be taken by virtue of paragraph (a) above as the value of part of a property shall not exceed the value of the whole of the property.

(4) The power to make orders under subsection (3) above shall be exercisable by statutory instrument, which shall be subject to annulment in pursuance of a resolution of the House of Commons.

(5) Where the person referred to in section 49(1) above is not entitled to any income of the property but is entitled, jointly or in common with one or more other persons, to the use and enjoyment of the property, his interest shall be taken to subsist in such part of the property as corresponds to the proportion which the annual value of his interest bears to the aggregate of the annual values of his interest and that or those of the other or others.

(6) Where, under section 43(3) above, a lease of property is to be treated as a settlement, the lessee's interest in the property shall be taken to subsist in the whole of the property less such part of it as corresponds to the proportion which the value of the lessor's interest (as determined under Part VI of this Act) bears to the value of the property.

51 Disposal of interest in possession

(1) Where a person beneficially entitled to an interest in possession in settled property disposes of his interest the disposal –

(a) is not a transfer of value, but

(b) shall be treated for the purposes of this Chapter as the coming to an end of his interest;

and tax shall be charged accordingly under section 52 below.

(2) Where a disposition satisfying the conditions of section 11 above is a disposal of an interest in possession in settled property, the interest shall not by virtue of subsection (1) above be treated as coming to an end.

(3) References in this section to any property or to an interest in any property include references to part of any property or interest.

52 Charge on termination of interest in possession

(1) Where at any time during the life of a person beneficially entitled to an interest in possession in settled property his interest comes to an end, tax shall be charged, subject to section 53 below, as if at that time he had made a transfer of value and the value transferred had been equal to the value of the property in which his interest subsisted.

(2) If the interest comes to an end by being disposed of by the person beneficially entitled to it and the disposal is for a consideration in money or money's worth, tax shall be chargeable under this section as if the value of the property in which the interest subsisted were reduced by the amount of the consideration; but in determining that amount the value of a reversionary interest in the property or of any interest in other property comprised in the same settlement shall be left out of account.

(3) Where a transaction is made between the trustees of the settlement and a person who is, or is connected with, –

(a) the person beneficially entitled to an interest in the property, or

(b) a person beneficially entitled to any other interest in that property or to any interest in any other property comprised in the settlement, or

(c) a person for whose benefit any of the settled property may be applied,

and, as a result of the transaction, the value of the first-mentioned property is less than it would be but for the transaction, a corresponding part of the interest shall be deemed for the purposes of this section to come to an end, unless the transaction is such that, were the trustees beneficially entitled to the settled property, it would not be a transfer of value.

(4) References in this section or section 53 below to any property or to an interest in any property include references to part of any property or interest; and –

(a) the tax chargeable under this section on the coming to an end of part of an interest shall be charged as if the value of the property (or part) in which the interest subsisted were a corresponding part of the whole; and

(b) if the value of the property (or part) to which or to an interest in which a person becomes entitled as mentioned in subsection (2) of section 53 below is less than the value on which tax would be chargeable apart from that subsection, tax shall be chargeable on a value equal to the difference.

53 Exceptions from charge under section 52

(1) Tax shall not be chargeable under section 52 above if the settled property is excluded property.

(2) Tax shall not be chargeable under section 52 above (except in the case mentioned in subsection (4)(b) of that section) if the person whose interest in the property comes to an end becomes on the same occasion beneficially entitled to the property or to another interest in possession in the property.

(3) Tax shall not be chargeable under section 52 above if the interest comes to an end during the settlor's life and on the same occasion the property in which the interest subsisted reverts to the settlor.

(4) Tax shall not be chargeable under section 52 above if on the occasion when the interest comes to an end –

(a) the settlor's spouse, or

(b) where the settlor has died less than two years earlier, the settlor's widow or widower,

becomes beneficially entitled to the settled property and is domiciled in the United Kingdom.

(5) Subsections (3) and (4) above shall not apply in any case where –

(a) the settlor or the spouse (or in a case within subsection (4)(b), the widow or widower) of the settlor had acquired a reversionary interest in the property for a consideration in money or money's worth, or

(b) their application depends upon a reversionary interest having been transferred into a settlement on or after 10th March 1981.

(6) For the purposes of subsection (5) above a person shall be treated as acquiring an interest for a consideration in money or money's worth if he becomes entitled to it as a result of transactions which include a disposition for such consideration (whether to him or another) of that interest or of other property. ...

54   Exceptions from charge on death

(1) Where a person is entitled to an interest in possession in settled property which on his death, but during the settlor's life, reverts to the settlor, the value of the settled property shall be left out of account in determining for the purposes of this Act the value of the deceased's estate immediately before his death.

(2) Where on the death of a person entitled to an interest in possession in settled property –

(a) the settlor's spouse, or

(b) if the settlor has died less than two years earlier, the settlor's widow or widower,

becomes beneficially entitled to the settled property and is domiciled in the United Kingdom, the value of the settled property shall be left out of account in determining for the purposes of this Act the value of the deceased's estate immediately before his death.

(3) Subsections (5) and (6) of section 53 above shall apply in relation to subsections (1) and (2) above as they apply in relation to section 53(3) and (4).

(4) For the purposes of this section, where it cannot be known which of two or more persons who have died survived the other or others they shall be assumed to have died at the same instant.

54A Special rate of charge where settled property affected by potentially exempt transfer

(1) If the circumstances fall within subsection (2) below, this section applies to any chargeable transfer made –

(a) under section 52 above, on the coming to an end of an interest in possession in settled property during the life of the person beneficially entitled to it, or

(b) on the death of a person beneficially entitled to an interest in possession in settled property;

and in the following provisions of this section the interest in possession mentioned in paragraph (a) or paragraph (b) above is referred as to 'the relevant interest'.

(2) The circumstances referred to in subsection (1) above are –

(a) that the whole or part of the value transferred by the transfer is attributable to property in which the relevant interest subsisted and which became settled property in which there subsisted an interest in possession (whether the relevant interest or any previous interest) on the making by the settlor of a potentially exempt transfer at any time on or after 17th March 1987 and within the period of seven years ending with the date of the chargeable transfer; and

(b) that the settlor is alive at the time when the relevant interest comes to an end; and

(c) that, on the coming to an end of the relevant interest, any of the property in which that interest subsisted becomes settled property in which no qualifying interest in possession (as defined in section 59 below) subsists, other than property to which section 71 below applies; and

(d) that, within six months of the coming to an end of the relevant interest, any of the property in which that interest subsisted has neither –

(i) become settled property in which a qualifying interest in possession subsists or to which section 71 below applies, nor

(ii) become property to which an individual is beneficially entitled.

(2) In the following provisions of this section 'the special rate property', in relation to a chargeable transfer to which this section applies, means the property in which the relevant interest subsisted or, in a case where –

(a) any part of that property does not fall within subsection (2)(a) above, or

(b) any part of that property does not become settled property of the kind mentioned in subsection (2)(c) above,

so much of that property as appears to the Board or, on appeal, to the Special Commissioners to be just and reasonable.

(4) Where this section applies to a chargeable transfer (in this section referred to as 'the relevant transfer'), the tax chargeable on the value transferred by the transfer shall be whichever is the greater of the tax that would have been chargeable apart from this section and the tax determined in accordance with subsection (5) below.

(5) The tax determined in accordance with this subsection is the aggregate of –

(a) the tax that would be chargeable on a chargeable transfer of the description specified in subsection (6) below, and

(b) so much (if any) of the tax that would, apart from this section, have been chargeable on the value transferred by the relevant transfer as is attributable to the value of property other than the special rate property.

(6) The chargeable transfer postulated in subsection (5)(a) above is one –

(a) the value transferred by which is equal to the value transferred by the relevant transfer or, where only part of that value is attributable to the special rate property, that part of that value;

(b) which is made at the time of the relevant transfer by a transferor who has in the preceding seven years made chargeable transfers having an aggregate value equal to the aggregate of the values transferred by any chargeable transfers made by the settlor in the period of seven years ending with the date of the potentially exempt transfer; and

(c) for which the applicable rate or rates are one-half of the rate or rates referred to in section 7(1) above.

(7) This section has settled subject to section 54B below.

54B Provisions supplementary to section 54A

(1) The death of the settlor, at any time after a chargeable transfer to which section 54A above applies, shall not increase the tax chargeable on the value transferred by the transfer unless, at the time of the transfer, the tax determined in accordance with subsection (5) of that section is greater than the tax that would be chargeable apart from that section.

(2) The death of the person who was beneficially entitled to the relevant interest, at any time after a chargeable transfer to which section 54A above

applies, shall not increase the tax chargeable on the value transferred by the transfer unless, at the time of the transfer, the tax that would be chargeable apart from that section is greater than the tax determined in accordance with subsection (5) of that section.

(3) Where the tax chargeable on the value transferred by a chargeable transfer to which section 54A above applies falls to be determined in accordance with subsection (5) of that section, the amount referred to in paragraph (a) of that subsection shall be treated for the purposes of this Act as tax attributable to the value of the property in which the relevant interest subsisted.

(4) Subsection (5) below shall apply if –

    (a) during the period of seven years preceding the date on which a chargeable transfer to which section 54A above applies ('the current transfer') is made, there has been another chargeable transfer to which that section applied, and

    (b) the person who is for the purposes of the current transfer the settlor mentioned in subsection (2)(a) of that section is the settlor for the purposes of the other transfer (whether or not the settlements are the same);

and in subsections (5) and (6) below the other transfer is referred to as the 'previous transfer'.

(5) Where this subsection applies, the appropriate amount in relation to the previous transfer (or, if there has been more than one previous transfer, the aggregate of the appropriate amounts in relation to each) shall, for the purposes of calculating the tax chargeable on the current transfer, be taken to be the value transferred by a chargeable transfer made by the settlor immediately before the potentially exempt transfer was made.

(6) In subsection (5) above 'the appropriate amount', in relation to a previous transfer, means so much of the value transferred by the previous transfer as was attributable to the value of property which was the special rate property in relation to that transfer.

(7) In this section –

    'the relevant interest' has the meaning given by subsection (1) of section 54A above; and

    'the special rate property' has the meaning given by subsection (3) of that section.

55 Reversionary interest acquired by beneficiary

(1) Notwithstanding section 5(1) above, where a person entitled to an interest (whether in possession or not) in any settled property acquires a reversionary interest expectant (whether immediately or not) on that interest, the reversionary interest is not part of his estate for the purposes of this Act

(2) Section 10(1) above shall not apply to a disposition by which a reversionary interest is acquired in the circumstances mentioned in subsection (1) above.

55A Purchased settlement powers

(1) Where a person makes a disposition by which he acquires a settlement power for consideration in money or money's worth –

(a) section 10(1) above shall not apply to the disposition;

(b) the person shall be taken for the purposes of this Act to make a transfer of value;

(c) the value transferred shall be determined without bringing into account the value of anything which the person acquires by the disposition; and

(d) sections 18 and 23 to 27 above shall not apply in relation to that transfer of value.

(2) For the purposes of this section, a person acquires a settlement power if he becomes entitled –

(a) to a settlement power,

(b) to exercise, or to secure or prevent the exercise of, a settlement power (whether directly or indirectly), or

(c) to restrict, or secure a restriction on, the exercise of a settlement power (whether directly or indirectly),

as a result of transactions which include a disposition (whether to him or another) of a settlement power or of any power of a kind described in paragraph (b) or (c) above which is exercisable in relation to a settlement power.

56 Exclusion of certain exemptions

(1) Sections 18 and 23 to 27 above shall not apply in relation to property which is given in consideration of the transfer of a reversionary interest if,

by virtue of section 55(1) above, that interest does not form part of the estate of the person acquiring it.

(2) Where a person acquires a reversionary interest in any settled property for a consideration in money or money's worth, section 18 above shall not apply in relation to the property when it becomes the property of that person on the termination of that interest on which the reversionary interest is expectant.

(3) Sections 23 to 27 above shall not apply in relation to any property if –

(a) the property is an interest in possession in settled property and the settlement does not come to an end in relation to that settled property on the making of the transfer of value, or

(b) immediately before the time when it becomes property of the exempt body it is comprised in a settlement and, at or before that time, an interest under the settlement is or has been acquired for a consideration in money or money's worth by that or another exempt body.

(4) in subsection (3)(b) above 'exempt body' means a charity, political party or other body within sections 23 to 25 above or the trustees of a settlement in relation to which a direction under paragraph 1 of Schedule 4 to this Act has effect; and for the purposes of subsection (3)(b) there shall be disregarded any acquisition from a charity, political party or body within sections 23 to 25.

(5) For the purposes of subsections (2) and (3) above, a person shall be treated as acquiring an interest for a consideration in money or money's worth if he becomes entitled to it as a result of transactions which include a disposition for such consideration (whether to him or another) of that interest or of other property.

(6) Nothing in this section shall apply to a transfer of value if or to the extent that it is a disposition whereby the use of money or other property is allowed by one person to another. ...

57 Application of certain exemptions

(1) Subject to subsection (3) below, references to transfers of value in sections 19 and 22 above shall be construed as including references to events on the happening of which tax is chargeable under section 52 above, and references to the transferor and (in section 22(3) and (4)) to a disposition shall be construed accordingly.

(2) For the purposes of its application, by virtue of subsection (1) above, to the termination of interests in possession in settled property, section 22 above shall have effect as if –

(a) references to transfers of value made by gifts in consideration of marriage were references to the termination of such interests in consideration of marriage;

(b) references to outright gifts were references to cases where the property ceases on the termination to be settled property; and

(c) references to cases where the property is settled by the gift were references to cases where it remains settled property after the termination.

(3) Subsection (1) above shall not apply to a transfer of value –

(a) unless the transferor has in accordance with subsection (4) below given to the trustees of the settlement a notice informing them of the availability of an exemption, and

(b) except to the extent specified in that notice.

(4) A notice under subsection (3) above shall be in such form as may be prescribed by the Board and shall be given before the end of the period of six months beginning with the date of the transfer of value.

(5) Section 27 above shall apply where the value transferred by a transfer of value is attributable to property which immediately after the transfer remains comprised in a settlement as it applies where a property becomes comprised in a settlement by virtue of the transfer.

CHAPTER III

SETTLEMENTS WITHOUT INTERESTS IN POSSESSION

58 Relevant property

(1) In this Chapter 'relevant property' means settled property in which no qualifying interest in possession subsists, other than –

(a) property held for charitable purposes only, whether for a limited time or otherwise;

(b) property to which section 71, 73, 74 or 86 below applies;

(c) property held on trusts which comply with the requirements mentioned in paragraph 3(1) of Schedule 4 to this Act [maintenance funds for historic buildings, etc] and in respect of which a direction given under paragraph 1 of that Schedule has effect;

(d) property which is part of or held for the purposes of a fund or scheme to which section 151 below [treatment of pension rights, etc] applies;

(e) property comprised in a trade or professional compensation fund; and

(f) excluded property.

(2) The reference in subsection (1)9d) above to property which is part of or held for the purposes of a fund or scheme does not include a reference to a benefit which, having become payable under the fund or scheme, becomes comprised in a settlement.

(3) In subsection (1)(e) above 'trade or professional compensation fund' means a fund which is maintained or administered by a representative association of persons carrying on a trade or profession and the only or main objects of which are compensation for or relief of losses or hardship that, through the default or alleged default of persons carrying on the trade or profession or of their agents or servants, are incurred or likely to be incurred by others.

59   Qualifying interest in possession

(1) In this Chapter 'qualifying interest in possession' means an interest in possession to which an individual, or where subsection (2) below applies a company, is beneficially entitled.

(2) This subsection applies where –

(a) the business of the company consists wholly or mainly in the acquisition of interests in settled property, and

(b) the company has acquired the interest for full consideration in money or money's worth from an individual who was beneficially entitled to it.

...

60   Commencement of settlement

In this Chapter references to the commencement of a settlement are references to the time when property first becomes comprised in it.

61   Ten-year anniversary

(1) In this Chapter 'ten-year anniversary' in relation to a settlement means the tenth anniversary of the date on which the settlement commenced and subsequent anniversaries at ten-yearly intervals, but subject to subsections (2) to (4) below.

(2) The ten-year anniversaries of a settlement treated as made under section 80 below shall be the dates that are (or would but for that section be) the ten-year anniversaries of the settlement first mentioned in that section.

(3) No date falling before 1st April 1983 shall be a ten-year anniversary.

(4) Where –

(a) the first ten-year anniversary of a settlement would apart from this subsection fall during the year ending with 31st March 1984, and

(b) during that year an event occurs in respect of the settlement which could not have occurred except as the result of some proceedings before a court, and

(c) the event is one on which tax was chargeable under Chapter II of Part IV of the Finance Act 1982 (or, apart from Part II of Schedule 15 to that Act, would have been so chargeable) [repealed],

the first ten-year anniversary shall be taken to be 1st April 1984 (but without affecting the dates of later anniversaries).

62   Related settlements

(1) For the purposes of this Chapter two settlements are related if and only if –

(a) the settlor is the same in each case, and

(b) they commenced on the same day,

but subject to subsection (2) below.

(2) Two settlements are not related for the purposes of this Chapter if all the property comprised in one or both of them was immediately after the settlement commenced held for charitable purposes only without limit of time (defined by a date or otherwise).

63   Minor interpretative provisions

In this Chapter, unless the context otherwise requires –

'payment' includes a transfer of assets other than money;

'quarter' means period of three months

64   Charge at ten-year anniversary

Where immediately before a ten-year anniversary all or any part of the property comprised in a settlement is relevant property, tax shall be charged at the rate applicable under sections 66 and 67 below on the value of the property or part at that time.

65 Charge at other times

(1) There shall be a charge to tax under this settlement –

(a) where the property comprised in a settlement or any part of that property ceases to be relevant property (whether because it ceases to be comprised in the settlement or otherwise); and

(b) in a case in which paragraph (a) above does not apply, where the trustees of the settlement make a disposition as a result of which the value of relevant property comprised in the settlement is less than it would be but for the disposition.

(2) The amount on which tax is charged under this section shall be –

(a) the amount by which the value of relevant property comprised in the settlement is less immediately after the event in question than it would be but for the event, or

(b) where the tax payable is paid out of relevant property comprised in the settlement immediately after the event, the amount which, after deducting the tax, is equal to the amount on which tax would be charged by virtue of paragraph (a) above.

(3) The rate at which tax is charged under this section shall be the rate applicable under section 68 [rate before first ten-year anniversary] or 69 [rate between ten-year anniversaries] below.

(4) Subsection (1) above does not apply if the event in question occurs in a quarter beginning with the day on which the settlement commenced or with a ten-year anniversary.

(5) Tax shall not be charged under this section in respect of –

(a) a payment of costs or expenses (so far as they are fairly attributable to relevant property), or

(b) a payment which is (or will be) income of any person for any of the purposes of income tax or would for any of those purposes be income of a person not resident in the United Kingdom if he were so resident,

or in respect of a liability to make such a payment.

(6) Tax shall not be charged under this section by virtue of subsection (1)(b) above if the disposition is such that, were the trustees beneficially entitled to the settled property, section 10 or section 16 [grants of tenancies of agricultural property] above would prevent the disposition from being a transfer of value.

(7) Tax shall not be charged under this section by reason only that property

comprised in a settlement ceases to be situated in the United Kingdom and thereby becomes excluded property by virtue of section 48(3)(a) above.

(8) If the settlor of a settlement was not domiciled in the United Kingdom when the settlement was made, tax shall not be charged under this section by reason only that property comprised in the settlement is invested in securities issued by the Treasury subject to a condition of the kind mentioned in section 6(2) above and thereby becomes excluded property by virtue of section 48(4)(b) above.

(9) For the purposes of this section trustees shall be treated as making a disposition if they omit to exercise a right (unless it is shown that the omission was not deliberate) and the disposition shall be treated as made at the time or latest time when they could have exercised the right.

66   Rate of ten-yearly charge

(1) Subject to subsection (2) below, the rate at which tax is charged under section 64 above at any time shall be three tenths of the effective rate (that is to say the rate found by expressing the tax chargeable as a percentage of the amount on which it is charged) at which tax would be charged on the value transferred by a chargeable transfer of the description specified in subsection (3) below.

(2) Where the whole or part of the value mentioned in section 64 above is attributable to property which was not relevant property, or was not comprised in the settlement, throughout the period of ten years ending immediately before the ten-year anniversary concerned, the rate at which tax is charged on that value or part shall be reduced by one-fortieth for each of the successive quarters in that period which expired before the property became, or last became, relevant property comprised in the settlement.

(3) The chargeable transfer postulated in subsection (1) above is one –

(a) the value transferred by which is equal to an amount determined in accordance with subsection (4) below;

(b) which is made immediately before the ten-year anniversary concerned by a transferor who has in the preceding seven years made chargeable transfers having an aggregate value determined in accordance with subsection (5) below; and

(c) on which tax is charged in accordance with section 7(2) of this Act.

(4) The amount referred to in subsection (3)(a) above is equal to the aggregate of –

(a) the value on which tax is charged under section 64 above;

(b) the value immediately after it became comprised in the settlement of any property which was not then relevant property and has not subsequently become relevant property while remaining comprised in the settlement; and

(c) the value, immediately after a related settlement commenced, of the property then comprised in it;

but subject to subsection (6) below.

(5) The aggregate value referred to in subsection (3)(b) above is equal to the aggregate of –

(a) the values transferred by any chargeable transfers made by the settlor in the period of seven years ending with the day on which the settlement commenced, disregarding transfers made on that day or before 27th March 1974, and

(b) the amounts on which any charges to tax were imposed under section 65 above in respect of the settlement in the ten years before the anniversary concerned;

but subject to subsection (6) and section 67 below.

(6) In relation to a settlement which commenced before 27th March 1974 –

(a) subsection (4) above shall have effect with the omission of paragraphs (b) and (c); and

(b) subsection (5) above shall have effect with the omission of paragraph (a);

and where tax is chargeable under section 64 above by reference to the first ten-year anniversary of a settlement which commenced before 9th March 1982, the aggregate mentioned in subsection (5) above shall be increased by the amounts of any distribution payments (determined in accordance with the rules applicable under paragraph 11 of Schedule 5 to the Finance Act 1975) made out of the settled property before 9th March 1982 (or, where paragraph 6, 7 or 8 of Schedule 15 to the Finance Act 1982 applied, 1st April 1983, or, as the case may be, 1st April 1984) and within the period of ten years before the anniversary concerned.

67   Added property, etc

(1) This subsection applies where, after the settlement commenced and after 8th March 1982, but before the anniversary concerned, the settlor made a chargeable transfer as a result of which the value of the property comprised in the settlement was increased.

(2) For the purposes of subsection (1) above, it is immaterial whether the amount of the property so comprised was increased as a result of the transfer, but a transfer as a result of which the value increased but the amount did not shall be disregarded if it is shown that the transfer –

(a) was not primarily interested to increase the value, and

(b) did not result in the value being greater immediately after the transfer by an amount exceeding five per cent of the value immediately before the transfer.

(3) Where subsection (1) above applies in relation to a settlement which commenced after 26th March 1974, section 66(5)(a) above shall have effect as if it referred to the greater of –

(a) the aggregate of the values there specified, and

(b) the aggregate of the values transferred by any chargeable transfers made by the settlor in the period of seven years ending with the day on which the chargeable transfer falling within subsection (1) above was made –

(i) disregarding transfers made on that day or before 27th March 1974, and

(ii) excluding the values mentioned in subsection (5) below;

and where the settlor made two or more chargeable transfers falling within subsection (1) above, paragraph (b) above shall be taken to refer to the transfer in relation to which the aggregate there mentioned is the greatest.

(4) Where subsection (1) above applies in relation to a settlement which commenced before 27th March 1974, the aggregate mentioned in section 66(5) above shall be increased (or further increased) by the aggregate of the values transferred by any chargeable transfers made by the settlor in the period of seven years ending with the day on which the chargeable transfer falling within subsection (1) above was made –

(a) disregarding transfers made on that day or before 27th March 1974, and

(b) excluding the values mentioned in subsection (5) below; and where the settlor made two or more chargeable transfers falling within subsection (1) above, this subsection shall be taken to refer to the transfer in relation to which the aggregate to be added is the greatest.

(5) The values excluded by subsections (3)(b)(ii) and (4)(b) above are –

(a) any value attributable to property whose value is taken into account in determining the amount mentioned in section 66(4) above; and

(b) any value attributable to property in respect of which a charge to tax has been made under section 65 above and by reference to which an amount mentioned in section 66(5)(b) above is determined.

(6) Where the property comprised in a settlement immediately before the ten-year anniversary concerned, or any part of that property, had on any occasion within the preceding ten years ceased to be relevant property then, if on that occasion tax was charged in respect of the settlement under section 65 above, the aggregate mentioned in section 66(5) above shall be reduced by an amount equal to the lesser of –

(a) the amount on which tax was charged under section 65 (or so much of that amount as is attributable to the part in question), and

(b) the value on which tax is charged under section 64 above (or so much of that value as is attributable to the part in question);

and if there were two or more such occasions relating to the property or the same part of it, this subsection shall have effect in relation to each of them.

(7) References in subsection (6) above to the property comprised in a settlement immediately before an anniversary shall, if part only of the settlement property was then relevant property, be construed as references to that part.

71 Accumulation and maintenance trusts

(1) Subject to subsection (2) below, this section applies to settled property if –

(a) one or more persons (in this section referred to as beneficiaries) will, on or before attaining a specified age not exceeding twenty-five, become beneficially entitled to it or to an interest in possession of it, and

(b) no interest in possession subsists in it and the income from it is to be accumulated so far as not applied for the maintenance, education or benefit of a beneficiary.

(2) This section does not apply to settled property unless either –

(a) not more than twenty-five years have elapsed since the commencement of the settlement or, if it was later, since the time (or latest time) when the conditions stated in paragraphs (a) and (b) of subsection (1) above became satisfied with respect to the property, or

(b) all the persons who are or have been beneficiaries are or were either –

(i) grandchildren of a common grandparent, or

(ii) children, widows or widowers of such grandchildren who were themselves beneficiaries but died before the time when, had they survived, they would have become entitled as mentioned in subsection (1)(a) above.

(3) Subject to subsections (4) and (5)below, there shall be a charge to tax under this section –

(a) where settled property ceased to be property to which this section applies, and

(b) in a case in which paragraph (a) above does not apply, where the trustees make a disposition as a result of which the value of settled property to which this section applies is less than it would be but for the disposition.

(4) Tax shall not be charged under this section –

(a) on a beneficiary's becoming beneficially entitled to, or to an interest in possession in, settled property on or before attaining the specified age, or

(b) on the death of a beneficiary before attaining the specified age.

(5) Subsections (3) to (8) and (10) of section 70 above shall apply for the purposes of this section as they apply for the purposes of that section (with the substitution of a reference to subsection (3)(b) above for the reference in section 70(4) to section 70(2)(b)).

(6) Where the conditions stated in paragraphs (a) and (b) of subsection (1) above were satisfied on 15th April 1976 with respect to property comprised in a settlement which commenced before that day, (2)(a) above shall have effect with the substitution of a reference to that day for the reference to the commencement of the settlement, and the condition stated in subsection (2)(b) above shall be treated as satisfied if –

(a) it is satisfied in respect of the period beginning with 15th April 1976, or

(b) it is satisfied in respect of the period beginning with 1st April 1977 and either there was no beneficiary living on 15th April 1976 or the beneficiaries on 1st April 1977 included a living beneficiary, or

(c) there is no power under the terms of the settlement whereby it could have become satisfied in respect of the period beginning with 1st April 1977, and the trusts of the settlement have not been varied at any time after 15th April 1976.

(7) In subsection (1) above 'persons' includes unborn persons; but the conditions stated in that subsection shall be treated as not satisfied unless there is or has been a living beneficiary.

(8) For the purposes of this section a person's children shall be taken to include his illegitimate children, his adopted children and his stepchildren.

76 Property becoming held for charitable purposes, etc

(1) Tax shall not be charged under this Chapter (apart from section 79 below) in respect of property which ceases to be relevant property, or ceases to be property to which section 70 [property leaving temporary charitable trusts], 71, 72 [property leaving employee trusts and newspaper trusts], 73 [pre-1978 protective trusts] or 74 [pre-1981 trusts for disabled persons] above or paragraph 8 of Schedule 4 to this Act [mainenance funds for historic buildings, etc] applies, on becoming –

(a) property held for charitable purposes only without limit of time (defined by a date or otherwise);

(b) the property of a political party qualifying for exemption under section 24 above; or

(c) the property of a body within Schedule 3 to this Act.

(3) If the amount on which tax would be charged apart from this section in respect of any property exceeds the value of the property immediately after it becomes property of a description specified in paragraphs (a) to (c) of subsection (1) above (less the amount of any consideration for its transfer received by the trustees), that subsection shall not apply but the amount on which tax is charged shall be equal to the excess.

(4) The reference in subsection (3) above to the amount on which tax would be charged is a reference to the amount on which it would be charged –

(a) assuming (if it is not in fact so) that the tax is not paid out of settled property, and

(b) apart from Chapters I and II of Part V of this Act;

and the reference in that subsection to the amount on which tax is charged is a reference to the amount on which it would be charged on that assumption and apart from those Chapters.

(5) Subsection (1) above shall not apply in relation to any property if the disposition by which it becomes property of the relevant description is defeasible; but for this purpose a disposition which has not been defeated at a time twelve months after the property concerned becomes property of the relevant description and is not defeasible after that time shall be treated as not being defeasible, whether or not it was capable of being defeated before that time.

(6) Subsection (1) above shall not apply in relation to any property if it or

any part of it may become applicable for purposes other than charitable purposes or purposes of a body mentioned in subsection (1)(b) or (c) above.

(7) Subsection (1) shall not apply in relation to any property if, at or before the time when it becomes property of the relevant description, an interest under the settlement is or has been acquired for a consideration in money or money's worth by an exempt body otherwise than for a charity or a body mentioned in subsection (1)(b) or (c) above.

(8) In subsection (7) above 'exempt body' means a charity or a body mentioned in subsection (1)(b) or (c) above; and for the purposes of subsection (7) above a body shall be treated as acquiring an interest for a consideration in money or money's worth if it becomes entitled to the interest as a result of transactions which include a disposition for such consideration (whether to that body or to another person) of that interest or of other property.

78 Conditionally exempt occasions

(1) A transfer of property or other event shall not constitute an occasion on which tax is chargeable under any provision of this Chapter other than section 64 if the property in respect of which the charge would have been made has been comprised in the settlement throughout the six years ending with the transfer or event, and –

(a) the property is, on a claim made for the purpose, designated by the Treasury under section 31 above, and

(b) the requisite undertaking described in that section is given with respect to the property by such person as the Treasury think appropriate in the circumstances of the case or (where the property is an area of land within subsection (1)(d) of that section) the requisite undertakings described in that section are given with respect to the property by such person or persons as the Treasury think appropriate in the circumstances of the case.

(1A) A claim under subsection (1) above must be made no more than two years after the date of the transfer or other event in question or within such longer period as the Board may allow.

(2) References in this Chapter to a conditionally exempt occasion are to –

(a) a transfer or event which by virtue of subsection (1) above does not constitute an occasion on which tax is chargeable under this chapter;

(b) a transfer or event which, by virtue of section 81(1) of the Finance Act 1976, did not constitute an occasion on which tax was chargeable under Chapter II of Part IV of the Finance Act 1982;

(c) a conditionally exempt distribution within the meaning given by section 81(2) of the Finance Act 1976 as it had effect in relation to events before 9th March 1982.

(3) Where there has been a conditionally exempt occasion in respect of any property, sections 32, 32A, 33(1), 33(3) to (7) [amount of charge under section 32] and 35(2) [conditional exemption of death before 7th April 1976] above shall have effect (and tax shall accordingly be chargeable under section 32 or 32A) as if –

(a) references to a conditionally exempt transfer and to such a transfer of property included references respectively to a conditionally exempt occasion and to such an occasion in respect of property;

(b) references to a disposal otherwise than by sale included references to any occasion on which tax is chargeable under any provision of this chapter other than section 64;

(c) references to an undertaking given under section 30 above included references to an undertaking given under this section;

and the references in section 33(5) above to the person who made a conditionally exempt transfer shall have effect in relation to a conditionally exempt occasion as references to the person who is the settlor of the settlement in respect of which the occasion occurred (or if there is more than one such person, whichever of them the Board may select).

(4) Where by virtue of subsection (3) above the relevant person for the purposes of section 33 above is the settlor of a settlement, the rate (or each of the rates) mentioned in section 33(1)(b)(i) or (ii) –

(a) shall, if the occasion occurred before the first ten-year anniversary to fall after the property became comprised in the settlement concerned, be 30 per cent of what it would be apart from this subsection, and

(b) shall, if the occasion occurred after the first and before the second ten-year anniversary to fall after the property became so comprised, be 60 per cent of what it would be apart from this subsection;

and the appropriate provision of section 7 for the purposes of section 33(1)(b)(ii) is, if the settlement was created on his death, subsection (1) and, if not, subsection (2). ...

(6) Section 34 [reinstatement of transferor's cumulative total] above shall not apply to a chargeable event in respect of property if the last conditionally exempt transfer of the property has been followed by a conditionally exempt occasion in respect of it.

79   Exemption from ten-yearly charge

(1) Where property is comprised in a settlement and there has been a conditionally exempt transfer of the property on or before the occasion on which it became comprised in the settlement, section 64 above shall not have effect in relation to the property on any ten-year anniversary falling before the first occurrence after the transfer of a chargeable event with respect to the property.

(2) Where property is comprised in a settlement and there has been, on or before the occasion on which it became comprised in the settlement, a disposal of the property in relation to which subsection (4) of section 258 of the 1992 Act (capital gains tax relief for works of art etc) had effect, section 64 above shall not have effect in relation to the property on any ten-year anniversary falling before the first occurrence after the disposal of an event on the happening of which the property is treated as sold under subsection (5) of the said section 258.

(3) Where property is comprised in a settlement and there has been no such transfer or disposal of the property as is mentioned in subsection (1) or (2) above on or before the occasion on which it became comprised in the settlement, then, if –

(a) the property has, on a claim made for the purpose, been designated by the Treasury under section 31 above,

(b) the requisite undertaking described in that section has been given with respect to the property by such person as the Treasury think appropriate in the circumstances of the case or (where the property is an area of land within subsection (1)(d) of that section) the requisite undertakings described in that section have been given with respect to the property by such person or persons as the Treasury think appropriate in the circumstances of the case, and

(c) the property is relevant property,

section 64 above shall not have effect in relation to the property; but there shall be a charge to tax under this subsection on the first occurrence of an event which, if there had been a conditionally exempt transfer of the property when the claim was made and the undertaking had been given under section 30 above, would be a chargeable event with respect to the property.

(4) Tax shall not be charged under subsection (3) above in respect of property if, after the occasion and before the occurrence there mentioned, there has been a conditionally exempt occasion in respect of the property.

(5) The amount on which tax is charged under subsection (3) above shall be an amount equal to the value of the property at the time of the event.

(6) The rate at which tax is charged under subsection (3) above shall be the aggregate of the following percentages –

(a) 0.25 per cent for each of the first forty complete successive quarters in the relevant period,

(b) 0.20 per cent for each of the next forty,

(c) 0.15 per cent for each of the next forty,

(d) 0.10 per cent for each of the next forty, and

(e) 0.05 per cent for each of the next forty.

(7) In subsection (6) above 'the relevant period' means the period beginning with the latest of –

(a) the day on which the settlement commenced,

(b) the date of the last ten-year anniversary of the settlement to fall before the day on which the property became comprised in the settlement, and

(c) 13th March 1975,

and ending with the day before the event giving rise to the charge.

(8) Subsection (9) below shall have effect where –

(a) by virtue of subsection (3) above, section 64 does not have effect in relation to property on the first ten-year anniversary of the settlement to fall after the making of the claim and the giving of the undertaking,

(b) on that anniversary a charge to tax falls to be made in respect of the settlement under section 64, and

(c) the property became comprised in the settlement, and the claim was made and the undertaking was given, within the period of ten years ending with that anniversary.

(9) In calculating the rate at which tax is charged under section 64 above, the value of the consideration given for the property on its becoming comprised in the settlement shall be treated for the purposes of section 66(5)(b) above as if it were an amount on which a charge to tax was imposed in respect of the settlement under section 65 above at the time of the property becoming so comprised.

(10) In subsection (1) above, the reference to a conditionally exempt transfer of any property includes a reference to a transfer of value in relation to which the value of any property has been left out of account under the

provisions of sections 31 to 34 of the Finance Act 1975 and, in relation to such property, the reference to a chargeable event includes a reference to an event on the occurrence of which tax becomes chargeable under Schedule 5 to this Act.

79A Variation of undertakings

(1) An undertaking given under section 78 or 79 above may be varied from time to time by agreement between the Board and the person bound by the undertaking.

(2) Where a Special Commissioner is satisfied that –

(a) the Board have made a proposal for the variation of such an undertaking to the person bound by the undertaking,

(b) that person has failed to agree to the proposed variation within six months after the date on which the proposal was made, and

(c) it is just and reasonable, in all the circumstances, to require the proposed variation to be made,

the Commissioner may direct that the undertaking is to have effect from a date specified by him as if the proposed variation had been agreed to by the person bound by the undertaking. ...

80   Initial interest of settlor or spouse

(1) Where a settlor or his spouse is beneficially entitled to an interest in possession in property immediately after it becomes comprised in the settlement, the property shall for the purposes of this Chapter be treated as not having become comprised in the settlement on that occasion; but when the property or any part of it becomes held on trusts under which neither of those persons is beneficially entitled to an interest in possession, the property or part shall for those purposes be treated as becoming comprised in a separate settlement made by that one of them who ceased (or last ceased) to be beneficially entitled to an interest in possession in it.

(2) References in subsection (1) above to the spouse of a settlor include references to the widow or widower of a settlor. ...

83   Property becoming settled on a death

Property which becomes comprised in a settlement in pursuance of a will or intestacy shall for the purposes of this Chapter be taken to have become comprised in it on the death of the testator or intestate (whether it occurred before or after the passing of this Act).

84 Income applied for charitable purposes

For the purposes of this Chapter (except sections 78 and 79) where the trusts on which settled property is held require part of the income of the property to be applied for charitable purposes, a corresponding part of the settled property shall be regarded as held for charitable purposes.

CHAPTER IV

MISCELLANEOUS

91 Administration period

(1) Where a person would have been entitled to an interest in possession in the whole or part of the residue of the estate of a deceased person had the administration of that estate been completed, the same consequences shall follow under this Act as if he had become entitled to an interest in possession in the unadministered estate and in the property (if any) representing ascertained residue, or in a corresponding part of it, on the date as from which the whole or part of the income of the residue would have been attributable to his interest had the residue been ascertained immediately after the death of the deceased person.

(2) In this section –

(a) 'unadministered estate' means all the property for the time being held by personal representatives as such, excluding property devolving on them otherwise than as assets for the payment of debts and excluding property that is the subject of a specific disposition, and making due allowance for outstanding charges on residue and for any adjustments between capital and income remaining to be made in due curse of administration;

(b) 'ascertained residue' means property which, having ceased to be held by the personal representatives as such, is held as part of the residue;

(c) 'charges on residue', and 'specific disposition' have the same meanings as in Part XVI of the Taxes Act 1988 and the reference to the completion of the administration of an estate shall be construed as if contained in that Part.

92   Survivorship clauses

(1) Where under the terms of a will or otherwise property is held for any person on condition that he survives another for a specified period of not more than six months this Act shall apply as if the dispositions taking effect at the end of the period or, if he does not survive until then, on his death (including any such disposition which has effect by operation of law or is a separate disposition of the income from the property) had had effect from the beginning of the period.

(2) Subsection (1) above does not affect the application of this Act in relation to any distribution or application of property occurring before the dispositions there mentioned take effect.

93   Disclaimers

Where a person becomes entitled to an interest in settled property but disclaims the interest, then, if the disclaimer is not made for the consideration in money or money's worth, this Act shall apply as if he had not become entitled to the interest.

PART V

MISCELLANEOUS RELIEFS

CHAPTER I

BUSINESS PROPERTY

103   Preliminary

(1) In this Chapter references to a transfer of value include references to an occasion on which tax is chargeable under Chapter III of Part III of this Act (apart from section 79), and

(a) references to the value transferred by a transfer of value include references to the amount on which tax is then chargeable, and

(b) references to the transferor include references to the trustees of the settlement concerned.

(2) For the purposes of this Chapter a company and all its subsidiaries are members of a group, and 'holding company' and 'subsidiary' have the meanings given by section 736 of the Companies Act 1985.

(3) In this Chapter 'business' includes a business carried on in the exercise

of a profession or vocation, but does not include a business carried on otherwise than for gain.

104 The relief

(1) Where the whole or part of the value transferred by a transfer of value is attributable to the value of any relevant business property, the whole or that part of the value transferred shall be treated as reduced –

(a) in the case of property falling within section 105(1)(a), (b) or (bb) below, by 100 per cent;

(b) in the case of other relevant business property, by 50 per cent;

but subject to the following provisions of this Chapter.

(2) For the purposes of this section, the value transferred by a transfer of value shall be calculated as a value on which no tax is chargeable.

105 Relevant business property

(1) Subject to the following provisions of this section and to sections 106, 108, 112(3) [exclusion of value of excepted assets] and 113 below, in this Chapter 'relevant business property' means, in relation to any transfer of value, –

(a) property consisting of a business or interest in a business;

(b) securities of a company which are unquoted and which (either by themselves or together with other such securities owned by the transferor and any unquoted shares so owned) gave the transferor control of the company immediately before the transfer;

(bb) any unquoted shares in a company;

(cc) shares in or securities of a company which are quoted and which (either by themselves or together with other such shares or securities owned by the transferor) gave the transferor control of the company immediately before the transfer;

(d) any land or building, machinery or plant which, immediately before the transfer, was used wholly or mainly for the purposes of a business carried on by a company of which the transferor then had control or by a partnership of which he then was a partner; and

(e) any land or building, machinery or plant which, immediately before the transfer, was used wholly or mainly for the purposes of a business carried on by the transferor and was settled property in which he was then beneficially entitled to an interest in possession.

(1ZA) In subsection (1) above 'quoted', in relation to any shares or securities, means listed on a recognised stock exchange and 'unquoted', in relation to any shares or securities, means not so listed.

(2) Shares in or securities of a company do not fall within subsection (1)(cc) above if –

(a) they would not have been sufficient, without other property, to give the transferor control of the company immediately before the transfer, and

(b) their value is taken by virtue of section 176 below to be less than the value previously determined.

(3) A business or interest in a business, or shares in or securities of a company, are not relevant business property if the business or, as the case may be, the business carried on by the company consists wholly or mainly of one or more of the following, that is to say, dealing in securities, stocks or shares, land or buildings or making or holding investments.

(4) Subsection (3) above –

(a) does not apply to any property if the business concerned is wholly that of a market maker or is that of a discount house and (in either case) is carried on in the United Kingdom, and

(b) does not apply to shares in or securities of a company if the business of the company consists wholly or mainly in being a holding company of one or more companies whose business does not fall within that subsection.

(5) Shares in or securities of a company are not relevant business property in relation to a transfer of value if at the time of the transfer a winding-up order has been made in respect of the company or the company has passed a resolution for voluntary winding-up or is otherwise in process of liquidation, unless the business of the company is to continue to be carried on after a reconstruction or amalgamation and the reconstruction or amalgamation either is the purpose of the winding-up or liquidation or take place not later than one year after the transfer of value.

(6) Land, a building, machinery or plant owned by the transferor and used wholly or mainly for the purposes of a business carried on as mentioned in subsection (1)(d) or (e) above is not relevant business property in relation to a transfer of value, unless the business or the transferor's interest in it is, or shares or securities of the company carrying on the business immediately before the transfer are, relevant business property in relation to the transfer.

(7) In this section 'market maker' means a person who –

(a) holds himself out at all normal times in compliance with the rules of The Stock Exchange as willing to buy and sell securities, stocks or shares at a price specified by him, and

(b) is recognised as doing so by the Council of The Stock Exchange.

106 Minimum period of ownership

Property is not relevant business property in relating to a transfer of value unless it was owned by the transferor throughout the two years immediately preceding the transfer.

107 Replacements

(1) Property shall be treated as satisfying the condition in section 106 above if –

(a) it replaced other property and it, that other property and any property directly or indirectly replaced by that other property were owned by the transferor for periods which together comprised at least two years falling within the five years immediately preceding the transfer of value, and

(b) any other property concerned was such that, had the transfer of value been made immediately before it was replaced, it would (apart from section 106) have been relevant business property in relation to the transfer.

(2) In a case falling within subsection (1) above relief under this Chapter shall not exceed what it would have been had the replacement or any one or more of the replacements not been made.

(3) For the purposes of subsection (2) above changes resulting from the formation, alteration or dissolution of a partnership, or from the acquisition of a business by a company controlled by the former owner of the business, shall be disregarded.

(4) Without prejudice to subsection (1) above, where any shares falling within section 105(1)(bb) above which are such shares owned by the transferor immediately before the transfer would under any of the provisions of sections 126 to 136 of the 1992 Act be identified with other shares previously owned by him his period of ownership of the first-mentioned shares shall be treated for the purposes of section 106 above as including his period of ownership of the other shares.

108 Successions

For the purposes of sections 106 and 107 above, where the transferor became entitled to any property on the death of another person –

(a) he shall be deemed to have owned it from the date of the death, and

(b) if that other person was his spouse he shall also be deemed to have owned it for any period during which the spouse owned it.

110 Value of business

For the purposes of this Chapter –

(a) the value of a business or of an interest in a business shall be taken to be its net value;

(b) the net value of a business is the value of the assets used in the business (including goodwill) reduced by the aggregate amount of any liabilities incurred for the purposes of the business;

(c) in ascertaining the net value of an interest in a business no regard shall be had to assets or liabilities other than those by reference to which the net value of the entire business would fall to be ascertained.

113A Transfers within seven years before death of transferor

(1) Where any part of the value transferred by a potentially exempt transfer which proves to be a chargeable transfer would (apart from this section) be reduced in accordance with the preceding provisions of this Chapter, it shall not be so reduced unless the conditions in subsection (3) below are satisfied.

(2) Where –

(a) any part of the value transferred by any chargeable transfer, other than a potentially exempt transfer, is reduced in accordance with the preceding provisions of this Chapter, and

(b) the transfer is made within seven years of the death of the transferor,

then, unless the conditions in subsection (3) below are satisfied, the additional tax chargeable by reason of the death shall be calculated as if the value transferred had not been so reduced.

(3) The conditions referred to in subsection (1) and (2) above are –

(a) that the original property was owned by the transferee throughout the period beginning with the date of the chargeable transfer and ending with the death of the transferor; and

(b) except to the extent that the original property consists of shares or securities to which subsection (3A) below applies that, in relation to a notional transfer of value made by the transferee immediately before the death, the original property would (apart form section 106 above) be relevant business property.

(3A) This subsection applies to shares or securities –

(a) which were quoted at the time of the chargeable transfer referred to in subsection (1) or subsection (2) above; or

(b) which fell within paragraph (b) or (bb) of section 105(1) above in relation to that transfer and were unquoted throughout the period referred to in subsection (3)(a) above.

(3B) In subsection (3A) above 'quoted', in relation to any shares or securities, means listed on a recognised stock exchange and 'unquoted', in relation to any shares or securities, means not so listed.

(4) If the transferee has died before the transferor, the reference in subsection (3) above to the death of the transferor shall have effect as a reference to the death of the transferee.

(5) If the conditions in subsection (3) above are satisfied only with respect to part of the original property, then, –

(a) in a case falling within subsection (1) above, only a proportionate part of so much of the value transferred as is attributable to the original property shall be reduced in accordance with the preceding provisions of this Chapter, and

(b) in a case falling within subsection (2) above, the additional tax shall be calculated as if only a proportionate part of so much of the value transferred as was attributable to the original property had been so reduced.

(6) Where any shares owned by the transferee immediately before the death in question –

(a) would under any of the provisions of sections 126 to 136 of the 1992 Act be identified with the original property (or part of it), or

(b) were issued to him in consideration of the transfer of a business or interest in a business consisting of the original property (or part of it),

they shall be treated for the purposes of this section as if they were the original property (or that part of it).

(7) This section has effect subject to section 113B below.

(7A) The provisions of this Chapter for the reduction of value transferred shall be disregarded in any determination for the purposes of this section of whether there is a potentially exempt or chargeable transfer in any case.

(8) In this section –

'the original property' means the property which was relevant business property in relation to the chargeable transfer referred to in subsection (1) or subsection (2) above; and

'the transferee' means the person whose property the original property became on that chargeable transfer or, where on the transfer the original property became or remained settled property in which no qualifying interest in possession (within the meaning of Chapter III of Part III of this Act) subsists, the trustees of the settlement.

113B Application of section 113A to replacement property

(1) Subject to subsection (2) below, this section applies where –

(a) the transferee has disposed of all or part of the original property before the death of the transferor; and

(b) the whole of the consideration received by him for the disposal has been applied by him in acquiring other property (in this section referred to as 'the replacement property').

(2) This section does not apply unless –

(a) the replacement property is acquired, or a binding contract for its acquisition is entered into, within the allowed period after the disposal of the original property (or, as the case may be, the part concerned); and

(b) the disposal and acquisition are both made in transactions at arm's length or on terms such as might be expected to be included in a transaction at arm's length.

(3) Where this section applies, the conditions in section 113A(3) above shall be taken to be satisfied in relation to the original property (or, as the case may be, the part concerned) if –

(a) the replacement property is owned by the transferee immediately before the death of the transferor; and

(b) throughout the period beginning with the date of the chargeable transfer and ending with the death (disregarding any period between the disposal and acquisition) either the original property or the replacement property was owned by the transferee; and

(c) in relation to a notional transfer of value made by the transferee immediately before the death, the replacement property would (apart from section 106 above) be relevant business property.

(4) If the transferee has died before the transferor, any reference in subsections (1) to (3) above to the death of the transferor shall have effect as a reference to the death of the transferee.

(5) In any case where –

(a) all or part of the original property has been disposed of before the death of the transferor or is excluded by section 113 above from being relevant business property in relation to the notional transfer of value referred to in section 113A(3)(b) above, and

(b) the replacement property is acquired, or a binding contract for its acquisition is entered into, after the death of the transferor but within the allowed period after the disposal of the original property or part, and

(c) the transferor dies before the transferee,

subsection (3) above shall have effect with the omission of paragraph (a), and as if any reference to a time immediately before the death of the transferor or to the death were a reference to the time when the replacement property is acquired.

(6) Section 113A(6) above shall have effect in relation to the replacement property as it has effect in relation to the original property.

(7) Where a binding contract for the disposal of any property is entered into at any time before the disposal of the property, the disposal shall be regarded for the purposes of subsections (2)(a) and (5)(b) above as taking place at that time.

(8) In this section 'the original property' and 'the transferee' have the same meaning as in section 113A above and 'allowed period' means the period of three years or such longer period as the Board may allow.

CHAPTER II

AGRICULTURAL PROPERTY

115 Preliminary

(1) In this Chapter references to a transfer of value include references to an occasion on which tax is chargeable under Chapter III of Part III of this Act (apart form section 79) and –

(a) references to the value transferred by a transfer of value include references to the amount on which tax is then chargeable, and

(b) references to the transferor include references to the trustees of the settlement concerned.

(2) In this Chapter 'agricultural property' means agricultural land or pasture and includes woodland and any building used in connection with the intensive rearing of livestock or fish if the woodland or building is occupied with agricultural land or pasture and the occupation is ancillary to that of the agricultural land or pasture; and also includes such cottages, farm buildings and farmhouses, together with the land occupied with them, as are of a character appropriate to the property.

(3) For the purposes of this Chapter the agricultural value of any agricultural property shall be taken to be the value which would be the value of the property if the property were subject to a perpetual covenant prohibiting its use otherwise than as agricultural property.

(4) For the purposes of this Chapter the breeding and rearing of horses on a stud farm and the grazing of horses in connection with those activities shall be taken to be agriculture and any buildings used in connection with those activities to be farm buildings.

(5) This Chapter applies to agricultural property only if it is in the United Kingdom, the Channel Islands or the Isle of Man.

116 The relief

(1) Where the whole or part of the value transferred by a transfer of value is attributable to the agricultural value of agricultural property, the whole or that part of the value transferred shall be treated as reduced by the appropriate percentage, but subject to the following provisions of this Chapter.

(2) The appropriate percentage is 100 per cent if –

(a) the interest of the transferor in the property immediately before the transfer carries the right to vac ant possession or the right to obtain it within the next twelve months, or

(b) the transferor has been beneficially entitled to that interest since before 10th March 1981 and the conditions set out in subsection (3) below are satisfied; or

(c) the interest of the transferor in the property immediately before the transfer does not carry either of the rights mentioned in paragraph (a) above because the property is let on a tenancy beginning on or after 1st September 1995;

and, subject to subsection (4) below, it is 50 per cent in any other case.

(3) The conditions referred to in subsection (2)(b) above are –

(a) that if the transferor had disposed of his interest by a transfer or value immediately before 10th March 1981 and duly made a claim under paragraph 1 of Schedule 8 to the Finance Act 1975, the value transferred would have been computed in accordance with paragraph 2 of that Schedule and relief would not have been limited by paragraph 5 of that Schedule (restriction to £250,000 or one thousand acres); and

(b) that the transferor's interest did not at any time during the period beginning with 10th March 1981 and ending with the date of the transfer carry a right mentioned in subsection (2)(a) above, and did not fail to do so by reason of any act or deliberate omission of the transferor during the period.

(4) Where the appropriate percentage would be 100 per cent but for a limitation on relief that would have been imposed (as mentioned in subsection (3)(a) above) by paragraph 5 of Schedule 8 to the Finance Act 1975, the appropriate percentage shall be 100 per cent in relation to a part of the value transferred equal to the amount which would have attracted relief under that Schedule and 50 per cent in relation to the remainder.

(5) In determining for the purposes of subsections (3)(a) and (4) above whether or to what extent relief under Schedule 8 to the Finance Act 1975 would have been limited by paragraph 5 of that Schedule, that paragraph shall be construed as if references to relief given under that Schedule in respect of previous chargeable transfers included references to –

(a) relief given under this Chapter by virtue of subsection (2)(b) or (4) above, and

(b) relief given under Schedule 14 to the Finance Act 1981 by virtue of paragraph 2(2)(b) or (4) of that Schedule,

in respect of previous chargeable transfers made on or after 10th March 1981.

(5A) Where, in consequence of the death on or after 1st September 1995 of the tenant or, as the case may be, the last surviving tenant of any property, the tenancy –

(a) becomes vested in a person, as a result of his being a person beneficially entitled under the deceased tenant's will or other testamentary writing or on his intestacy, and

(b) is or becomes binding on the landlord and that person as landlord and tenant respectively,

subsection (2)(c) above shall have effect as if the tenancy so vested had been a tenancy beginning on the date of the death.

(5B) Where in consequence of the death on or after 1st September 1995 of the tenant or, as the case may be, the last surviving tenant of any property, a tenancy of the property or of any property comprising the whole or part of it –

(a) is obtained by a person under or by virtue of an enactment, or

(b) is granted to a person in circumstances such that he is already entitled under or by virtue of an enactment to obtain such a tenancy, but one which takes effect on a later date, or

(c) is granted to a person who is or has become the only or only remaining applicant, or the only or only remaining person eligible to apply, under a particular enactment for such a tenancy in the particular case,

subsection (2)(c) above shall have effect as if the tenancy so obtained or granted had been a tenancy beginning on the date of the death.

(5C) Subsection (5B) above does not apply in relation to property situated in Scotland.

(5D) If, in a case where the transferor dies on or after 1st September 1995, –

(a) the tenant of any property has, before the death, given notice of intention to retire in favour of a new tenant, and

(b) the tenant's retirement in favour of the new tenant takes place after the death but not more than thirty months after the giving of the notice,

subsection (2)(c) above shall have effect as if the tenancy granted or assigned to the new tenant had been a tenancy beginning immediately before the transfer of value which the transferor is treated by section 4(1) above as making immediately before his death.

(5E) In subsection (5D) above and this subsection –

'the new tenant' means –

(a) the person or persons identified in a notice of intention to retire in favour of a new tenant as the person or persons who it is desired should become the tenant of the property to which that notice relates; or

(b) the survivor or survivors of the persons so identified, whether alone or with any other person or persons;

'notice of intention to retire in favour of a new tenant' means, in the case of any property, a notice or other written intimation given to the landlord by the tenant, or (in the case of a joint tenancy or tenancy in common) all of the tenants, of the property indicating, in whatever terms, his or their wish that one or more persons identified in the notice or intimation should become the tenant of the property;

'the retiring tenant's tenancy' means the tenancy of the person or persons giving the notice of intention to retire in favour of a new tenant;

'the tenant's retirement in favour of the new tenant' means –

(a) the assignment ... of the retiring tenant's tenancy to the new tenant in circumstances such that the tenancy is or becomes binding on the landlord and the new tenant as landlord and tenant respectively; or

(b) the grant of a tenancy of the property which is the subject of the retiring tenant's tenancy, or of any property comprising the whole or part of that property, to the new tenant and the acceptance of that tenancy by him;

and ... 'grant' and 'acceptance' in paragraph (b) above respectively include the deemed grant, and the deemed acceptance, of a tenancy under or by virtue of any enactment.

(6) For the purposes of this Chapter the interest of one of two or more joint tenants or tenants in common ... shall be taken to carry a right referred to in subsection (2)(a) above if the interests of all of them together carry that right.

(7) For the purposes of this section, the value transferred by a transfer of value shall be calculated as a value on which no tax is chargeable.

117 Minimum period of occupation or ownership

Subject to the following provisions of this Chapter, section 116 above does not apply to any agricultural property unless –

(a) it was occupied by the transferor for the purposes of agriculture throughout the period of two years ending with the date of the transfer, or

(b) it was owned by him throughout the period of seven years ending with that date and was throughout that period occupied (by him or another) for the purposes of agriculture.

118 Replacements

(1) Where the agricultural property occupied by the transferor on the date of the transfer replaced other agricultural property, the condition stated in section 117(a) above shall be treated as satisfied if it, the other property and any agricultural property directly or indirectly replaced by the other property were occupied by the transferor for the purposes of agriculture for periods which together comprised at least two years falling within the five years ending with that date.

(2) Where the agricultural property owned by the transferor on the date of the transfer replaced other agricultural property, the condition stated in section 117(b) above shall be treated as satisfied if it, the other property and any agricultural property directly or indirectly replaced by the other property were, for periods which together comprised at least seven years falling within the ten years ending with that date, both owned by the transferor and occupied (by him or another) for the purposes of agriculture.

(3) In a case falling within subsection (1) or (2) above relief under this chapter shall not exceed what it would have been had the replacement or any one or more of the replacements not been made.

(4) For the purposes of subsection (3) above changes resulting from the formation, alteration or dissolution of a partnership shall be disregarded.

119 Occupation by company ...

(1) For the purposes of sections 117 and 118 above, occupation by a company which is controlled by the transferor shall be treated as occupation by the transferor. ...

120 Successions

(1) For the purposes of section 117 above, where the transferor became entitled to any property on the death of another person –

(a) he shall be deemed to have owned it (and, if he subsequently occupies it, to have occupied it) from the date of the death, and

(b) if that other person was his spouse he shall also be deemed to have occupied it for the purposes of agricultural for any period for which it was so occupied by his spouse, and to have owned it for any period for which his spouse owned it.

(2) Where the transferor became entitled to his interest on the death of his spouse on or after 10th March 1981 –

(a) he shall for the purposes of section 116(2)(b) above be deemed to have been beneficially entitled to it for any period for which his spouse was beneficially entitled to it;

(b) the condition set out in section 116(3)(a) shall be taken to be satisfied if and only if it is satisfied in relation to his spouse; and

(c) the condition set out in section 116(3)(b) shall be taken to be satisfied only if it is satisfied both in relation to him and in relation to his spouse.

124A   Transfers within seven years before death of transferor

(1) Where any part of the value transferred by a potentially exempt transfer which proves to be a chargeable transfer would (apart from this section) be reduced in accordance with the preceding provisions of this Chapter, it shall not be so reduced unless the conditions in subsection (3) below are satisfied.

(2) Where –

(a) any part of the value transferred by any chargeable transfer, other than a potentially exempt transfer, is reduced in accordance with the preceding provisions of this chapter, and

(b) the transfer is made within seven years of the death of the transferor,

then, unless the conditions in subsection (3) below are satisfied, the additional tax chargeable by reason of the death shall be calculated as if the value transferred had not been so reduced.

(3) The conditions referred to in subsections (1) and (2) above are –

(a) that the original property was owned by the transferee throughout the period beginning with the date of the chargeable transfer and ending with the death of the transferor (in this subsection referred to as 'the relevant period') and it is not at the time of the death subject to a binding contract for sale; and

(b) except in a case falling within paragraph (c) below, that the original property is agricultural property immediately before the death and has been occupied (by the transferee or another) for the purposes of agriculture throughout the relevant period; and

(c) where the original property consists of shares in or securities of a company, that throughout the relevant period the agricultural property to which section 116 above applied by virtue of section 122(1) above on the chargeable transfer was owned by the company and occupied (by the company or another) for the purposes of agriculture.

(4) If the transferee has died before the transferor, the reference in

subsection (3) above to the death of the transferor shall have effect as a reference to the death of the transferee.

(5) If the conditions in subsection (3) above are satisfied only with respect to part of the original property, then, –

(a) in a case falling within subsection (1) above, only a proportionate part of so much of the value transferred as is attributable to the original property shall be reduced in accordance with the preceding provisions of this Chapter, and

(b) in a case falling within subsection (2) above, the additional tax shall be calculated as if only a proportionate part of so much of the value transferred as was attributable to the original property has been so reduced.

(6) Where any shares owned by the transferee immediately before the death in question –

(a) would under any of the provisions of sections 126 to 136 of the 1992 Act be identified with the original property (or part of it), or

(b) were issued to him in consideration of the transfer of agricultural property consisting of the original property (or part of it),

his period of ownership of the original property shall be treated as including his period of ownership of the shares.

(7) This section has effect subject to section 124B below.

(7A) The provisions of this Chapter for the reduction of value transferred shall be disregarded in any determination for the purposes of this section of whether there is a potentially exempt or chargeable transfer in any case.

(8) In this section –

'the original property' means the property which, in relation to the chargeable transfer referred to in subsection (1) or subsection (2) above, was either agricultural property to which section 116 above applied or shares or securities of a company owning agricultural property to which that section applied by virtue of section 122(1) above, and

'the transferee' means the person whose property the original property became on that chargeable transfer or, where on the transfer the original property became or remained settled property in which no qualifying interest in possession (within the meaning of Chapter III of Part III of this Act) subsists, the trustees of the settlement.

124B Application of section 124A to replacement property

(1) Subject to subsection (2) below, this section applies where –

(a) the transferee has disposed of all or part of the original property before the death of the transferor; and

(b) the whole of the consideration received by him for the disposal has been applied by him in acquiring other property (in this section referred to as 'the replacement property').

(2) This section does not apply unless –

(a) the replacement property is acquired, or a binding contract for its acquisition is entered into, within the allowed period after the disposal of the original property (or, as the case may be, the part concerned); and

(b) the disposal and acquisition are both made in transactions at arm's length or on terms such as might be expected to be included in a transaction at arm's length.

(3) Where this section applies, the conditions in section 124A(3) above shall be taken to be satisfied in relation to the original property (or, as the case may be, the part concerned) if –

(a) the replacement property is owned by the transferee immediately before the death of the transferor and is not at that time subject to a binding contract for sale; and

(b) throughout the period beginning with the date of the chargeable transfer and ending with the disposal, the original property was owned by the transferee and occupied (by the transferee or another) for the purposes of agriculture; and

(c) throughout the period beginning with the date when the transferee acquired the replacement property and ending with the death, the replacement property was owned by the transferee and occupied (by the transferee or another) for the purposes of agriculture; and

(d) the replacement property is agricultural property immediately before the death.

(4) If the transferee has died before the transferor, any reference in subsections (1) to (3) above to the death of the transferor shall have effect as a reference to the death of the transferee.

(5) In any case where –

(a) all or part of the original property has been disposed of before the death of the transferor or is subject to a binding contract for sale at the time of the death, and

(b) the replacement property is acquired, or a binding contract for its acquisition is entered into, after the death of the transferor but within the allowed period after the disposal of the original property or part, and

(c) the transferor dies before the transferee,

subsection (3) above shall have effect with the omission of paragraphs (a) and (c), and as if any reference to a time immediately before the death of the transferor were a reference to the time when the replacement property is acquired.

(6) Section 124A(6) above shall have effect in relation to the replacement property as it has effect in relation to the original property.

(7) Where a binding contract for the disposal of any property is entered into at any time before the disposal of the property, the disposal shall be regarded for the purposes of subsections (2)(a) and (5)(b) above as taking place at that time.

(8) In this section 'the original property' and 'the transferee' have the same meaning as in section 124A above and 'allowed period' means the period of three years or such longer period as the Board may allow.

124C   Land in habitat schemes

(1) For the purposes of this Chapter, where any land is in a habitat scheme –

(a) the land shall be regarded as agricultural land;

(b) the management of the land in accordance with the requirements of the scheme shall be regarded as agriculture; and

(c) buildings used in connection with such management shall be regarded as farm buildings.

(2) For the purposes of this section land is in a habitat scheme at any time if –

(a) an application for aid under one of the enactments listed in subsection (3) below has been accepted in respect of the land; and

(b) the undertakings to which the acceptance relates have neither been terminated by the expiry of the period to which they relate nor been treated as terminated.

(3) Those enactments are –

(a) regulation 3(1) of the Habitat (Water Fringe) Regulations 1994;

(b) the Habitat (Former Set-Aside Land) Regulations 1994;

(c) the Habitat (Salt-Marsh) Regulations 1994; ...

(4) The Treasury may by order made by statutory instrument amend the list of enactments in subsection (3) above. ...

(6) This section has effect –

(a) in relation to any transfer of value made on or after 26th November 1996; and

(b) in relation to transfers of value made before that date, for the purposes of any charge to tax, or to extra tax, which arises by reason of an event occurring on or after 26th November 1996.

CHAPTER III

WOODLANDS

125 The relief

(1) This section applies where –

(a) part of the value of a person's estate immediately before his death is attributable to the value of land in the United Kingdom on which trees or underwood are growing but which is not agricultural property within the meaning of Chapter II of this Part of this Act, and

(b) either he was beneficially entitled to the land throughout the five years immediately preceding his death, or he became beneficially entitled to it otherwise than for a consideration in money or money's worth.

(2) Where this section applies and the person liable for the whole or part of the tax so elects –

(a) the value of the trees or underwood shall be left out of account in determining the value transferred on the death, but

(b) tax shall be charged in the circumstances mentioned in section 126 below.

(3) An election under this section must be made by notice in writing to the Board within two years of the death or such longer time as the Board may allow.

126 Charge to tax on disposal of trees or underwood

(1) Where under section 125 above the value of any trees or underwood has

been left out of account in determining the value transferred on the death of any person, and the whole or any part of the trees or underwood is disposed of (whether together with or apart from the land on which they were growing) then, if the disposal occurs before any part of the value transferred on the death of any other person is attributable to the value of that land, tax shall be charged in accordance with sections 127 and 128 below.

(2) Subsection (1) above shall not apply to a disposal made by any person to his spouse.

(3) Where tax has been charged under this section on the disposal of any trees or underwood tax shall not again be charged in relation to the same death on a further disposal of the same trees or underwood.

127 Amount subject to charge

(1) The amount on which tax is charged under section 126 above on a disposal of trees or underwood shall be –

(a) if the disposal is a sale for full consideration in money or money's worth, an amount equal to me net proceeds of the sale, and

(b) in any other case, an amount equal to the net value of the trees or underwood at the time of the disposal.

(2) Where, if the value of the trees or underwood had not been left out of account in determining the value transferred on the death of the person in question –

(a) it would have been taken into account in determining the value of any relevant business property for the purposes of relief under Chapter I of this Part of this Act in relation to the transfer of value made on his death, or

(b) it would have been so taken into account if this Act had then been in force,

the amount on which tax is charged under section 126 above shall be reduced by 50 per cent.

128 Rate of charge

Tax charged under section 126 above on an amount determined under section 127 above shall be charged at the rate or rates at which it would have been charged on the death first mentioned in section 126 if –

(a) that amount, and any amount on which tax was previously charged under section 126 in relation to that death, had been included in the value transferred on death, and

(b) the amount on which the tax is charged had formed the highest part of that value.

129 Credit for tax charged

Where a disposal on which tax is chargeable under section 126 above is a chargeable transfer, the value transferred by it shall be calculated as if the value of the trees or underwood had been reduced by the tax chargeable under that section.

130 Interpretation

(1) In this Chapter –

(a) references to the value transferred on a death are references to the value transferred by the chargeable transfer made on that death;

(b) references to the net proceeds of sale or the net value of any trees or underwood are references to the proceeds of sale or value after deduction of any expenses allowable under this Chapter so far as those expenses are not allowable for the purposes of income tax; and

(c) references to the disposal of any trees or underwood include references to the disposal of any interest in the trees or underwood (and references to a disposal of the same trees or underwood shall, where the case so requires, be construed as referring to a disposal of the same interest).

(2) The expenses allowable under this Chapter are, in relation to any trees or underwood the value of which has been left out of account on any death, –

(a) the expenses incurred in disposing of the trees or underwood; and

(b) the expenses incurred in replanting within three years of a disposal (or such longer time as the Board may allow) to replace the trees or underwood disposed of; and

(c) the expenses incurred in replanting to replace trees or underwood previously disposed of, so far as not allowable on the previous disposal.

CHAPTER IV

TRANSFER WITHIN [SEVEN] YEARS BEFORE DEATH

131 The relief

(1) Subject to section 132 below, this section applies where because of the transferor's death within seven years of the transfer, tax becomes chargeable in respect of the value transferred by a potentially exempt transfer or (by virtue of section 7(4) above) additional tax becomes chargeable in respect of the value transferred by any other chargeable transfer and (in either case) all or part of the value transferred is attributable to the value of property ('the transferred property') which –

(a) is, at the date of the death, the property of the person ('the transferee') whose property it became on the transfer or of his spouse, or

(b) has, before that date, been sold by the transferee or his spouse by a qualifying sale;

and in the following provisions of this section 'the relevant date' means, in a case within paragraph (a) above, the date of the death, and in a case within paragraph (b), the date of the qualifying sale.

(2) If –

(a) the market value of the transferred property at the time of the chargeable transfer exceeds its market value on the relevant date, and

(b) a claim is made by a person liable to pay the whole or part of the tax or, as the case may be, additional tax,

the tax or, as the case may be, additional tax shall be calculated as if the value transferred were reduced by the amount of the excess.

(2A) Where so much of the value transferred as is attributable to the value, or agricultural value, of the transferred property is reduced by any percentage (in this subsection referred to as 'the appropriate percentage'), in accordance with Chapter I or Chapter II of this Part of this Act, references in subsection (2) above to the market value of the transferred property at any time shall have effect –

(a) in a case within Chapter I, as references to that market value reduced by the appropriate percentage; and

(b) in a case within Chapter II, as references to that market value less the appropriate percentage of the agricultural value of the transferred property at that time.

(3) A sale is a qualifying sale for the purposes of this section if –

(a) it is at arm's length for a price freely negotiated at the time of the sale, and

(b) no person concerned as vendor (or as having an interest in the proceeds of the sale) is the same as or connected with any person concerned as purchaser (or as having an interest in the purchase), and

(c) no provision is made, in or in connection with the agreement for the sale, that the vendor (or any person having an interest in the proceeds of sale) is to have any right to acquire some or all of the property sold or some interest in or created out of it.

132 Wasting assets

(1) Section 131 above shall not apply if the transferred property is tangible movable property that is a wasting asset.

(2) The transferred property is a wasting asset for the purposes of this section if, immediately before the chargeable transfer, it had a predictable useful life not exceeding fifty years, having regard to the purpose for which it was held by the transferor; and plant and machinery shall in every case be regarded as having a predictable useful life of less than fifty years.

133 Shares – capital receipts

(1) If the transferred property consists of shares and at any time before the relevant date the transferee or his spouse becomes entitled to a capital payment in respect of them, then for the purposes of section 131 above the market value of the transferred property on the relevant date shall (except where apart from this section it reflects a right to the payment) be taken to be increased by an amount equal to the payment.

(2) If at any time before the relevant date the transferee or his spouse receives or becomes entitled to receive in respect of the transferred property a provisional allotment of shares and disposes of the rights, the amount of the consideration for the disposal shall be treated for the purposes of this section as a capital payment in respect of the transferred property.

(3) In this section 'capital payment' means any money or money's worth which does not constitute income for the purposes of income tax.

137 Interests in land

(1) Where the transferred property is an interest in land in relation to which

the conditions mentioned in subsection (2) below are not satisfied, then, subject to subsections (3)and (4)below, the market value of the transferred property on the relevant date shall for the purposes of section 131 above be taken to be increased by an amount equal to the difference between –

(a) the market value of the interest at the time of the chargeable transfer, and

(b) what that market value would have been if the circumstances prevailing on the relevant date and by reason of which the conditions are not satisfied had prevailed at the time of the chargeable transfer.

(2) The conditions referred to in subsection (1) above are –

(a) that the interest was the same in all respects and with the same incidents at the time of the chargeable transfer and on the relevant date, and

(b) that the land in which the interest subsists was in the same state and with the same incidents at the time of the chargeable transfer and on the relevant date.

(3) If after the date of the chargeable transfer but before the relevant date compensation becomes payable under any enactments to the transferee or his spouse –

(a) because of the imposition of a restriction on the use or development of the land in which the interest subsists, or

(b) because the value of the interest is reduced for any other reason,

the imposition of the restriction or the other cause of the reduction in value shall be ignored for the purposes of subsections (1) and (2) above, but the market value of the interest on the relevant date shall be taken to be increased by an amount equal to the amount of the compensation.

(4) Where the market value of the interest at the time of the chargeable transfer is less than it would have been as mentioned in subsection (1) above, that subsection shall apply as if, instead of providing for an increase, it provided for the market value on the relevant date to be reduced to what it would have been if the change in circumstances by reason of which the conditions mentioned in subsection (2) above are not satisfied had not occurred.

139 Other property

(1) Where the transferred property is neither shares nor an interest in land and the condition mentioned in subsection (2) below is not satisfied inn relation to it, then, subject to subsections (3) and (4) below, the market

value of the property on the relevant date shall for the purposes of section 131 above to be taken to be increased by an amount equal to the difference between –

(a) the market value of the property at the time of the chargeable transfer, and

(b) what that value would have been if the circumstances prevailing at the relevant date and by reason of which the condition is not satisfied had prevailed at the time of the chargeable transfer.

(2) The condition referred to in subsection (1) above is that the transferred property was the same in all respects at the time of the chargeable transfer and on the relevant date.

(3) Where the market value of the transferred property at the time of the chargeable transfer is less than it would have been as mentioned in subsection (1) above, that subsection shall apply as if, instead of providing for an increase, it provided for the market value on the relevant date to be reduced to what it would have been if the property had remained the same in all respects as it was at the time of the chargeable transfer.

(4) Where the transferred property is neither shares nor an interest in land and during the period between the time of the chargeable transfer and the relevant date benefits in money or money's worth are derived form it which exceed a reasonable return on its market value at the time of the chargeable transfer, then –

(a) any effect of the benefits on the transferred property shall be ignored for the purposes of the preceding provisions of this section, but

(b) the market value of the transferred property on the relevant date shall be taken for the purposes of section 131 above to be increased by an amount equal to the said excess.

140 Interpretation

(1) In this Chapter –

'close company' has the same meaning as in Part IV of this Act;

'interest in land' does not include any estate, interest or right by way of mortgage or other security;

'shares' includes securities;

and 'the relevant date', 'the transferee' and 'the transferred property' shall be construed in accordance with section 131(1) above.

(2) For the purposes of this Chapter the market value at any time of any

property is the price which the property might reasonably be expected to fetch if sold in the open market at that time; but –

(a) that price shall not be assumed to be reduced on the ground that the whole property is on the market at one and the same time, and

(b) in the case of unquoted shares, it shall be assumed that in that market there is available to any prospective purchaser of the shares all the information which a prudent prospective purchaser might reasonably require if he were proposing to purchase them from a willing vendor by private treaty and at arm's length.

CHAPTER V

MISCELLANEOUS

141 Two or more transfers within five years

(1) Where the value of a person's estate was increased by a chargeable transfer ('the first transfer') made not more than five years before –

(a) his death, or

(b) a chargeable transfer which is made by him otherwise than on his death and as to which the conditions specified in subsection (2) below are satisfied,

the tax chargeable on the value transferred by the transfer made on his death or, as the case may be, referred to in paragraph (b) above ('the later transfer') shall be reduced by an amount calculated in accordance with subsection (3) below.

(2) The conditions referred to in subsection (1)(b) above are –

(a) that the value transferred by the later transfer falls to be determined by reference to the value of settled property in which there subsists an interest in possession to which the transferor is entitled;

(b) that the value transferred by the first transfer also fell to be determined by reference to the value of that property; and

(c) that the first transfer either was or included the making of the settlement or was made after the making of the settlement.

(3) The amount referred to in subsection (1) above is a percentage of the tax charged on so much of the value transferred by the first transfer as is attributable to the increase mentioned in that subsection; and the percentage is –

(a) 100 per cent if the period beginning with the date of the first transfer and ending with the date of the later does not exceed one year;

(b) 80 per cent if it exceeds one year but does not exceed two years;

(c) 60 per cent if it exceeds two years but does not exceed three years;

(d) 40 per cent if it exceeds three years but does not exceed four years; and

(e) 20 per cent if it exceeds four years.

(4) Where in relation to the first transfer there is more than one later transfer, the reduction provided for by this section shall be given only n respect of the earliest of them, unless the reduction represents less than the whole of the tax charged as mentioned in subsection (3) above; and in that case a reduction may be made in respect of subsequent transfers (in chronological order) until reductions representing the whole of that tax have been made.

(5) For the purposes of subsection (4) above, a reduction made in accordance with paragraph (a) of subsection (3) above represents an equivalent amount of tax, a reduction made in accordance with paragraph (b) represents the amount of tax of which it is 80 per cent, and so on.

(6) In determining for the purposes of this section whether or to what extent the value of the transferor's estate was increased by a chargeable transfer, there shall be disregarded any excluded property consisting of a reversionary interest to which he became entitled on the occasion of or before the chargeable transfer.

(7) Where –

(a) the value of the transferor's estate was increased in consequence of –

(i) a gift inter vivos, or

(ii) a disposition or determination of a beneficial interest in possession in property comprised in a settlement, and

(b) tax under section 22(5) of the Finance Act 1975 was by reason of the gift or interest payable on a subsequent death,

this section shall apply as if the increase had been by the chargeable transfer made on the occasion of the death.

142 Alteration of dispositions taking effect on death

(1) Where within the period of two years after a person's death –

(a) any of the dispositions (whether effected by will, under the law relating to intestacy or otherwise) of the property comprised in his estate immediately before his death are varied, or

(b) the benefit conferred by any of those dispositions is disclaimed,

by an instrument in writing made by the persons or any of the persons who benefit or would benefit under the dispositions, this Act shall apply as if the variation had been effected by the deceased or, as the case may be, the disclaimed benefit had never been conferred.

(2) Subsection (1) above shall not apply to a variation unless the instrument contains a statement, made by all the relevant persons, to the effect that they intend the subsection to apply to the variation.

(2A) For the purposes of subsection (2) above the relevant persons are –

(a) the person or persons making the instrument, and

(b) where the variation results in additional tax being payable, the personal representatives.

Personal representatives may decline to make a statement under subsection (2) above only if no, or no sufficient, assets are held by them in that capacity for discharging the additional tax.

(3) Subsection (1) above shall not apply to a variation or disclaimer made for any consideration in money or money's worth other than consideration consisting of the making, in respect of another of the dispositions, of a variation or disclaimer to which that subsection applies.

(4) Where a variation to which subsection (1) above applies results in property being held in trust for a person for a period which ends not more than two years after the death, this Act shall apply as if the disposition of the property that takes effect at the end of the period had had effect from the beginning of the period; but this subsection shall not affect the application of this Act in relation to any distribution or application of property occurring before the disposition takes effect.

(5) For the purposes of subsection (1) above the property comprised in a person's estate includes any excluded property but not any property to which he is treated as entitled by virtue of section 49(1) above or section 102 of the Finance Act 1986.

(6) Subsection (1) above applies whether or not the administration of the estate is complete or the property concerned has been distributed in accordance with the original dispositions.

(7) In the application of subsection (4) above to Scotland, property which is subject to a proper liferent shall be deemed to be held in trust for the liferenter.

143 Compliance with testator's request

Where a testator expresses a wish that property bequeathed by his will should be transferred by the legatee to other persons, and the legatee transfers any of the property in accordance with that wish within the period of two years after the death of the testator, this Act shall have effect as if the property transferred had been bequeathed by the will to the transferee.

144 Distribution, etc from property settled by will

(1) This section applies where property comprised in a person's estate immediately before his death is settled by his will and, within the period of two years after his death and before any interest in possession has subsisted in the property, there occurs –

(a) an event on which tax would (apart form this section) be chargeable under any provision, other than section 64 or 79, of Chapter II of Part III of this Act, or

(b) an event on which tax would be so chargeable but for section 75 or 76 [property becoming subject to employee trusts] above or paragraph 16(1) of Schedule 4 [property becoming comprised in maintenance funds] to this Act.

(2) Where this section applies by virtue of an event within paragraph (a) of subsection (1) above, tax shall not be charged under the provision in question on that event; and in every case in which this section applies in relation to an event, this Act shall have effect as if the will had provided that on the testator's death the property should be held as it is held after the event.

145 Redemption of surviving spouse's life interest

Where an election is made by a surviving spouse under section 47A of the Administration of Estates Act 1925, this Act shall have effect as if the surviving spouse, instead of being entitled to the life interest, had been entitled to a sum equal to the capital value mentioned in that section.

146 Inheritance (Provision for Family and Dependants) Act 1975

(1) Where an order is made under section 2 of the Inheritance (Provision for Family and Dependants) Act 1975 ('the 1975 Act') in relation to any property forming part of the net estate of a deceased person, then, without prejudice to section 19(1) of that Act, the property shall for the purposes of this Act be treated as if it had on his death devolved subject to the provisions of the order.

(2) Where an order is made under section 10 of the 1975 Act requiring a person to provide any money or other property by reason of a disposition made by the deceased, then –

(a) if that disposition was a chargeable transfer and the personal representatives of the deceased make a claim for the purpose –

(i) tax paid or payable on the value transferred by that chargeable transfer (whether or not by the claimants) shall be repaid to them by the Board or, as the case may be, shall not be payable, and

(ii) the rate or rates of tax applicable to the transfer of value made by the deceased on his death shall be determined as if the values previously transferred by chargeable transfers made by him were reduced by that value;

(b) the money or property shall be included in the deceased's estate for the purpose of the transfer of value made by him on his death.

(3) Where the money or other property ordered to be provided under section 10 of the 1975 Act is less than the maximum permitted by that section, subsection (2)(a) above shall have effect in relation to such part of the value there mentioned as is appropriate.

(4) The adjustment in consequence of the provisions of this section or of section 19(1) of the 1975 Act of the tax payable in respect of the transfer of value made by the deceased on his death shall not affect –

(a) the amount of any deduction to be made under section 8 of that Act in respect of tax borne by the person mentioned in subsection (3) of that section, or

(b) the amount of tax to which regard is to be had under section 9(2) of that Act;

and where a person is ordered under that Act to make a payment or transfer property by reason of his holding property treated as part of the deceased's net estate under section 8 or 9 and tax borne by him is taken into account for the purposes of the order, any repayment of that tax shall be made to the personal representatives of the deceased and not to that person.

(5) Tax repaid under paragraph (a)(i) of subsection (2) above shall be included in the deceased's estate for the purposes of the transfer of value made by him on his death; and tax repaid under that paragraph or under subsection (4) above shall form part of the deceased's net estate for the purposes of the 1975 Act.

(6) Anything which is done in compliance with an order under the 1975 Act or occurs on the coming into force of such an order, and which would (apart

from this subsection) constitute an occasion on which tax is chargeable under any provision, other than section 79, of Chapter III of Part III of this Act, shall not constitute such an occasion; and where an order under the 1975 Act provides for property to be settled or for the variation of a settlement, and (apart from this subsection) tax would be charged under section52(1) above on the coming into force of the order, section 52(1) shall not apply.

(7) In subsections (2)(a) and (5) above references to tax include references to interest on tax.

(8) Where an order is made staying or dismissing proceedings under the 1975 Act on terms set out in or scheduled to the order, this section shall have effect as if any of those terms which could have been included in an order under section 2 or 10 of that Act were provisions of such an order. ...

150 Voidable transfers

(1) Where on a claim made for the purpose it is shown that the whole or any part of a chargeable transfer ('the relevant transfer') has by virtue of any enactment or rule of law been set aside as voidable or otherwise defeasible –

> (a) tax paid or payable by the claimant (in respect of the relevant transfer or any other chargeable transfer made before the claim) that would not have been payable if the relevant transfer had been void ab initio shall be repaid to him by the Board, or as the case may be shall not be payable, and

> (b) the rate or rates of tax applicable to any chargeable transfer made after the claim by the person who made the relevant transfer shall be determined as if that transfer or that part of it had been void as aforesaid.

(2) In subsection (1)(a) above the reference to tax includes a reference to interest on tax.

154 Death on active service, etc

(1) Section 4 above shall not apply in relation to the death of a person in whose cases it is certified by the Defence Council or the Secretary of State –

> (a) that he died from a wound inflicted, accident occurring or disease contracted at a time when the conditions specified in subsection (2) below were satisfied, or

> (b) that he died from a disease contracted at some previous time, the

death being due to or hastened by the aggravation of the disease during a period when those conditions were satisfied.

(2) The conditions referred to in subsection (1) above are that the deceased was a member of any of the armed forces of the Crown or (not being a member of any of those forces) was subject to the law governing any of those forces by reason of association with or accompanying any body of those forces and (in any case) was either –

(a) on active service against an enemy, or

(b) on other service of a warlike nature or which in the opinion of the Treasury involved the same risks as service of a warlike nature. ...

PART VI

VALUATION

CHAPTER I

GENERAL

160 Market value

Except as otherwise provided by this Act, the value at any time of any property shall for the purposes of this Act be the price which the property might reasonably be expected to fetch if sold in the open market at that time; but that price shall not be assumed to be reduced on the ground that the whole property is to be placed on the market at one and the same time.

161 Related property

(1) Where the value of any property comprised in a person's estate would be less than the appropriate portion of the value of the aggregate of that and any related property, it shall be the appropriate portion of the value of that aggregate.

(2) For the purposes of this section, property is related to the property comprised in a person's estate if –

(a) it is comprised in the estate of his spouse; or

(b) it is or has within the preceding five years been –

(i) the property of a charity, or held on trust for charitable purposes only, or

(ii) the property of a body mentioned in section 24, 24A or 25 above, and became so on a transfer of value which was made by him or his spouse after 15th April 1976 and was exempt to the extent that the value transferred was attributable to the property.

(3) The appropriate portion of the value of the aggregate mentioned in subsection (1) above is such portion thereof as would be attributable to the value of the first-mentioned property if the value of that aggregate were equal to the sums of the values of that and any related property, the value of each property being determined as if it did not form part of that aggregate.

(4) For the purposes of subsection (3) above the proportion which the value of a smaller number of shares of any claim bears to the value of a greater number shall be taken to be that which the smaller number bears to the greater; and similarly with stock, debentures and units of any other description of property.

(5) Shares shall not be treated for the purposes of subsection (4) above as being of the same class unless they are so treated by the practice of a recognised stock exchange or would be so treated if dealt with on such a stock exchange.

162 Liabilities

(1) A liability in respect of which there is a right to reimbursement shall be taken into account only to the extent (if any) that reimbursement cannot reasonably be expected to be obtained.

(2) Subject to subsection (3) below, where a liability falls to be discharged after the time at which it is to be taken into account it shall be valued as at the time at which it is to be taken into account.

(3) In determining the value of a transferor's estate immediately after a transfer of value, his liability for capital transfer tax shall be computed –

(a) without making any allowance for the fact that the tax will not be due immediately, and

(b) as if any tax recovered otherwise than from the transferor (or a person liable for it under section 203(1) below) were paid in discharge of a liability in respect of which the transferor had a right to reimbursement.

(4) A liability which is an incumbrance on any property shall, as far as possible, be taken to reduce the value of that property.

(5) Where a liability taken into account is a liability to a person resident outside the United Kingdom which neither –

(a) falls to be discharged in the United Kingdom, nor

(b) is an incumbrance on property in the United Kingdom,

it shall, so far as possible, be taken to reduce the value of property outside the United Kingdom.

163 Restriction on freedom to dispose

(1) Where, by a contract made at any time, the right to dispose of any property has been excluded or restricted, then, in determining the value of the property for the purpose of the first relevant event happening after that time, –

(a) the exclusion or restriction shall be taken into account only to the extent (if any) that consideration in money or money's worth was given for it, but

(b) if the contract was a chargeable transfer or was part of associated operations which together were a chargeable transfer, an allowance shall be made for the value transferred thereby (calculated as if not tax had been chargeable on it) or for so much of the value transferred as is attributable to the exclusion or restriction. ...

(3) In this section 'relevant event', in relation to any property, means –

(a) a chargeable transfer in the case of which the whole or part of the value transferred is attributable to the value of the property; and

(b) anything which would be such a chargeable transfer but for this section.

164 Transferor's expenses

In determining the value transferred by a transfer of value, expenses incurred by the transferor in making the transfer (but not his liability for capital transfer tax) –

(a) shall, if borne by him, be left out of account;

(b) shall, if borne by a person benefiting from the transfer, be treated as reducing the value transferred.

165 Tax on capital gains

(1) Where a chargeable transfer is or includes a disposal of an asset and on the disposal a gain accrues to the transferor for the purposes of the [Taxation of Chargeable Gains Act 1992], then if –

(a) the whole or part of the gain is a chargeable gain or a development gain, and

(b) the whole or part of any capital gains tax or income tax chargeable on the gain is borne by the donee (within the meaning of section 282 of that Act),

the amount of the tax so borne shall be treated as reducing the value transferred by the chargeable transfer.

(2) Subsection (1) above shall not apply where the chargeable transfer is made under Part III of this Act and the gain accrues to the trustees of the settlement; but if in such a case any capital gains tax chargeable on the gain is borne by a person who becomes absolutely entitled to the settled property concerned, the amount of the tax so borne shall be treated as reducing the value transferred by the chargeable transfer.

(3) In any case where –

(a) payment of an amount of capital gains tax is postponed by virtue of Schedule 14 to the Finance Act 1984, and

(b) any of that capital gains tax becomes payable in accordance with paragraph 11 of that Schedule by reason of the receipt of a capital payment by a close relative of the beneficiary, as mentioned in sub-paragraph (3) of that paragraph, and

(c) all or part of the capital gains tax becoming so payable is paid by the close relative,

the payment by the close relative shall be treated for the purposes of this Act as made in satisfaction of a liability of his.

166 Creditor's rights

In determining the value of a right to receive a sum due under any obligation it shall be assumed that the obligation will be duly discharged, except if or to the extent that recovery of the sum is impossible or not reasonably practicable and has not become so by any act or omission of the person to whom the sum is due.

167 Life policies, etc

(1) In determining in connection with a transfer of value of a policy of insurance on a person's life or of a contract for an annuity payable on a person's death, that value shall be taken to be not less than –

(a) the total of the premiums or other consideration which, at any time before the transfer of value, has been paid under the policy or contract or any policy or contract for which it was directly or indirectly substituted, less

(b) any sum which, at any time before the transfer of value, has been paid under, or in consideration for the surrender of any right conferred by, the policy or contract or a policy or contract for which it was directly or indirectly substituted.

(2) Subsection (1) above shall not apply in the case of –

(a) the transfer of value which a person makes on his death, or

(b) any other transfer of value which does not result in the policy or contract ceasing to be part of the transferor's estate.

(3) Subsection (1) above shall not apply where the policy is one –

(a) under which the sum assured becomes payable only if the person whose life is insured dies before the expiry of a specified term or both before the expiry of a specified term and during the life of a specified person, and

(b) which, if that specified term ends, or can, under the policy, be extended so as to end, more than three years after the making of the insurance, satisfies the condition that, if neither the person whose life is insured nor the specified person dies before the expiry of the specified term –

(i) the premiums are payable during at least two-thirds of that term and at yearly or shorter intervals, and

I99) the premiums payable in any one period of twelve months are not more than twice the premiums payable in any other such period.

(4) Where the policy is one under which –

(a) the benefit secured is expressed in units the value of which is published and subject to fluctuation, and

(b) the payment of each premium secures the allocation to the policy of a specified number of such units,

then, if the value, at the time of the transfer of value, of the units allocated to the policy on the payment of premiums is less than the aggregate of what the respective values of those units were at the time of allocation, the value to be taken under subsection (1) above as a minimum shall be reduced by the amount of the difference.

(5) References in subsections (1) and (4) above to a transfer of value shall be construed as including references to an event on which there is a charge

to tax under Chapter III of Part III of this Act (apart from section 79), other than an event on which tax is chargeable in respect of the policy or contract by reason only that its value (apart from this section) is reduced.

CHAPTER II

ESTATE ON DEATH

171 Changes occurring on death

(1) In determining the value of a person's estate immediately before his death changes in the value of his estate which have occurred by reason of the death and fall within subsection (2) below shall be taken into account as if they had occurred before the death.

(2) A change falls within this subsection if it is an addition to the property comprised in the estate or an increase or decrease of the value of any property so comprised, other than a decrease resulting from such an alteration as is mentioned in section 98(1) above [alteration of close company's capital], but the termination on the death of any interest or the passing of any interest by survivorship does not fall within this subsection.

172 Funeral expenses

In determining the value of a person's estate immediately before his death, allowance shall be made for reasonable funeral expenses.

176 Related property, etc – sales

(1) This section has effect where, within three years after the death of any person, there is a qualifying sale of any property ('the property concerned') comprised in his estate immediately before his death and valued for the purposes of this Act –

   (a) in accordance with section 161 above, or

   (b) in conjunction with property which was also comprised in the estate but has not at any time since the death been vested in the vendors.

(2) If a claim is made for relief under this section the value of the property concerned immediately before the death shall be taken to be what it would have been if it had not been determined as mentioned in subsection (1) above.

(3) For the purposes of subsection (1) above a sale is a qualifying sale if –

(a) the vendors are the persons in whom the property concerned vested immediately after the death or the deceased's personal representatives; and

(b) it is at arm's length for a price freely negotiated at the time of the sale and is not made in conjunction with a sale of any of the related property taken into account as mentioned in subsection (1)(a) above or any of the property mentioned in subsection (1)(b) above; and

(c) no person concerned as vendor (or as having an interest in the proceeds of sale) is the same as or connected with any person concerned as purchaser (or as having an interest in the purchase); and

(d) neither the vendors nor any other person having an interest in the proceeds of sale obtain in connection with the sale a right to acquire the property sold or any interest in or created out of it.

(4) Subsection (2) above shall not apply unless the price obtained on the sale, with any adjustment needed to take account of any difference in circumstances at the date of the sale and at the date of the death, is less than the value which, apart from this section and apart from Chapter IV of this Part of this Act, would be the value of the property concerned determined as mentioned in subsection (1) above. ...

CHAPTER III

SALE OF SHARES, ETC FROM THE DECEASED'S ESTATE

178 Preliminary

(1) In this Chapter –

'the appropriate person', in relation to any qualifying investments comprised in a person's estate immediately before his death, means the person liable for inheritance tax attributable to the value of those investments or, if there is more than one such person, and one of them is in fact paying the tax, that person;

'the loss on sale' means the amount determined in accordance with section 179(1) below;

'qualifying investments' means (subject to subsection (2) below [listing or dealing suspended]) shares or securities which are quoted at the date of the death in question, holdings in a unit trust which at that date is an authorised unit trust, shares in an open-ended investment company and shares in any common investment fund established under section 42 of the Administration of Justice Act 1982;

'relevant proportion', in relation to the investments to which a claim relates, or any of them, means the proportion by which the loss on sale is reduced under section 180 below;

'sale value', in relation to any qualifying investments, means their value for the purposes of section 179(1)(b) below;

'value on death', in relation to any qualifying investments, means their value for the purposes of section 179(1)(a) below. ...

(3) Any reference in this Chapter to the investments to which a claim relates is a reference to all the qualifying investments which, on the making of the claim, are taken into account under section 179(1) below in determining the loss on sale.

(4) For the purposes of this Chapter –

(a) the personal representatives of the deceased, and

(b) the trustees of a settlement,

shall each be treated as a single and continuing body of persons (distinct from the persons who may from time to time be the personal representatives or trustees).

(5) In any case where, for the purposes of this Chapter, it is necessary to determine the price at which any investments were purchased or sold or the best consideration that could reasonably have been obtained on the sale of any investments, no account shall be taken of expenses (whether by way of commission, stamp duty or otherwise) which are incidental to the sale or purchase.

179 The relief

(1) On a claim being made in that behalf by the appropriate person there shall be determined for the purposes of this Chapter the amount (if any) by which –

(a) aggregate of the values which, apart from this Chapter, would be the values for the purposes of tax of all the qualifying investments comprised in a person's estate immediately before his death which are sold by the appropriate person within the period of twelve months immediately following the date of the death;

exceeds

(b) the aggregate of the values of those investments at the time they were so sold, taking the value of any particular investments for this purpose as the price for which they were so sold or, if it is greater, the best consideration which could reasonably have been obtained for them at the time of the sale.

(2) Subject to the following provisions of this Chapter, in determining the tax chargeable on the death in question, the value of the investments to which the claim relates shall be treated as reduced by an amount equal to the loss on sale.

(3) A claim made by the appropriate person under this Chapter shall specify the capacity in which he makes the claim, and the reference in subsection (1) above to qualifying investments which are sold by him is a reference to investments which, immediately before their sale, were held by him in the capacity in which he makes the claim.

180 Effect of purchases

(1) If a claim is made under this Chapter and, at any time during the period beginning on the date of the death in question and ending two months after the date of the last sale made as mentioned in section 179(1)(a) above, the person making the claim purchases any qualifying investments in the same capacity as that in which he makes the claim, the loss on sale of the investments to which the claim relates shall be treated for the purposes of section 179(2) above as reduced by the proportion which the aggregate of the purchase prices of all the qualifying investments so purchased bears to the aggregate of the values referred to in section 179(1)(b) above (or, if the aggregate of those purchase prices equals or exceeds the aggregate of those values, the loss on sale shall be extinguished). ...

CHAPTER IV

SALE OF LAND FROM DECEASED'S ESTATE

190 Preliminary

(1) In this Chapter –

'the appropriate person', in relation to any interest in land comprised in a person's estate immediately before his death, means the person liable for inheritance tax attributable to the value of that interest or, if there is more than one such person and one of them is in fact paying the tax, that person;

'interest in land' does not include any estate, interest or right by way of mortgage or other security;

'sale price', in relation to any interest in land, means the price for which it is sold or, if greater, the best consideration that could reasonably have been obtained for it at the time of the sale;

'sale value', in relation to any interest in land, means its sale price as increased or reduced under the following provisions of this Chapter;

'value on death', in relation to any interest in land comprised in a person's estate immediately before his death, means the value which, apart from this Chapter, (and apart from section 176 above) would be its value as part of that estate for the purposes of this Act.

(2) Any reference in this Chapter to the interests to which a claim relates is a reference to the interests to which section 191(1) below applies by virtue of the claim.

(3) For the purposes of this Chapter –

(a) the personal representatives of the deceased, and

(b) the trustees of a settlement,

shall each be treated as a single and continuing body of persons (distinct from the persons who may from time to time be the personal representatives or trustees).

(4) In any case where, for the purposes of this Chapter, it is necessary to determine the price at which any interest was purchased or sold or the best consideration that could reasonably have been obtained on the sale of any interest, no account shall be taken of expenses (whether by way of commission, stamp duty or stamp duty land tax or otherwise) which are incidental to the sale or purchase.

191 The relief

(1) Where –

(a) an interest in land is comprised in a person's estate immediately before his death and is sold by the appropriate person within the period of three years immediately following the date of the death, and

(b) the appropriate person makes a claim under this Chapter stating the capacity in which he makes it,

the value for the purposes of this Act of that interest and of any other interest in land comprised in that estate and sold within that period by the person making the claim acting in the same capacity shall, subject to the following provisions of this Chapter, be its sale value.

(2) Subsection (1) above shall not apply to an interest if its sale value would differ from its value on death by less than the lower of –

(a) £1,000, and

(b) 5 per cent of its value on death.

(3) Subsection (1) above shall not apply to an interest if its sale is –

(a) a sale by a personal representative or trustee to –

(i) a person who, at any time between the death and the sale, has been beneficially entitled to, or to an interest in possession in, property comprising the interest sold, or

(ii) the spouse or a child or remoter descendant of a person within sub-paragraph (i) above, or

(iii) trustees of a settlement under which a person within sub-paragraph (i) or (ii) above has an interest in possession in property comprising the interest sold; or

(b) a sale in connection with which the vendor or any person within sub-paragraph (i), (ii) or (iii) of paragraph (a) above obtains a right to acquire the interest sold or any other interest in the same land;

and for the purposes of this subsection a person shall be treated as having in the property comprised in an unadministered estate (within the meaning of section 91(2) above) the same interest as he would have if the administration of the estate had been completed.

PART VII

LIABILITY

199 Dispositions by transferor

(1) The persons liable for the tax on the value transferred by a chargeable transfer made by a disposition (including any omission treated as a disposition under section 3(3) above) of the transferor are –

(a) the transferor;

(b) any person the value of whose estate is increased by the transfer;

(c) so far as the tax is attributable to the value of any property, any person in whom the property is vested (whether beneficially or otherwise) at any time after the transfer, or who at any such time is beneficially entitled to an interest in possession in the property;

(d) where by the chargeable transfer any property becomes comprised in a settlement, any person for whose benefit any of the property or income from it is applied.

(2) Subsection (1)(a) above shall apply in relation to –

(a) the tax on the value transferred by a potentially exempt transfer; and

(b) so much of the tax on the value transferred by any other chargeable transfer made within seven years of the transferor's death as exceeds what it would have been had the transferor died more than seven years after the transfer,

with the substitution for the reference to the transferor of a reference to his personal representatives.

(3) A purchaser of property, and a person deriving title from or under such a purchaser, shall not by virtue of subsection (1)(c) above be liable for tax attributable to the value of the property unless the property is subject to an Inland Revenue charge.

(4) For the purposes of this section –

(a) any person who takes possession of or intermeddles with, or otherwise acts in relation to, property so as to become liable as executor or trustee ... and

(b) any person to whom the management of property is entrusted on behalf of a person not of full legal capacity,

shall be treated as a person in whom the property is vested.

(5) References in this section to any property include references to any property directly or indirectly representing it.

200 Transfer on death

(1) The persons liable for the tax on the value transferred by a chargeable transfer made (under section 4 above) on the death of any person are –

(a) so far as the tax is attributable to the value of property which either –

(i) was not immediately before the death comprised in a settlement, or

(ii) was so comprised and consists of land in the United Kingdom which devolves upon or vests in the deceased's personal representatives,

the deceased's personal representatives;

(b) so far as the tax is attributable to the value of property which, immediately before the death, was comprised in a settlement, the trustees of the settlement;

(c) so far as the tax is attributable to the value of any property, any person in whom the property is vested (whether beneficially or otherwise) at any time after the death, or who at any such time is beneficially entitled to an interest in possession in the property;

(d) so far as the tax is attributable to the value of any property which, immediately before the death, was comprised in a settlement, any person for whose benefit any of the property or income from it is applied after the death.

(2) A purchaser of property, and a person deriving title from or under such a purchaser, shall not by virtue of subsection (1)(c) above be liable for tax attributable to the value of the property unless the property is subject to an Inland Revenue charge.

(3) For the purposes of subsection (1) above a person entitled to part only of the income of any property shall, notwithstanding anything in section 50 above, be deemed to be entitled to an interest n the whole of the property.

(4) Subsections (4) and (5) of section 199 above shall have effect for the purposes of this section as they have effect for the purposes of that section.

201 Settled property

(1) The persons liable for the tax on the value transferred by a chargeable transfer made under Part III of this Act are –

(a) the trustees of the settlement;

(b) any person entitled (whether beneficially or not) to an interest in possession in the settled property;

(c) any person for whose benefit any of the settled property or income from it is applied at or after the time of the transfer;

(d) where the transfer is made during the life of the settlor and the trustees are not for the time being resident in the United Kingdom, the settlor.

(2) Where the chargeable transfer is made within seven years of the transferor's death but it is not a potentially exempt transfer, subsection (1)(d) above shall not apply in relation to so much of the tax as exceeds what it would have been had the transferor died more than seven years after the transfer. ...

(4) Where more than one person is a settlor in relation to a settlement and the circumstances so require, subsection (1)(d) above shall have effect in relation to it as if the settled property were comprised in separate settlements.

(5) For the purposes of this section trustees of a settlement shall be regarded as not resident in the United Kingdom unless the general administration of the settlement is ordinarily carried on in the United Kingdom and the trustees or a majority of them (and, where there is more than one class of trustees, a majority of each class) are for the time being resident in the United Kingdom.

(6) References in this section to any property include references to any property directly or indirectly representing it.

203 Liability of spouse

(1) Where –

(a) a transferor is liable for any tax on the value transferred by a chargeable transfer, and

(b) by another transfer of value made by him on or after 27th March 1974 ('the spouse transfer') any property became the property of a person ('the transferee') who at the time of both transfers was his spouse,

the transferee is liable for so much of the tax as does not exceed the market value of the property at the time of the spouse transfer or, in a case where subsection (2) below applies the lower market value mentioned in paragraph (c) of that subsection.

(2) This subsection applies where –

(a) the chargeable transfer is made after the spouse transfer; and

(b) the property ('the transferred property') which became the property of the transferee either remains the transferee's property at the date of the chargeable transfer or has before that date been sold by the transferee by a qualifying sale; and

(c) the market value of the transferred property on the relevant date (that is to say, the date of the chargeable transfer or, as the case may be, of the qualifying sale) is lower than its market value at the time of the spouse transfer; and

(d) the transferred property is not tangible movable property.

(3) In this section 'qualifying sale' has the same meaning as in section 131 above; and, subject to subsection (4) below sections 133 to 140 above shall have effect for the purposes of this section as they have effect for the purposes of section 131.

(4) In their application by virtue of subsection (3) above, sections 133 to 140 above shall have effect as if –

(a) references to the chargeable transfer were references to the spouse transfer,

(b) references to the transferee's spouse were omitted, and

(c) references to section 131 above were references to this section.

204 Limitation of liability

(1) A person shall not be liable under section 200(1)(a) above for any tax as a personal representative of a deceased person, except to the extent of the following assets, namely –

(a) so far as the tax is attributable to the value of any property other than such as is mentioned in paragraph (b) below, the assets (other than property so mentioned) which he has received as personal representative or might have so received but for his own neglect or default; and

(b) so far as the tax is attributable to property which, immediately before the death, was comprised in a settlement and consists of land in the United Kingdom, so much of that property as is at any time available in his hands for the payment of the tax, or might have been so available but for his own neglect or default.

(2) A person shall not be liable for tax as trustee in relation to any property, except to the extent of –

(a) so much of the property as he has actually received or disposed of or as he has become liable to account for to the persons beneficially entitled thereto, and

(b) so much of any other property as is for the time being available in his hands as trustee for the payment of the tax or might have been so available but for his own neglect or default.

(3) A person not liable as mentioned in subsection (1) or (2) above but liable for tax as a person in whom property is vested or liable for tax as a person entitled to a beneficial interest in possession in any property shall not be liable for the tax except to the extent of that property.

(5) A person liable for tax as a person for whose benefit any settled property, or income from any settled property, is applied, shall not be liable for the tax except to the extent of the amount of the property or income (reduced in the case of income by the amount of any income tax borne by him in respect of it, and in the case of other property in respect of which he has borne income tax by virtue of section 739 or 740 of the Taxes Act 1988 by the amount of that tax).

(6) Where a person is liable for any tax –

(a) under section 199 above otherwise than as transferor or personal representative of the transferor, or

(b) under section 201 above otherwise than as trustee of the settlement,

he shall be liable only if the tax remains unpaid after it ought to have been paid and, in a case where any part of the value transferred is attributable to the tax on it, shall be liable to no greater extent than he would have been had the value transferred been reduced by the tax remaining unpaid.

(7) Where the tax exceeds what it would have been had the transferor died more than seven years after the transfer, subsection (6) above shall not apply in relation to the excess.

(8) A person liable by virtue of section 199(2) above for any tax as personal representative of the transferor shall be liable only to the extent that either –

(a) in consequence of subsections (2), (3) and (5) above, no person falling within paragraphs (b) to (d) of section 199(1) above is liable for the tax, or

(b) the tax remains unpaid twelve months after the end of the month in which the death of the transferor occurs,

and, subject to that, shall be liable only to the extent of the assets mentioned in subsection (1) above.

(9) Where by virtue of subsection (3) of section 102 of the Finance Act 1986 the estate of a deceased person is treated as including property which would not apart from that subsection form part of his estate, a person shall be liable under section 200(1)(a) above as personal representative for tax attributable to the value of that property only if the tax remains unpaid twelve months after the end of the month in which the death occurs and, subject to that, only to the extent of the assets mentioned in subsection (1) above.

205 More than one person liable

Except as otherwise provided, where under this Act two or more persons are liable for the same tax, each of them shall be liable for the whole of it.

207 Conditional exemption, etc

(1) Where tax is chargeable under section 32 above on the occurrence of an event which is a chargeable event with respect to any property by virtue of subsection (2) or subsection (3)(a) of that section, the person liable for the tax is the person who, if the property were sold –

(a) in a case within subsection (2) of that section, at the time the tax becomes chargeable, and

(b) in a case within subsection (3)(a), immediately after the death,

would be entitled to receive (whether for his benefit or not) the proceeds of sale or any income arising from them.

(2) Where tax is chargeable under section 32 above on the occurrence of an event which is a chargeable event with respect to any property by virtue of subsection (3)(b) of that section, the person liable for the tax is the person by whom or for whose benefit the property is disposed of.

(2A) Where tax is chargeable under section 32A above on the occurrence of an event which is a chargeable event with respect to any property by virtue of subsection (3) or subsection (4)(a) of that section, the person liable for the tax is the person who, if the property were sold –

(a) in a case within subsection (3) of that section, at the time the tax becomes chargeable, and

(b) in a case within subsection (4)(a), immediately after the death,

would be entitled to receive (whether for his benefit or not) the proceeds of sale or any income arising from them.

(2B) Where tax is chargeable under section 32A above on the occurrence of an event which is a chargeable event with respect to any property by virtue of subsection (4)(b) of that section, the person liable for the tax is the person by whom or for whose benefit the property is disposed of.

(3) The persons liable for tax charged under section 79(3) above are –

(a) the trustees of the settlement concerned, and

(b) any person for whose benefit any of the property or income from it is applied at or after the time of the event occasioning the charge. ...

208 Woodlands

The person liable for tax chargeable under section 126 above in relation to a disposal is the person who is entitled to the proceeds of sale or would be so entitled if the disposal were a sale.

211 Burden of tax on death

(1) Where personal representatives are liable for tax on the value transferred by a chargeable transfer made on death, the tax should be treated as part of the general testamentary and administration expenses

of the estate, but only so far as it is attributable to the value of property in the United Kingdom which –

(a) vests in the deceased's personal representatives, and

(b) was not immediately before the death comprised in a settlement.

(2) Subsection (1) above shall have effect subject to any contrary intention shown by the deceased in his will.

(3) Where any amount of tax paid by personal representatives on the value transferred by a chargeable transfer made on death does not fall to be borne as part of the general testamentary and administration expenses of the estate, that amount shall, where occasion requires, be repaid to them by the person in whom the property to the value of which the tax is attributable is vested.

(4) References in this section to tax include references to interest on tax.

PART VIII

ADMINISTRATION AND COLLECTION MANAGEMENT

215 General

The tax shall be under the care and management of the Board.

216 Delivery of accounts

(1) Except as otherwise provided by this section or by regulations under section 256 below, the personal representatives of a deceased person and every person who –

(a) is liable as transferor for tax on the value transferred by a chargeable transfer, or would be so liable if tax were chargeable on that value, or

(b) is liable as trustee of a settlement for tax on the value transferred by a transfer of value, or would be so liable if tax were chargeable on that value, or

(bb) is liable under section 199(1)(b) above for tax on the value transferred by a potentially exempt transfer which proves to be a chargeable transfer, or would be so liable if tax were chargeable on that value, or

(bc) is liable under section 200(1)(c) above for tax on the value transferred by a chargeable transfer made on death, so far as the tax is attributable to the value of property which, apart from section 102(3) of the Finance Act 1986, would not form part of the deceased's estate, or would be so liable if tax were chargeable on the value transferred on the death, or

(bd) is liable under section 201(1)(b), (c) or (d) above for tax on the value transferred by a potentially exempt transfer which is made under section 52 above and which proves to be a chargeable transfer, or would be so liable if tax were chargeable on that value, or

(c) is liable as trustee of a settlement for tax on an occasion on which tax is chargeable under Chapter III of Part III of this Act (apart from section 79), or would be so liable if tax were chargeable on the occasion,

shall deliver to the Board an account specifying to the best of his knowledge and belief all appropriate property and the value of that property.

(2) Where in the case of the estate of a deceased person no grant of representation or confirmation has been obtained in the United Kingdom before the expiration of the period of twelve months from the end of the month in which the death occurred –

(a) every person in whom any of the property forming part of the estate vests (whether beneficially or otherwise) on or at any time after the deceased's death or who at any such time is beneficially entitled to an interest in possession in any such property, and

(b) where any of the property is at any such time comprised in a settlement and there is no person beneficially entitled to an interest in possession in that property, every person for whose benefit any of that property (or income from it) is applied at any such time,

shall deliver to the Board an account specifying to the best of his knowledge and belief the appropriate property vested in him, in which he has an interest or which (or income from which) is applicable for his benefit and the value of that property.

(3) Subject to subsections (3A) and (3B) below, where an account is to be delivered by personal representatives (but not where it is to be delivered by a person who is an executor of the deceased only in respect of settled land in England and Wales), the appropriate property is –

(a) all property which formed part of the deceased's estate immediately before his death, other than property which would not, apart from section 102(3) of the Finance Act 1986, form part of his estate; and

(b) all property to which was attributable the value transferred by any chargeable transfers made by the deceased within seven years of his death.

(3A) If the personal representatives, after making the fullest enquiries that are reasonably practicable in the circumstances, are unable to ascertain the exact value of any particular property, their account shall in the first instance be sufficient as regards that property if it contains –

(a) a statement to that effect;

(b) a provisional estimate of the value of the property; and

(c) an undertaking to deliver a further account of it as soon as its value is ascertained.

(3B) The Board may from time to time give such general or special directions as they think fit for restricting the property to be specified in pursuance of subsection (3) above by any class of personal representatives.

(4) Where subsection (3) above does not apply the appropriate property is any property to the value of which the tax is or would be attributable.

(5) Except in the case of an account to be delivered by personal representatives, a person shall not be required to deliver an account under this section with respect to any property if a full and property account of the property, specifying its value, has already been delivered to the Board by some other person who –

(a) is or would be liable for the tax attributable to the value of the property, and

(b) is not or would not be liable with him jointly as trustee;

and a person within subsection (2) above shall not be required to deliver an account under that subsection if he or another person within that subsection has satisfied the Board that an account will in due course be delivered by the personal representatives.

(6) An account under the preceding provisions of this section shall be delivered –

(a) in the case of an account to be delivered by personal representatives, before the expiration of the period of twelve months from the end of the month in which the death occurs, or, if it expires later, the period of three months beginning with the date on which the personal representatives first act as such;

(aa) in the case of an account to be delivered by a person within subsection (1)(bb) or (bd) above, before the expiration of the period of twelve months from the end of the month in which the death of the transferor occurs;

(ab) in the case of an account to be delivered by a person within subsection (1)(bc) above, before the expiration of the period of twelve months from the end of the month in which the death occurs;

(b) in the case of an account to be delivered by a person within subsection (2) above, before the expiration of the period of three months from the time when he first has reason to believe that he is required to deliver an account under that subsection;

(c) in the case of an account to be delivered by any other person, before the expiration of that period of twelve months from the end of the month in which the transfer is made or, if it expires later, the period of three months beginning with the date on which he first becomes liable for tax.

(7) A person liable for tax under section 32, 32A, 79 or 126 above or under Schedule 5 [Conditional exemption: deaths before 7th April 1976] to this Act shall deliver an account under this section before the expiration of the period of six months from the end of the month in which the event by reason of which the tax is chargeable occurs.

217 Defective accounts

If a person who has delivered an account under section 216 above discovers at any time that the account is defective in a material respect by reason of anything contained in or omitted from it he shall, within six months of that time, deliver to the Board a further account containing such information as may be necessary to remedy the defect.

218A Instruments varying dispositions taking effect on death

(1) Where –

(a) an instrument is made varying any of the dispositions of the property comprised in the estate of a deceased person immediately before his death,

(b) the instrument contains a statement under subsection (2) of section 142 above, and

(c) the variation results in additional tax being payable,

the relevant persons (within the meaning of that subsection) shall, within six months after the day on which the instrument is made, deliver a copy of it to the Board and notify them of the amount of the additional tax.

(2) To the extent that any of the relevant persons comply with the requirements of this section, the others are discharged from the duty to comply with them.

219 Power to require information

(1) The Board may by notice in writing require any person to furnish them within such time, not being less than thirty days, as may be specified in the notice with such information as the Board may require for the purposes of this Act.

(1A) A notice under this section is not to be given except with the consent of a Special Commissioner and the Commissioner is to give his consent only on being satisfied that in all the circumstances the Board are justified in proceeding under this section.

(2) A notice under this section may be combined with one relating to income tax.

(3) Subject to subsection (4) below, a barrister or solicitor shall not be obliged in pursuance of a notice under this section to disclose, without his client's consent, any information with respect to which a claim to professional privilege could be maintained.

(4) A solicitor may be obliged in pursuance of a notice under this section to disclose the name and address of his client; ...

219A Power to call for documents, etc

(1) An officer of the Board may by notice in writing require any person who has delivered, or is liable to deliver, an account under section 216 or 217 above, within such time as may be specified in the notice –

   (a) to produce to the officer such documents as are in the person's possession or power and as the officer may reasonably require for any of the purposes mentioned in subsection (2) below; and

   (b) to furnish the officer with such accounts or particulars as he may reasonably require for any of those purposes.

(2) The purposes are –

   (a) enquiring into an account under section 216 or 217 above (including any claim or election included in the account);

   (b) determining whether and, if so, the extent to which such an account is incorrect or incomplete; and

   (c) making a determination for the purposes of a notice under section 221 below. ...

219B   Appeal against requirement to produce documents, etc

(1) An appeal may be brought against any requirement imposed by a notice under section 219A(1) above to produce any document or to furnish any accounts or particulars.

(2) Subject to the following provisions of this section, the provisions of this Act relating to appeals shall have effect in relation to an appeal under this section as they have effect in relation to an appeal against a determination specified in a notice under section 221 below.

(3) An appeal under this section must be brought within the period of thirty days beginning with the date on which the notice under section 219A(1) above is given. …

221   Notices of determination

(1) Where it appears to the Board that a transfer of value has been made or where a claim under this Act is made to the Board in connection with a transfer of value, the Board may give notice in writing to any person who appears to the Board to be the transferor or the claimant or to be liable for any of the tax chargeable on the value transferred, stating that they have determined the matters specified in the notice. …

222   Appeals against determinations

(1) A person on whom a notice under section 221 above has been served may, within thirty days of the service, appeal against any determination specified in it by notice in writing given to the Board and specifying the grounds of appeal.

(2) Subject to the following provisions of this section the appeal shall be to the Special Commissioners.

(3) Where –

   (a) it is so agreed between the appellant and the Board, or
   (b) the High Court, on an application made by the appellant, is satisfied that the matters to be decided on the appeal are likely to be substantially confined to questions of law and gives leave for that purpose,

the appeal may be to the High Court.

(4) An appeal on any question as to the value of land in the United Kingdom may be to the appropriate tribunal.

(4A) If and so far as the question in dispute on any appeal under this section to the Special Commissioners or the High Court is a question as to the value of land in the United Kingdom, the question shall be determined on a reference to the appropriate tribunal.

(4B) In this section 'the appropriate tribunal' means –

(a) where the land is in England or Wales, the Lands Tribunal; ...

223 Appeals out of time

An appeal under section 222 above may be brought out of time with the consent of the Board or the Special Commissioners; and the Board –

(a) shall give that consent if satisfied, on an application for the purpose, that there was a reasonable excuse for not bringing the appeal within the time limited and that the application was made thereafter without unreasonable delay, and

(b) shall, if not so satisfied, refer the application for determination by the Special Commissioners.

225 Appeals from Special Commissioners

(1) Any party to an appeal, if dissatisfied in point of law with the determination of that appeal by the Special Commissioners, may appeal against that determination to the High Court.

(2) The High Court shall hear and determine any question of law arising on an appeal under subsection (1) above and may reserve, affirm or vary the determination appealed against, or remit the matter to the Special Commissioners with the court's opinion on it, or make such other order in relation to the matter as the court thinks fit. ...

226 Payment: general rules

(1) Except as otherwise provided by the following provisions of this Part of this Act, the tax on the value transferred by a chargeable transfer shall be due six months after the end of the month in which the chargeable transfer is made or, in the case of a transfer made after 5th April and before 1st October in any year otherwise than on death, at the end of April in the next year.

(2) Personal representatives shall, on delivery of their account, pay all the tax for which they are liable and may, on delivery of that account, also pay

any part of the tax chargeable on the death for which they are not liable, if the persons liable for it request them to make the payment. ...

230 Acceptance of property in satisfaction of tax

(1) The Board may, if they think fit and the Secretary of State agrees, on the application of any person liable to pay tax or interest payable under section 233 below, accept in satisfaction of the whole or any part of it any property to which this section applies.

(2) This section applies to any such land as may be agreed upon between the Board and the person liable to pay tax.

(3) This section also applies to any objects which are or have been kept in any building –

(a) if the Board have determined to accept or have accepted that building in satisfaction or part satisfaction of tax or of estate duty, or

(b) if the building or any interest in it belongs to Her Majesty in right of the Crown or of the Duchy of Lancaster, or belongs to the Duchy of Cornwall or belongs to a Government department or is held for the purposes of a Government department, or

(c) if the building is one of which the Secretary of State is guardian under the Ancient Monuments and Archaeological Areas Act 1979 ..., or

(d) if the building belongs to any body within Schedule 3 to this Act,

in any case where it appears to the Secretary of State desirable for the objects to remain associated with the building.

(4) This section also applies to –

(a) any picture, print, book, manuscript, work of act, scientific object or other thing which the Secretary of State is satisfied is pre-eminent for its national, scientific, historic or artistic interest, and

(b) any collection or group of pictures, prints, books, manuscripts, works of art, scientific objects or other things if the Secretary of State is satisfied that the collection or group, taken as a whole, is pre-eminent for its national, scientific, historic or artistic interest.

(5) In this section –

'national interest' includes interest within any part of the United Kingdom;

and in determining under subsection (4) above whether any object or collection or group of objects is pre-eminent, regard shall be had to any significant association of the object, collection or group with a particular place. ...

239 Certificates of discharge

(1) Where application is made to the Board by a person liable for any tax on the value transferred by a chargeable transfer which is attributable to the value of property specified in the application, the Board, on being satisfied that the tax so attributable has been or will be paid, may give a certificate to that effect, and shall do so if the chargeable transfer is one made on death or the transferor has died.

(2) Where tax is or may be chargeable on the value transferred by a transfer of value and –

(a) application is made to the Board after the expiration of two years from the transfer (or, if the Board think fit to entertain the application, at an earlier time) by a person who is or might be liable for the whole or part of the tax, and

(b) the applicant delivers to the Board, if the transfer is one made on death, a full statement to the best of his knowledge and belief of all property included in the estate of the deceased immediately before his death and, in any other case, a full and proper account under this Part of this Act,

the Board may, as the case requires, determine the amount of the tax or determine that no tax is chargeable; and subject to the payment of any tax so determined to be chargeable the Board may give a certificate of their determination, and shall do so if the transfer of value is one made on death or the transferor has died.

(2A) An application under subsection (1) or (2) above with respect to tax which is or may become chargeable on the value transferred by a potentially exempt transfer may not be made before the expiration of two years from the date of the transferor (except where the Board think fit to entertain the application at an earlier time after the death).

(3) Subject to subsection (4) below, –

(a) a certificate under subsection (1) above shall discharge the property shown in it from the Inland Revenue charge on its acquisition by a purchaser, and

(b) a certificate under subsection (2) above shall discharge all persons from any further claim for the tax on the value transferred by the chargeable transfer concerned and extinguish any Inland Revenue charge for that tax.

(4) A certificate under this section shall not discharge any person from tax in case of fraud or failure to disclose material facts and shall not affect any further tax –

(a) that may afterwards be shown to be payable by virtue of section 93, 142, 143, 144 or 145 above, or

(b) that may be payable if any further property is afterwards shown to have been included in the estate of a deceased person immediately before his death;

but in so far as the certificate shows any tax to be attributable to the value of any property it shall remain valid in favour of a purchaser of that property without notice of any fact invalidating the certificate.

(5) References in this section to a transfer of value, or to the value transferred by a transfer of value, shall be construed as including references to an occasion on which tax is chargeable under Chapter III of Part III of this Act (apart from section 79) or to the amount on which tax is then chargeable.

PART IX

MISCELLANEOUS AND SUPPLEMENTARY

269 Control of company

(1) For the purposes of this Act a person has control of a company at any time if he then has the control of powers of voting on all questions affecting the company as a whole which if exercised would yield a majority of the votes capable of being exercised on them.

(2) For the purposes of this Act shares or securities shall be deemed to give a person control of a company if, together with any shares or securities which are related property within the meaning of section 161 above, they would be sufficient to give him control of the company (as defined in subsection (1) above).

(3) Where shares or securities are comprised in a settlement, any powers of voting which they give to the trustees of the settlement shall for the purposes of subsection (1) above be deemed to be given to the person beneficially entitled in possession to the shares or securities (except in a case where no individual is so entitled).

(4) Where a company has shares or securities of any class giving powers of voting limited to either or both of –

(a) the question of winding up the company, and

(b) any question primarily affecting shares or securities of that class,

the reference in subsection (1) above to all questions affecting the company as a whole shall have effect as a reference to all such questions except any in relation to which those powers are capable of being exercised.

270 Connected persons

For the purposes of this Act any question whether a person is connected with another shall be determined as, for the purposes of the 1992 Act, it falls to be determined under section 286 of that Act, but as if in that section 'relative' included uncle, aunt, nephew and niece and 'settlement', 'settlor' and 'trustee' had the same meanings as in this Act.

272 General interpretation

In this Act, except where the context otherwise requires, –

'amount' includes value;

'authorised unit trust' means a scheme which is a unit trust scheme for the purposes of section 469 of the Taxes Act 1988 (see subsection (7) of that section) and in the case of which an order under section 243 of the Finance Services and Markets Act 2000 is in force;

'barrister' includes a member of the Faculty of Advocates;

'the Board' means the Commissioners of Inland Revenue;

'charity' and 'charitable' have the same meanings as in the Income Tax Acts;

'conditionally exempt transfer' shall be construed in accordance with section 30(2) above;

'disposition' includes a disposition effected by associated operations;

'estate' shall be construed in accordance with sections 5, 55 and 151(4) above;

'estate duty' includes estate duty under the law of Northern Ireland;

'excluded property' shall be construed in accordance with sections 6 and 48 above; ...

'incumbrance' includes any heritable security, or other debt or payment secured upon heritage;

'Inland Revenue charge' means a charge imposed by virtue of section 237 above;

'land' does not include any estate interest or right by way of mortgage or other security;

'local authority' has the meaning given by section 842A of the Taxes Act 1988;

'mortgage' includes a heritable security and a security constituted over any interest in movable property;

'open-ended investment company' means an open-ended investment company within the meaning given by section 236 of the Financial Services and Markets Act 2000 which is incorporated in the United Kingdom;

'personal representatives' includes any person by whom or on whose behalf an application for a grant of administration or for the resealing of a grant made outside the United Kingdom is made, and any such person as mentioned in section 199(4)(a) above;

'property' includes rights and interests of any description but does not include a settlement power;

'purchaser' means a purchaser in good faith for consideration in money or money's worth other than a nominal consideration and includes a lessee, mortgagee or other person who for such consideration acquires an interest in the property in question;

'quoted', in relation to any shares or securities, means listed on a recognised stock exchange or dealt in on the Unlisted Securities Market and 'unquoted', in relation to any shares or securities, means neither so listed nor so dealt in;

'reversionary interest' has the meaning given by section 47 above;

'settlement' and 'settled property' shall be construed in accordance with section 43 above;

'settlement power' has the meaning given by section 47A above;

'settlor' shall be construed in accordance with section 44 above;

'Special Commissioners' has the same meaning as in the Taxes Management Act 1970;

'tax' means inheritance tax;

'the Taxes Act 1970' means the Income and Corporation Taxes Act 1970;

'the Taxes Act 1988' means the Income and Corporation Taxes Act 1988;

'trustee' shall be construed in accordance with section 45 above; and

'the 1992 Act' means the Taxation of Chargeable Gains Act 1992.

SCHEDULE 1

TABLE OF RATES OF TAX [2004–05]

Portion of value		Rate of tax
Lower Limit (£)	Upper Limit (£)	Per cent
0	263,000	NIL
263,000	–	40

SCHEDULE 2

PROVISIONS APPLYING ON REDUCTION OF TAX

1. In this Schedule –

(a) references to a reduction are to a reduction of tax by the substitution of a new Table in Schedule 1 to this Act, and

(b) references to something happening before or after a reduction are to its happening before or, as the case may be, on or after the date on which the Table giving effect to the reduction comes into force.

1A. Where a person who has made a potentially exempt transfer before a reduction dies after that reduction (or after that and one or more subsequent reductions) and within the period of seven years beginning with the date of the transfer, tax shall be chargeable by reason of the transfer proving to be a chargeable transfer only if, and to the extent that, it would have been so chargeable if the Table in Schedule 1 as substituted by that reduction (or by the most recent of those reductions) had applied to that transfer.

2. Where a person who has made a chargeable transfer (other than a potentially exempt transfer) before a reduction dies after that reduction (or after that and one or more subsequent reductions) and within seven years of the transfer, additional tax shall be chargeable by reason of his death only if, and to the extent that, it would have been so chargeable if the Table in Schedule 1 as substituted by that reduction (or by the most recent of those reductions) had applied to that transfer.

3. Where tax is chargeable under section 65 of this Act on any occasion after a reduction and the rate at which it is charged is determined under section 69 by reference to the rate that was (or would have been) charged under section 64 on an occasion before that reduction (or before that and one or more other reductions), the rate charged on the later occasion shall be determined as if the Table in Schedule 1 as substituted by that reduction (or

by the most recent of those reductions) had been in force on the earlier occasion.

4. Where the value of any trees or underwood has been left out of account under Chapter III of Part V of this Act in determining the value transferred by the chargeable transfer made on a death before a reduction and tax is chargeable under section 126 on a disposal of the trees or underwood after that reduction (or after that and one or more subsequent reductions) the rate or rates mentioned in section 128 shall be determined as if the Table in Schedule 1 as substituted by that reduction (or by the most recent of those reductions) had applied to that transfer.

5. Where tax is chargeable under section 32 or 32A of this Act by reason of a chargeable event occurring after a reduction and the rate or rates at which it is charged fall to be determined under the provisions of section 33(1)(b)(ii) by reference to a death which occurred before that reduction (or before that and one or more other reductions) those provisions shall apply as if the Table in Schedule 1 as substituted by that reduction (or by the most recent of those reductions) had been in force at the time of the death. ...

SCHEDULE 3

GIFTS FOR NATIONAL PURPOSES, ETC

The National Gallery.

The British Museum.

The National Museums of Scotland.

The National Museum of Wales.

The Ulster Museum.

Any other similar national institution which exists wholly or mainly for the purpose of preserving for the public benefit a collection of scientific, historic or artistic interest and which is approved for the purposes of this Schedule by the Treasury.

Any museum or art gallery in the United Kingdom which exists wholly or mainly for that purpose and is maintained by a local authority or university in the United Kingdom.

Any library the main function of which is to serve the needs of teaching and research at a university in the United Kingdom.

The Historic Buildings and Monuments Commission for England.

The National Trust for Places of Historic Interest or Natural Beauty.

The National Trust for Scotland for Places of Historic Interest or Natural Beauty.

The National Art Collection Fund.

The Trustees of the National Heritage Memorial Fund.

The National Endowment for Science, Technology and the Arts.

The Friends of the National Libraries.

The Historic Churches Preservation Trust.

English Nature.

Scottish Natural Heritage.

Countryside Council for Wales.

Any local authority.

Any Government department (including the National Debt Commissioners).

Any university or university college of the United Kingdom.

A health service body, within the meaning of section 519A of the Income and Corporation Taxes Act 1988.

NB As to the short title of this Act and the use of the expression 'inheritance tax', see s100 of the Finance Act 1986.

Extra-statutory concession F1 *Mourning: As a funeral expense*: A reasonable amount for mourning for the family and servants is allowed as a funeral expense

As amended by the Companies Consolidation (Consequential Provisions) Act 1985, s30, Schedule 2; National Heritage (Scotland) Act 1985, s24(1), Schedule 2, Pt I, para 4; Finance Act 1985, ss94, 98(6), Schedule 26, paras 1–5, 8–11, Schedule 27, Pt XI; Finance Act 1986, ss100, 101(1), (3), 106(1)–(3), 105, 114(6), Schedule 19, Pt I, paras 1–3, 5–11, 16, 17, 19, 21–24, 26–29, 35, 37, Schedule 23, Pt X; Finance Act 1987, s58, Schedule 8, paras 1, 4, 5, 8, 9, 11, 13, 17; Finance (No 2) Act 1987, ss96 (1)–(3), (5)–(7), 104(4), Schedule 7, paras 1, 3, 4, Schedule 9, Pt III; Income and Corporation Taxes Act 1988, s844(1), Schedule 29, para 32; Finance Act 1988, ss137, 148, Schedule 14, Pt X; Companies Act 1989, s144(4), Schedule 18, para 30(1), (3); Finance Act 1989, s171(1), (2), (4), (6); Transfer of Functions (Economic Statistics) Order 1989, art 6(4), Schedule 2, para 5(2)(b); Finance Act 1990, ss124, 127(3), (4), Schedule 18, para 4; National Health Service and Community Care Act 1990, s61(5); Environmental Protection Act 1990, s128, Schedule 6, para 25; National Heritage (Scotland) Act 1991, s4(10), Schedule 2, para 9; Taxation of Chargeable Gains Act 1992, s290(1), Schedule 10, para 8(1)–(3), (5), (8), (12), (13); Finance (No 2) Act 1992, s73, Schedule 14, paras 1–4; Transfer of Functions (National Heritage) Order 1992, art 12(2), Schedule 2, para 6;

Finance Act 1993, ss197, 200(1), (3); Finance Act 1994, s247(1)–(3); General and Special Commissioners (Amendment of Enactments) Regulations 1994, reg 2(1), Schedule 1, paras 1, 21; Finance Act 1995, ss52(4), (5), 155, 162, Schedule 29, Pt XI; Finance Act 1996, ss154(7), 184(1)–(7), 199, 205, Schedule 28, paras 7, 8, Schedule 38, paras 2, 4,(1), (3), Schedule 41, Pts IV, VI; Transfer of Functions (Registration and Statistics) Order 1996, art 5(1), Schedule 2, para 21; Housing Act 1996 (Consequential Provisions) Order 1996, art 5, Schedule 2, para 12; Finance Act 1997, ss93, 94; National Lottery Act 1998, s24(3); Finance Act 1998, ss142, 143(1)–(6), 144, 165, Schedule 25, paras 2–6, 7(1)–(7), 8, Schedule 27, Pt IV; Finance Act 1999, ss105, 106; Inheritance Tax (Indexation) Order 2000; Countryside and Rights of Way Act 2000, s73(4), Schedule 8, para 1(i); Finance Act 2002, ss119, 120(1), (2), (4); Finance Act 2003, ss123, 186, 216, Schedule 18, para 2, Schedule 43, Pt 4(1).

ADMINISTRATION OF JUSTICE ACT 1985
(1985 c 61)

48 Power of High Court to authorise action to be taken in reliance on counsel's opinion

(1) Where –

(a) any question of construction has arisen out of the terms of a will or a trust; and

(b) an opinion in writing given by a person who has a ten year High Court qualification, within the meaning of section 71 of the Courts and Legal Services Act 1990, has been obtained on that question by the personal representatives or trustees under the will or trust,

the High Court may, on the application of the personal representatives or trustees and without hearing argument, make an order authorising those persons to take such steps in reliance on the said opinion as are specified in the order.

(2) The High Court shall not make an order under subsection (1) if it appears to the court that a dispute exists which would make it inappropriate for the court to make the order without hearing argument.

49 Powers of High Court on compromise of probate action

(1) Where on a compromise of a probate action in the High Court –

(a) the court is invited to pronounce for the validity of one or more wills, or against the validity of one or more wills, or for the validity of one or more wills and against the validity of one or more other wills; and

(b) the court is satisfied that consent to the making of the pronouncement or, as the case may be, each of the pronouncements in question has been given by or on behalf of every relevant beneficiary,

the court may without more pronounce accordingly.

(2) In this section –

'probate action' means an action for the grant of probate of the will, or letters of administration of the estate, of a deceased person or for the revocation of such a grant or for a decree pronouncing for or against the validity of an alleged will, not being an action which is non-contentious or common form probate business; and

'relevant beneficiary', in relation to a pronouncement relating to any will or wills of a deceased person, means –

(a) a person who under any such will is beneficially interested in the deceased's estate; and

(b) where the effect of the pronouncement would be to cause the estate to devolve as on an intestacy (or partial intestacy), or to prevent it from so devolving, a person who under the law relating to intestacy is beneficially interested in the estate.

50   Power of High Court to appoint substitute for, or to remove, personal representative

(1) Where an application relating to the estate of a deceased person is made to the High Court under this subsection by or on behalf of a personal representative of the deceased or a beneficiary of the estate, the court may in its discretion –

(a) appoint a person (in this section called a substituted personal representative) to act as personal representative of the deceased in place of the existing personal representative or representatives of the deceased or any of them; or

(b) if there are two or more existing personal representatives of the deceased, terminate the appointment of one or more, but not all, of those persons.

(2) Where the court appoints a person to act as a substituted personal representative of a deceased person, then –

(a) if that person is appointed to act with an executor or executors the appointment shall (except for the purposes of including him in any chain of representation) constitute him executor of the deceased as from the date of the appointment; and

(b) in any other case the appointment shall constitute that person administrator of the deceased's estate as from the date of the appointment.

(3) The court may authorise a person appointed as a substituted personal representative to charge remuneration for his services as such, on such

terms (whether or not involving the submission of bills of charges for taxation by the court) as the court may think fit.

(4) Where an applicant relating to the estate of a deceased person is made to the court under subsection (1), the court may, if it thinks fit, proceed as if the application were, or included, an application for the appointment under the Judicial Trustees Act 1896 of a judicial trustee in relation to that estate.

(5) In this section 'beneficiary', in relation to the estate of a deceased person, means a person who under the will of the deceased or under the law relating to intestacy is beneficially interested in the estate.

As amended by the Courts and Legal Services Act 1990, s71(2), Schedule 10, para 63.

FINANCE ACT 1986
(1986 c 41)

100 Capital transfer tax to be known as inheritance tax

(1) On and after the passing of this Act, the tax charged under the Capital Transfer Tax Act 1984 (in this Part of this Act referred to as 'the 1984 Act') shall be known as inheritance tax and, accordingly, on and after that passing, –

(a) the 1984 Act may be cited as the Inheritance Tax Act 1984; and

(b) subject to subsection (2) below, any reference to capital transfer tax in the 1984 Act, in any other enactment passed before or in the same Session as this Act or in any document executed, made, served or issued on or before the passing of this Act or at any time thereafter shall have effect as a reference to inheritance tax.

(2) Subsection (1)(b) above does not apply where the reference to capital transfer tax relates to a liability to tax arising before the passing of this Act.

(3) In the following provisions of this Part of this Act, any reference to tax except where it is a reference to a named tax is a reference to inheritance tax and, in so far as it occurs in a provision which relates to a time before the passing of this Act, includes a reference to capital transfer tax.

102 Gifts with reservation

(1) Subject to subsections (5) and (6) below, this section applies where, on or after 18th March 1986, an individual disposes of any property by way of gift and either –

(a) possession and enjoyment of the property is not bona fide assumed by the donee at or before the beginning of the relevant period; or

(b) at any time in the relevant period the property is not enjoyed to the entire exclusion, or virtually to the entire exclusion, of the donor and of any benefit to him by contract or otherwise;

and in this section 'the relevant period' means a period ending on the date of the donor's death and the beginning seven years before that date or, if it is later, on the date of the gift.

(2) If and so long as –

(a) possession and enjoyment of any property is not bona fide assumed as mentioned in subsection (1)(a) above, or

(b) any property is not enjoyed as mentioned in subsection (1)(b) above,

the property is referred to (in relation to the gift and the donor) as property subject to a reservation.

(3) If, immediately before the death of the donor, there is any property which, in relation to him, is property subject to a reservation then, to the extent that the property would not, apart from this section, form part of the donor's estate immediately before his death, that property shall be treated for the purposes of the 1984 Act as property to which he was beneficially entitled immediately before his death.

(4) If, at a time before the end of the relevant period, any property ceases to be property subject to a reservation, the donor shall be treated for the purposes of the 1984 Act as having at that time made a disposition of the property by a disposition which is a potentially exempt transfer.

(5) This section does not apply if or, as the case may be, to the extent that the disposal of property by way of gift is an exempt transfer by virtue of any of the following provisions of Part II of the 1984 Act, –

(a) section 18 (transfers between spouses), except as provided by subsections (5A) and (5B) below;

(b) section 20 (small gifts);

(c) section 22 (gifts in consideration of marriage);

(d) section 23 (gifts to charities);

(e) section 24 (gifts to political parties);

(ee) section 24A (gifts to housing associations);

(f) section 25 (gifts for national purposes, etc);

(h) section 27 (maintenance funds for historic buildings); and

(i) section 28 (employee trusts).

(5A) Subsection (5)(a) above does not prevent this section from applying if or, as the case may be, to the extent that –

(a) the property becomes settled property by virtue of the gift,

(b) by reason of the donor's spouse ('the relevant beneficiary') becoming beneficially entitled to an interest in possession in the settled property, the disposal is or, as the case may be, is to any extent an exempt transfer by virtue of section 18 of the 1984 Act in consequence of the operation of section 49 of that Act (treatment of interests in possession),

(c) at some time after the disposal, but before the death of the donor, the relevant beneficiary's interest in possession comes to an end, and

(d) on the occasion on which that interest comes to an end, the relevant beneficiary does not become beneficially entitled to the settled property or to another interest in possession in the settled property.

(5B) If or, as the case may be, to the extent that this section applies by virtue of subsection (5A) above, it has effect as if the disposal by way of gift had been made immediately after the relevant beneficiary's interest in possession came to an end.

(5C) For the purposes of subsections (5A) and (5B) above –

(a) section 51(1)(b) of the 1984 Act (disposal of interest in possession treated as coming to end of interest) applies as it applies for the purposes of Chapter 2 of Part 3 of that Act; and

(b) references to any property or an interest in any property include references to part of any property or interest.

(6) This section does not apply if the disposal of property by way of gift is made under the terms of a policy issued in respect of an insurance made before 18th March 1986 unless the policy is varied on or after that date so as to increase the benefits secured or to extend the term of the insurance; and, for this purpose, any change in the terms of the policy which is made in pursuance of an option or other power conferred by the policy shall be deemed to be a variation of the policy.

(7) If a policy issued as mentioned in subsection (6) above confers an option or other power under which benefits and premiums may be increased to take account of increases in the retail prices index (as defined in section 8(3) of the 1984 Act) or any similar index specified in the policy, then, to the extent that the right to exercise that option or power would have been lost if it had not been exercised on or before 1st August 1986, the exercise of that option or power before that date shall be disregarded for the purposes of subsection (6) above.

(8) Schedule 20 to this Act has effect for supplementing this section.

102A   Gifts with reservation: interest in land

(1) This section applies where an individual disposes of an interest in land by way of gift on or after 9th March 1999.

(2) At any time in the relevant period when the donor or his spouse enjoys a significant right or interest, or is party to a significant arrangement, in relation to the land –

(a) the interest disposed of is referred to (in relation to the gift and the donor) as property subject to a reservation; and

(b) section 102(3) and (4) above shall apply.

(3) Subject to subsections (4) and (5) below, a right, interest or arrangement in relation to land is significant for the purposes of subsection (2) above and if (and only if) it entitles or enables the donor to occupy all or part of the land, or to enjoy some right in relation to all or part of the land, otherwise than for full consideration in money or money's worth.

(4) A right, interest or arrangement is not significant for the purposes of subsection (2) above if –

(a) it does not and cannot prevent the enjoyment of the land to the entire exclusion, or virtually to the entire exclusion, of the donor; or

(b) it does not entitle or enable the donor to occupy all or part of the land immediately after the disposal, but would do so were it not for the interest disposed of.

(5) A right or interest is not significant for the purposes of subsection (2) above if it was granted or acquired before the period of seven years ending with the date of the gift.

(6) Where an individual disposes of more than one interest in land by way of gift, whether or not at the same time or to the same donee, this section shall apply separately in relation to each interest.

102B   Gifts with reservation: share of interest in land

(1) This section applies where an individual disposes, by way of gift on or after 9th March 1999, of an undivided share of an interest in land.

(2) At any time in the relevant period, except where subsection (3) or (4) below applies –

(a) the share disposed of is referred to (in relation to the gift and the donor) as property subject to a reservation; and

(b) section 102(3) and (4) above shall apply.

(3) This subsection applies when the donor –

(a) does not occupy the land; or

(b) occupies the land to the exclusion of the donee for full consideration in money or money's worth.

(4) This subsection applies when–

(a) the donor and the donee occupy the land; and

(b) the donor does not receive any benefit, other than a negligible one, which is provided by or at the expense of the donee for some reason connected with the gift.

102C   Sections 102A and 102B: supplemental

(1) In sections 102A and 102B above 'the relevant period' has the same meaning as in section 102 above.

(2) An interest or share disposed of is not property subject to a reservation under section 102A(2) or 102B(2) above if or, as the case may be, to the extent that the disposal is an exempt transfer by virtue of any of the provisions listed in section 102(5) above.

(3) In applying sections 102A and 102B above no account shall be taken of –

(a) occupation of land by a donor, or

(b) an arrangement which enables land to be occupied by a donor,

in circumstances where the occupation, or occupation pursuant to the arrangement, would be disregarded in accordance with paragraph 6(1)(b) of Schedule 20 to this Act.

(4) The provisions of Schedule 20 to this Act, apart from paragraph 6, shall have effect for the purposes of sections 102A and 102B above as they have effect for the purposes of section 102 above; and any question which falls to be answered under section 102A or 102B above in relation to an interest in land shall be determined by reference to the interest which is at that time treated as property comprised in the gift.

(5) Where property other than an interest in land is treated by virtue of paragraph 2 of that Schedule as property comprised in a gift, the provisions of section 102 above shall apply to determine whether or not that property is property subject to a reservation.

(6) Sections 102 and 102A above shall not apply to a case to which section 102B above applies.

(7) Section 102A above shall not apply to a case to which section 102 above applies.

103 Treatment of certain debts and incumbrances

(1) Subject to subsection (2) below, if, in determining the value of a person's estate immediately before his death, account would be taken, apart from this subsection, of a liability consisting of a debt incurred by him or an incumbrance created by a disposition made by him, that liability shall be subject to an abatement to an extent proportionate to the value of any of the consideration given for the debt or incumbrance which consisted of –

(a) property derived from the deceased; or

(b) consideration (not being property derived from the deceased) given by any person who was at any time entitled to, or amongst whose resources there was at any time included, any property derived from the deceased.

(2) If, in a case where the whole or a part of the consideration given for a debt or incumbrance consisted of such consideration as is mentioned in subsection (1)(b) above, it is shown that the value of the consideration given, or of that part thereof, as the case may be, exceeded that which could have been rendered available by application of all the property derived from the deceased, other than such (if any) of that property –

(a) as is included in the consideration given, or

(b) as to which it is shown that the disposition of which it, or the property which it represented, was the subject matter was not made with reference to, or with a view to enabling or facilitating, the giving of the consideration or the recoupment in any manner of the cost thereof,

no abatement shall be made under subsection (1) above in respect of the excess.

(3) In subsections (1) and (2) above 'property derived from the deceased' means, subject to subsection (4) below, any property which was the subject matter of a disposition made by the deceased, either by himself alone or in concert or by arrangement with any other person or which represented any of the subject matter of such a disposition, whether directly or indirectly, and whether by virtue of one or more intermediate dispositions.

(4) If the disposition first-mentioned in subsection (3) above was not a transfer of value and it is shown that the disposition was not part of associated operations which included –

(a) a disposition by the deceased, either alone or in concert or by arrangement with any other person, otherwise than for full consideration in money or money's worth paid to the deceased for his own use or benefit; or

(b) a disposition by any other person operating to reduce the value of the property of the deceased,

that first-mentioned disposition shall be left out of account for the purposes of subsections (1) to (3) above.

(5) If, before a person's death but on or after 18th March 1986, money or money's worth is paid or applied by him –

(a) in or towards the satisfaction or discharge of a debt or incumbrance in the case of which subsection (1) above would have effect on his death if the debt or incumbrance had not been satisfied or discharged, or

(b) in reduction of a debt or incumbrance in the case of which that subsection has effect on his death,

the 1984 Act shall have effect as if, at the time of the payment or application, the person concerned had made a transfer of value equal to the money or money's worth and that transfer were a potentially exempt transfer.

(6) Any reference in this section to a debt incurred is a reference to a debt incurred on or after 18th March 1986 and any reference to an incumbrance created by a disposition is a reference to an incumbrance created by a disposition made on or after that date; and in this section 'subject matter' includes, in relation to any disposition, any annual or periodical payment made or payable under or by virtue of the disposition.

(7) In determining the value of a person's estate immediately before his death, no account shall be taken (by virtue of section 5 of the 1984 Act) of any liability arising under or in connection with a policy of life insurance issued in respect of an insurance made on or after 1st July 1986 unless the whole of the sums assured under that policy form part of that person's estate immediately before his death.

As amended by the Finance Act 1989, s171(5), (6); Finance Act 1998, s165, Schedule 27, Pt IV; Finance Act 1999, s104; Finance Act 2003, s185.

FAMILY LAW REFORM ACT 1987
(1987 c 42)

1   General principle

(1) In this Act and enactments passed and instruments made after the coming into force of this section, references (however expressed) to any relationship between two persons shall, unless the contrary intention appears, be construed without regard to whether or not the father and mother of either of them, or the father and mother of any person through whom the relationship is deduced, have or had been married to each other at any time.

(2) In this Act and enactments passed after the coming into force of this section, unless the contrary intention appears –

    (a) references to a person whose father and mother were married to each other at the time of his birth include; and

    (b) references to a person whose father and mother were not married to each other at the time of his birth do not include,

references to any person to whom subsection (3) below applies, and cognate references shall be construed accordingly.

(3) This subsection applies to any person who –

    (a) is treated as legitimate by virtue of section 1 of the Legitimacy Act 1976;

    (b) is a legitimated person within the meaning of section 10 of that Act;

    (c) is an adopted child within the meaning of Part IV of the Adoption Act 1976; or

    (d) is otherwise treated in law as legitimate.

(4) For the purpose of construing references falling within subsection (2) above, the time of a person's birth shall be taken to include any time during the period beginning with –

    (a) the insemination resulting in his birth; or

(b) where there was no such insemination, his conception,

and (in either case) ending with his birth.

18   Succession on intestacy

(1) In Part IV of the Administration of Estates Act 1925 (which deals with the distribution of the estate of an intestate), references (however expressed) to any relationship between two persons shall be construed in accordance with section 1 above.

(2) For the purposes of subsection (1) above and that Part of that Act, a person whose father and mother were not married to each other at the time of his birth shall be presumed not to have been survived by his father, or by any person related to him only through his father, unless the contrary is shown.

(3) In section 50(1) of that Act (which relates to the construction of documents), the reference to Part IV of that Act, or to the foregoing provisions of that Part, shall in relation to an instrument inter vivos made, or a will or codicil coming into operation, after the coming into force of this section (but not in relation to instruments inter vivos made or wills or codicils coming into operation earlier) be construed as including references to this section.

(4) This section does not affect any rights under the intestacy of a person dying before the coming into force of this section.

19   Dispositions of property

(1) In the following dispositions, namely –

(a) dispositions inter vivos made on or after the date on which this section comes into force; and

(b) dispositions by will or codicil where the will or codicil is made on or after that date,

references (whether express or implied) to any relationship between two persons shall be construed in accordance with section 1 above.

(2) It is hereby declared that the use, without more, of the word 'heir' or 'heirs' or any expression purporting to create an entailed interest in real or personal property does not show a contrary intention for the purposes of section 1 as applied by subsection (1) above.

(3) In relation to the dispositions mentioned in subsection (1) above, section 33 of the Trustee Act 1925 (which specifies the trust implied by a direction

that income is to be held on protective trusts for the benefit of any person) shall have effect as if any reference (however expressed) to any relationship between two persons were construed in accordance with section 1 above.

(4) Where under any disposition of real or personal property, any interest in such property is limited (whether subject to any preceding limitation or charge or not) in such a way that it would, apart from this section, devolve (as nearly as the law permits) along with a dignity or title of honour, then –

(a) whether or not the disposition contains an express reference to the dignity or title of honour; and

(b) whether or not the property or some interest in the property may in some event become severed from it,

nothing in this section shall operate to sever the property or any interest in it from the dignity or title, but the property or interest shall devolve in all respects as if this section had not been enacted.

(5) This section is without prejudice to section 42 of the Adoption Act 1976 (construction of dispositions in cases of adoption).

(6) In this section 'disposition' means a disposition, including an oral disposition, of real or personal property whether inter vivos or by will or codicil.

(7) Notwithstanding any rule of law, a disposition made by will or codicil executed before the date on which this section comes into force shall not be treated for the purposes of this section as made on or after that date by reason only that the will or codicil is confirmed by a codicil executed on or after that date.

21 Entitlement to grant of probate, etc

(1) For the purpose of determining the person or persons who would in accordance with probate rules be entitled to a grant of probate or administration in respect of the estate of a deceased person, the deceased shall be presumed, unless the contrary is shown, not to have been survived –

(a) by any person related to him whose father and mother were not married to each other at the time of his birth; or

(b) by any person whose relationship with him is deduced through such a person as is mentioned in paragraph (a) above.

(2) In this section 'probate rules' means rules of court made under section 127 of the Supreme Court Act 1981.

(3) This section does not apply in relation to the estate of a person dying before the coming into force of this section.

As amended by the Trusts of Land and Appointment of Trustees Act 1996, s25(1), Schedule 3, para 25.

INCOME AND CORPORATION TAXES ACT 1988

(1988 c1)

PART I

THE CHARGE TO TAX

1   The charge to income tax

(1) Income tax is charged in accordance with the Income Tax Acts on –

(a) all amounts which, under those Acts, are charged to tax under any of Schedules A, D and F (set out in sections 15, 18 and 20),

(b) all amounts which are charged to tax under any of the following provisions of [the Income Tax (Earnings and Pensions) Act] 2003 –

(i) Part 2 (employment income),

(ii) Part 9 (pension income), and

(iii) Part 10 (social security income), and

(c) any other amounts which, under the Income Tax Acts, are charged to income tax.

(2) Where any Act enacts that income tax shall be charged for any year, income tax shall be charged for that year –

(aa) in respect of so much of an individual's total income as does not exceed £2,020, at such rate as Parliament may determine to be the starting rate for that year;

(a) in respect of any income which does not fall within paragraph (aa) above or paragraph (b) below, as such rate as Parliament may determine to be the basic rate for that year;

(b) in respect of so much of an individual's total income as exceeds £31,400, at such higher rate as Parliament may determine;

but this subsection has effect subject to any provision of the Income Tax Acts providing for income tax to be charged at a different rate in certain cases.

(2A) The amount up to which an individual's income is by virtue of subsection (2) above chargeable for any year at the starting rate shall be known as the starting rate limit.

(3) The amount up to which an individual's income is by virtue of subsection (2) above chargeable for any year at the starting rate or the basic rate shall be known as the basic rate limit.

(4) If the retail prices index for the month of September preceding a year of assessment is higher than it was for the previous September, then, unless Parliament otherwise determines, subsection (2) above shall apply for that year as if for each of the amounts specified in that subsection as it applied for the previous year (whether by virtue of this subsection or otherwise) there were substituted an amount arrived at by increasing the amount for the previous year by the same percentage as the percentage increase in the retail prices index and –

> (a) if the result in the case of the amount specified in subsection (2)(aa) above is not a multiple of £10, rounding it up to the nearest amount which is such a multiple, and

> (b) if the result in the case of the amount specified in subsection (2)(b) above is not a multiple of £100, rounding it up to the nearest amount which is such a multiple. ...

(6) The Treasury shall before each year of assessment make an order specifying the amounts which by virtue of subsection (4) above will be treated as specified for that year in subsection (2) above.

(6A) Where income tax at the basic rate has been borne on income chargeable at the starting rate any necessary repayment of tax shall be made on the making of a claim. ...

PART XVI

ESTATES OF DECEASED PERSONS IN COURSE OF ADMINISTRATION

695 Limited interests in residue

(1) The following provisions of this section shall have effect in relation to a person who, during the period commencing on the death of a deceased person and ending on the completion of the administration of his estate ('the administration period') or during a part of that period, has a limited interest in the residue of the estate or in a part thereof.

(2) When any sum has been paid during the administration period in respect

of that limited interest, the amount of that sum shall be deemed for all tax purposes to have been paid to that person as income for the year of assessment in which that sum was paid or, in the case of a sum paid in respect of an interest that has ceased, for the last year of assessment in which it was subsisting.

(3) Where, on the completion of the administration of the estate, there is an amount which remains payable in respect of that limited interest, that amount shall be deemed for all tax purposes to have been paid to that person as income for the year of assessment in which the administration period ends or, in the case of a sum which is deemed to be paid in respect of an interest that ceased before the end of that period, for the last year of assessment in which that interest was subsisting.

(4) Any amount which is deemed to have been paid to that person as income for any year by virtue of this section shall –

  (a) in the case of a United Kingdom estate, be deemed to be income of such an amount as would after deduction of income tax for that year be equal to the amount deemed to have been so paid, and to be income which has borne income tax at the applicable rate; ...

696 Absolute interests in residue

(1) The following provisions of this section shall have effect in relation to a person who, during the administration period or during a part of that period, has an absolute interest in the residue of the estate of a deceased person or in a part thereof.

(2) There shall be ascertained in accordance with section 697 the amount of the residuary income of the estate for each whole year of assessment, and for each broken part of a year of assessment, during which –

  (a) the administration period was current, and
  (b) that person had that interest;

and the amount so ascertained in respect of any year or part of a year or, in the case of a person having an absolute interest in a part of a residue, a proportionate part of that amount, is in this Part referred to as the 'residuary income' of that person for that year of assessment.

(3) When any sum has been paid during the administration period in respect of that absolute interest, that sum, except so far as it is excluded from the operation of this subsection, shall be deemed for all tax purposes to have been paid to that person as income for the year of assessment in which it was actually paid.

(3A) A payment shall be excluded from the operation of subsection (3) above to the extent (if any) that the aggregate of that sum and all the sums which –

(a) have been paid previously during the administration period in respect of that absolute interest, ...

exceeds the aggregated income entitlement of that person for the year of assessment in which the sum is paid.

(3B) For the purposes of this section the aggregated income entitlement of that person for any year of assessment is the amount which would be the aggregate of the amounts received for that year of assessment and all previous years of assessment in respect of the interest if that person had a right in each year to receive, and had received –

(a) in the case of a United Kingdom estate, his residuary income for that year less income tax at the applicable rate for that year; and

(b) in the case of a foreign estate, his residuary income for that year.

(4) In the case of a United Kingdom estate, any amount which is deemed to have been paid to that person as income for any year by virtue of subsection (3) above shall be deemed to be income of such an amount as would, after deduction of income tax for that year, be equal to the amount deemed to have been so paid, and to be income that has borne income tax at the applicable rate.

(5) Where, on the completion of the administration of the estate, the aggregate of all the sums which, apart from this subsection –

(a) have been paid during the administration period in respect of that absolute interest, and

(b) fall under this section to be treated as paid to that person as income,

is exceeded by the aggregated income entitlement of that person for the year of assessment in which the administration of the estate is completed, then an amount equal to the amount of the excess shall be treated for the purposes of subsections (3) to (4) above as having been actually paid, immediately before the end of the administration period, in respect of that interest. ...

(8) For the purposes of any charge to corporation tax under this section, the residuary income of a company shall be computed in the first instance by reference to years of assessment, and the residuary income for any such year shall be apportioned between the accounting periods (if more than one) comprising that year.

697 Supplementary provisions as to absolute interests in residue

(1) The amount of the residuary income of an estate for any year of assessment shall be ascertained by deducting from the aggregate income of the estate for that year –

(a) the amount of any annual interest, annuity or other annual payment for that year which is a charge on residue and the amount of any payment made in that year in respect of any such expenses incurred by the personal representatives as such in the management of the assets of the estate as, in the absence of any express provision in a will, would be properly chargeable to income, but excluding any such interest, annuity or payment allowed or allowable in computing the aggregate income of the estate; and

(b) the amount of any of the aggregate income of the estate for that year to which a person has on or after assent become entitled by virtue of a specific disposition either for a vested interest during the administration period or for a vested or contingent interest on the completion of the administration.

(1A) For the purpose of ascertaining under subsection (1) above the residuary income of an estate for any year, where the amount of the deductions falling to be made from the aggregate income of the estate for that year (including any falling to be made by virtue of this subsection) exceeds the amount of that income, the excess shall be carried forward and treated for that purpose as an amount falling to be deducted from the aggregate income of the estate for the following year.

(2) In the event of its appearing, on the completion of the administration of an estate in the residue of which, or in a part of the residue of which, a person had an absolute interest at the completion of the administration, that the aggregate of the benefits received in respect of that interest does not amount to as much as the aggregate for all years of the residuary income of the person having that interest, section 696 shall have effect as if the amount of the deficiency were to be applied in reducing the amount taken to be his residuary income for the year in which the administration of the estate is completed and, in so far as the deficiency exceeds that income, in reducing the amount taken to be his residuary income for the previous year, and so on.

(3) In subsection (2) above 'benefits received' in respect of an absolute interest means the following amounts in respect of all sums paid before, or payable on, the completion of the administration in respect of that interest, that is to say –

(a) as regards a sum paid before the completion of the administration, in the case of a United Kingdom estate such an amount as would, after deduction of income tax for the year of assessment in which that sum was paid, be equal to that sum, or in the case of a foreign estate the amount of that sum; and

(b) as regards a sum payable on the completion of the administration, in the case of a United Kingdom estate such an amount as would, after deduction of income tax for the year of assessment in which the administration is completed, be equal to that sum, or in the case of a foreign estate the amount of that sum.

(4) In the application of subsection (2) above to a residue or a part of a residue in which a person other than the person having an absolute interest at the completion of the administration had an absolute interest at any time during the administration period, the aggregates mentioned in that subsection shall be computed in relation to those interests taken together, and the residuary income of that other person also shall be subject to reduction under that subsection.

700 Adjustments and information

(1) Where on the completion of the administration of an estate any amount is deemed by virtue of this Part to have been paid to any person as income for any year of assessment and –

(a) that amount is greater than the amount that has previously been deemed to have been paid to him as income for that year by virtue of this Part; or

(b) no amount has previously been so deemed to have been paid to him as income for that year;

an assessment may be made upon him for that year and tax charged accordingly or, on a claim being made for the purpose, any relief or additional relief to which he may be entitled shall be allowed accordingly.

(2) Where on the completion of the administration of an estate any amount is deemed by virtue of this Part to have been paid to any person as income for any year of assessment, and that amount is less than the amount that has previously been so deemed to have been paid to him, then –

(a) if an assessment has already been made upon him for that year, such adjustments shall be made in that assessment as may be necessary for the purpose of giving effect to the provisions of this Part which take effect on the completion of the administration, and any tax overpaid shall be repaid; and

(b) if –

(i) any relief has been allowed to him by reference to the amount which has been previously deemed by virtue of this Part to have been paid to him as income for that year, and

(ii) the amount of that relief exceeds the amount of relief which could have been given by reference to the amount which, on the completion of the administration, is deemed to have been paid to him as income for that year,

the relief so given in excess may, if not otherwise made good, be charged under Case VI of Schedule D and recovered from that person accordingly.

(3) Notwithstanding anything in the Tax Acts, the time within which an assessment may be made for the purposes of this Part, or an assessment may be adjusted for those purposes, or a claim for relief may be made by virtue of this Part, shall not expire before the end of the period of three years beginning with the 31st January next following the year of assessment in which the administration of the estate is question was completed.

(4) An inspector may by notice require any person being or having been a personal representative of a deceased person, or having or having had an absolute or limited interest in the residue of the estate of a deceased person or in a part of such residue, to furnish him within such time as he may direct (not being less than 28 days) with such particulars as he thinks necessary for the purposes of this Part.

(5) It shall be the duty of a personal representative of a deceased person, if a request to do so is made in writing by a person who has, or has had, an absolute or limited interest in the residue of the estate of the deceased or by a person to whom any of the income of the residue of that estate has been paid in the exercise of any discretion, to furnish the person making the request with a statement in writing setting out –

(a) in respect of every amount which has been, or is treated as having been, actually paid to that person in respect of that interest or in the exercise of that discretion, the amount (if any) deemed under this Part to have been paid to him as income for a year of assessment; and

(b) the amount of any tax at the applicable rate which any amount falling within paragraph (a) above is deemed to have borne;

and, where an amount deemed to have been paid as income to any person for any year of assessment is deemed for any of the purposes of this Part to have borne tax on different parts of it at different applicable rates, the matters to be set out in pursuance of paragraphs (a) and (b) above shall set out separately as respects each part of that amount.

(6) The duty imposed by subsection (5) above shall be enforceable at the suit or instance of the person making the request.

701 Interpretation

(1) The following provisions of this section shall have effect for the purpose of the interpretation of sections 695 to 700.

(2) A person shall be deemed to have an absolute interest in the residue of the estate of a deceased person, or in a part of such residue, if and so long as the capital of the residue or of that part would, if the residue had been ascertained, be properly payable to him, or to another in his right, for his benefit, or is properly so payable, whether directly by the personal representatives or indirectly through a trustee or other person.

(3) A person shall be deemed to have a limited interest in the residue of the estate of a deceased person, or in a part of such residue, during any period, being a period during which he has not an absolute interest in the residue or in that part, where the income of the residue or of that part for that period would, if the residue had been ascertained at the commencement of that period, be properly payable to him, or to another in his right, for his benefit, whether directly by the personal representatives or indirectly through a trustee or other person.

(3A) 'Applicable rate', in relation to any amount which a person is deemed by virtue of this Part to receive or to have a right to receive, means the basic rate, the lower rate or the Schedule F ordinary rate according as the income of the residue of the estate out of which that amount is or would be paid bears tax at the basic rate, the lower rate or the Schedule F ordinary rate; and in determining for the purposes of this Part whether or how much of any payment is or would be deemed to be made out of income that bears tax at one rate rather than another –

  (a) such apportionments of the amounts bearing tax at different rates shall be made between different persons with interests in the residue of the estate as are just and reasonable in relation to their different interests; and

  (b) subject to paragraph (a) above, it shall be assumed –

    (i) that payments are to be made out of income bearing tax at the basic rate before they are made out of income bearing tax at the lower rate or the Schedule F ordinary rate; and

    (ii) that payments are to be made out of income bearing tax at the lower rate before they are made out of income bearing tax at the Schedule F ordinary rate.

(4) 'Personal representatives' means, in relation to the estate of a deceased person, his personal representatives as defined in relation to England and Wales by section 55 of the Administration of Estates Act 1925, and persons having in relation to the deceased under the law of another country any functions corresponding to the functions for administration purposes under the law of England and Wales of personal representatives as so defined; and references to 'personal representatives as such' shall be construed as references to personal representatives in their capacity as having such functions.

(5) 'Specific disposition' means a specific devise or bequest made by a testator, and includes the disposition of personal chattels made by section 46 of the Administration of Estates Act 1925 and any disposition having, whether by virtue of any enactment or otherwise, under the law of another country an effect similar to that of a specific devise or bequest under the law of England and Wales. Real estate included (either by specific or general description) in a residuary gift made by the will of a testator shall be deemed to be a part of the residue of his estate and not to be the subject of a specific disposition.

(6) Subject to subsection (7) below, 'charges on residue' means, in relation to the estate of a deceased person, the following liabilities, properly payable thereout and interest payable in respect of those liabilities, that is to say –

(a) funeral, testamentary and administration expenses and debts, and

(b) general legacies, demonstrative legacies, annuities and any sum payable out of residue to which a person is entitled under the law of intestacy of any part of the United Kingdom or any other country, and

(c) any other liabilities of his personal representatives as such.

(7) Where, as between persons interested under a specific disposition or in a general or demonstrative legacy or in an annuity and persons interested in the residue of the estate, any such liabilities as are mentioned in subsection (6) above fall exclusively or primarily upon the property that is the subject of the specific disposition or upon the legacy or annuity, only such part (if any) of those liabilities as falls ultimately upon the residue shall be treated as charges on residue.

(8) References to the aggregate income of the estate of a deceased person for any year of assessment shall be construed as references to the aggregate income from all sources for that year of the personal representatives of the deceased as such, treated as consisting of –

(a) any such income which is chargeable to United Kingdom income tax by deduction or otherwise, such income being computed at the amount on which that tax falls to be borne for that year; and

(b) any such income which would have been so chargeable if it had arisen in the United Kingdom to a person resident and ordinarily resident there, such income being computed at the fall amount thereof actually arising during that year, less such deductions as would have been allowable if it had been charged to United Kingdom income tax;

but excluding any income from property devolving on the personal representatives otherwise than as assets for payment of the debts of the deceased. This subsection has effect subject to sections 249(5) [issue of share capital], 421(2) [loans or advances] and 547(1)(c) [rights conferred by policy or contract].

(9) 'United Kingdom estate' means, as regards any year of assessment, an estate the income of which comprises only income which either –

(a) has borne United Kingdom income tax by deduction, or

(b) in respect of which the personal representatives are directly assessable to United Kingdom income tax,

not being an estate any part of the income of which is income in respect of which the personal representatives are entitled to claim exemption from United Kingdom income tax by reference to the fact that they are not resident, or not ordinarily resident, in the United Kingdom. ...

(11) In a case in which different parts of the estate of a deceased person are the subjects respectively of different residuary dispositions, this Part shall have effect in relation to each of those parts with the substitution –

(a) for references to the estate of references to that part of the estate; and

(b) for references to the personal representatives of the deceased as such of references to his personal representatives in their capacity as having the functions referred to in subsection (4) above in relation to that part of the estate.

(12) In this Part –

(a) references to sums paid include references to assets that are transferred or that are appropriated by a personal representative to himself, and to debts that are set off or released;

(b) references to sums payable include references to assets as to which an obligation to transfer or a right of a personal representative to appropriate to himself is subsisting on the completion of the administration and to debts as to which an obligation to release or set off, or a right of a personal representative so to do in his own favour, is then subsisting; and

(c) references to amount shall be construed, in relation to such assets as are referred to in paragraph (a) or (b) above, as references to their value at the date on which they were transferred or appropriated, or at the completion of the administration, as the case may require, and, in relation to such debts as are so referred to, as references to the amount thereof.

(13) In this Part references to the administration period shall be construed in accordance with section 695(1).

NB For the year 2004–05 the starting, basic and higher rates of income tax were 10, 22 and 40 per cent respectively.

As amended by the Finance Act 1988, ss24(2)(a), (b), 148, Schedule 14, Pts IV, V; Finance Act 1989, s187(1), Schedule 17, Pt V; Finance Act 1992, s9; Finance Act 1993, ss79(1), 107(1), (2), (8), 213, Schedule 6, paras 11(1), 25(1), Schedule 23, Pt III(10); Finance Act 1995, ss75, 162, Schedule 18, paras 1–4, 6, 7, Schedule 29, Pt VIII(10); Finance Act 1996, s79(2), 135(1), (2), Schedule 7, paras 1, 2, 32, Schedule 21, para 20; Finance Act 1997, s54(2); Finance (No 2) Act 1997, ss33(7)–(9), 36, 52, Schedule 6, para 13; Finance Act 1999, s22(1)–(6), (12); Income Tax (Earnings and Pensions) Act 2003, s722, Schedule 6, Pt 1, paras 1, 2(1), (2); Income Tax (Indexation) Order 2004.

COPYRIGHT, DESIGNS AND PATENTS ACT 1988
(1988 c 48)

90   Assignment and licences

(1) Copyright is transmissible by assignment, by testamentary disposition or by operation of law, as personal or moveable property.

(2) An assignment or other transmission of copyright may be partial, that is, limited so as to apply –

(a) to one or more, but not all, of the things the copyright owner has the exclusive right to do;

(b) to part, but not the whole, of the period for which the copyright is to subsist ...

93   Copyright to pass under will with unpublished work

Where under a bequest (whether specific or general) a person is entitled, beneficially or otherwise, to –

(a) an original document or other material thing recording or embodying a literary, dramatic, musical or artistic work which was not published before the death of the testator, or

(b) an original material thing containing a sound recording or film which was not published before the death of the testator,

the bequest shall, unless a contrary intention is indicated in the testator's will or a codicil to it, be construed as including the copyright in the work in so far as the testator was the owner of the copyright immediately before his death.

CHILDREN ACT 1989
(1989 c 41)

5   Appointment of guardians ...

(3) A parent who has parental responsibility for his child may appoint another individual to be the child's guardian in the event of his death.

(4) A guardian of a child may appoint another individual to take his place as the child's guardian in the event of his death.

(5) An appointment under subsection (3) or (4) shall not have effect unless it is made in writing, is dated and is signed by the person making the appointment or –

> (a) in the case of an appointment made by a will which is not signed by the testator, is signed at the direction of the testator in accordance with the requirements of section 9 of the Wills Act 1837; or

> (b) in any other case, is signed at the direction of the person making the appointment, in his presence and in the presence of two witnesses who each attest the signature.

(6) A person appointed as a child's guardian under this section shall have parental responsibility for the child concerned ...

(10) Nothing in this section shall be taken to prevent an appointment under subsection (3) or (4) being made by two or more persons acting jointly ...

6   Guardians: revocation and disclaimer

(1) An appointment under section 5(3) or (4) revokes an earlier such appointment (including one made in an unrevoked will or codicil) made by the same person in respect of the same child, unless it is clear (whether as the result of an express provision in the later appointment or by any necessary implication) that the purpose of the later appointment is to appoint an additional guardian.

(2) An appointment under section 5(3) or (4) (including one made in an

unrevoked will or codicil) is revoked if the person who made the appointment revokes it by a written and dated instrument which is signed –

(a) by him; or

(b) at his direction, in his presence and in the presence of two witnesses who each attest the signature ...

(3A) An appointment under section 5(3) or (4) (including one made in an unrevoked will or codicil) is revoked if the person appointed is the spouse of the person who made the appointment and either –

(a) a decree of a court of civil jurisdiction in England and Wales dissolves or annuls the marriage, or

(b) the marriage is dissolved or annulled and the divorce or annulment is entitled to recognition in England and Wales by virtue of Part II of the Family Law Act 1986,

unless a contrary intention appears by the appointment.

(4) For the avoidance of doubt, an appointment under section 5(3) or (4) made in a will or codicil is revoked if the will or codicil is revoked.

(5) A person who is appointed as a guardian under section 5(3) or (4) may disclaim his appointment by an instrument in writing signed by him and made within a reasonable time of his first knowing that the appointment has taken effect ...

(7) Any appointment of a guardian under section 5 may be brought to an end at any time by order of the court –

(a) on the application of any person who has parental responsibility for the child;

(b) on the application of the child concerned, with leave of the court; or

(c) in any family proceedings, if the court considers that it should be brought to an end even though no application has been made.

As amended by the Law Reform (Succession) Act 1995, s4.

TAXATION OF CHARGEABLE GAINS ACT 1992

(1992 c 12)

PART I

CAPITAL GAINS TAX AND CORPORATION TAX ON CHARGEABLE GAINS

1 The charge to tax

(1) Tax shall be charged in accordance with this Act in respect of capital gains, that is to say chargeable gains computed in accordance with this Act and accruing to a person on the disposal of assets.

(2) Companies shall be chargeable to corporation tax in respect of chargeable gains accruing to them in accordance with section 6 of the Taxes Act and the other provisions of the Corporation Tax Acts.

(3) Without prejudice to subsection (2), capital gains tax shall be charged for all years of assessment in accordance with the following provisions of this Act.

2 Persons and gains chargeable to capital gains tax, and allowable losses

(1) Subject to any exceptions provided by this Act, and without prejudice to sections 10 and 276, a person shall be chargeable to capital gains tax in respect of chargeable gains accruing to him in a year of assessment during any part of which he is resident in the United Kingdom, or during which he is ordinarily resident in the United Kingdom.

(2) Capital gains tax shall be charged on the total amount of chargeable gains accruing to the person chargeable in the year of assessment, after deducting –

(a) any allowable losses accruing to that person in that year of assessment, and

(b) so far as they have not been allowed as a deduction from chargeable gains accruing in any previous year of assessment, any allowable losses accruing to that person in any previous year of assessment (not earlier than the year 1965–66).

(3) Except as provided by section 62, an allowable loss accruing in a year of assessment shall not be allowable as a deduction from chargeable gains accruing in any earlier year of assessment, and relief shall not be given under this Act more than one in respect of any loss or part of a loss, and shall not be given under this Act if and so far as relief has been or may be given in respect of it under the Income Tax Acts.

(4) Where any amount is treated by virtue of any of sections 77, 86 [attribution of gains to settlors with interest in non-resident or dual resident settlements], 87 [attribution of gains to beneficiaries], and 89(2) [migrant settlements, etc] (read, where applicable, with section 10A [temporary non-residents]) as an amount of chargeable gains accruing to any person in any year of assessment –

(a) that amount shall be disregarded for the purposes of subsection (2) above; and

(b) the amount on which that person shall be charged to capital gains tax for that year (instead of being the amount given by that subsection) shall be the sum of the amounts specified in subsection (5) below.

(5) Those amounts are –

(a) the amount which after –

(i) making any deductions for which subsection (2) provides, and

(ii) applying any reduction in respect of taper relief under section 2A,

is the amount given for the year of assessment by the application of that subsection in accordance with subsection (4)(a) above;

(aa) every amount which is treated by virtue of sections 77 and 86 as an amount of chargeable gains accruing to the person in question for that year, reduced as follows –

(i) first, by making the deductions for which subsection (2) provides in respect of any allowable losses accruing to that person;

(ii) then, where taper relief would be deductible by the trustees of the settlement in question but for section 77(1)(b)(i) or 86(1)(e)(ii), by applying reductions in respect of taper relief under section 2A at the rates that would be applicable in the case of the trustees; and

(b) every amount which is treated by virtue of sections 87 and 89(2) (read, where applicable, with section 10A) as an amount of chargeable gains accruing to the person in question in that year.

(6) Allowable losses must (notwithstanding section 2A(6)) be deducted under paragraph (a)(i) of subsection (5) above before any may be deducted under paragraph (aa)(i) of that subsection.

(7) Where any year of assessment –

(a) there are amounts treated as accruing to a person by virtue of section 77 or 86,

(b) two or more of those amounts, or elements of them –

(i) relate to different settlements, and

(ii) attract taper relief (by virtue of subsection (5)(aa)(ii) above) at the same rate, or are not eligible for taper relief, and

(c) losses are deductible from the amounts or elements mentioned in paragraph (b) above ('the equal-tapered amounts') but are not enough to exhaust them all,

the deduction applicable to each of the equal-tapered amounts shall be the appropriate proportion of the aggregate of those losses. The 'appropriate proportion' is that given by dividing the equal-tapered amount in question by the total of the equal-tapered amounts.

(8) The references to section 86 in subsection (5)(aa) above (in the opening words) and subsection (7)(a) above include references to that section read with section 10A.

2A Taper relief

(1) This section applies where, for any year of assessment –

(a) there is, in any person's case, an excess of the total amount referred to in subsection (2) of section 2 over the amounts falling to be deducted from that amount in accordance with that subsection; and

(b) the excess is or includes an amount representing the whole or a part of any chargeable gain that is eligible for taper relief.

(2) The amount on which capital gains tax is taken to be charged by virtue of section 2(2) shall be reduced to the amount computed by –

(a) applying taper relief to so much of every chargeable gain eligible for that relief as is represented in the excess;

(b) aggregating the results; and

(c) adding to the aggregate of the results so much of every chargeable gain not eligible for taper relief as is represented in the excess.

(3) Subject to the following provisions of this Act, a chargeable gain is eligible for taper relief if –

(a) it is a gain on the disposal of a business asset with a qualifying holding period of at least one year; or

(b) it is a gain on the disposal of a non-business asset with a qualifying holding period of at least three years.

(4) Where taper relief falls to be applied to the whole or any part of a gain on the disposal of a business or non-business asset, that relief shall be applied by multiplying the amount of that gain or part of a gain by the percentage given by the table in subsection (5) below for the number of whole years in the qualifying holding period of that asset.

(5) That table is as follows –

Gains on disposals of business assets			Gains on disposals of non-business assets	
Number of whole years in qualifying holding period	Percentage of gain chargeable		Number of whole years in qualifying holding period	Percentage of gain chargeable
1	50		–	–
2 or more	25		–	–
			3	95
			4	90
			5	85
			6	80
			7	75
			8	70
			9	65
			10 or more	60

(6) The extent to which the whole or any part of a gain on the disposal of a business or non-business asset is to be treated as represented in the excess mentioned in subsection (1) above shall be determined by treating deductions made in accordance with section 2(2)(a) and (b) as set against chargeable gains in such order as results in the largest reduction under this section of the amount charged to capital gains tax under section 2. ...

3   Annual exempt amount

(1) An individual shall not be chargeable to capital gains tax in respect of so much of his taxable amount for any year of assessment as does not exceed the exempt amount for the year.

(2) Subject to subsection (3) below, the exempt amount for any year of assessment shall be [£8,200 for 2004–05].

(3) If the retail prices index for the month of September preceding a year of assessment is higher than it was for the previous September, then, unless Parliament otherwise determines, subsection (2) above shall have effect for that year as if for the amount specified in that subsection as it applied for the previous year (whether by virtue of this subsection or otherwise) there were substituted an amount arrived at by increasing the amount for the previous year by the same percentage as the percentage increase in the retail prices index and, if the result is not a multiple of £100, rounding it up to the nearest amount which is such a multiple.

(4) The Treasury shall, before each year of assessment, make an order specifying the amount which by virtue of this section is the exempt amount for that year.

(5) For the purposes of this section an individual's taxable amount for any year of assessment is the amount which, after –

(a) making every deduction for which section 2(2) provides,

(b) applying any reduction in respect of taper relief under section 2A, and

(c) adding any amounts falling to be added by virtue of section 2(5)(b),

is (apart from this section) the amount for that year on which that individual is chargeable to capital gains tax in accordance with section 2.

(5A) Where, in the case of any individual, the amount of the adjusted net gains for any year of assessment is equal to or less than the exempt amount for that year, no deduction shall be made for that year in respect of –

(a) any allowable losses carried forward from a previous year; or

(b) any allowable losses carried back from a subsequent year in which the individual dies.

(5B) Where, in the case of any individual, the amount of the adjusted net gains for any year of assessment exceeds the exempt amount for the year, the deductions made for that year in respect of allowable losses falling within subsection (5A)(a) or (b) above shall not be greater than the excess.

(5C) In subsections (5A) and (5B) above the references, in relation to any individual's case, to the adjusted net gains for any year are references to the amount given in his case by –

(a) taking the amount for that year from which the deductions for which section s2(2)(a) and (b) provides are to be made;

(b) deducting only the amounts falling to be deducted in accordance with section 2(2)(a); and

(c) in a year in which any amount falls to be brought into account by virtue of section 2(5)(b), adding whichever is the smaller of the exempt amount for that year and the amount falling to be so brought into account.

(7) For the year of assessment in which an individual dies and for the next 2 following years, subsections (1) to (5C) above shall apply to his personal representatives as they apply to an individual.

(7A) As they apply by virtue of subsection (7) above –

(a) subsection (5A) has effect with the omission of paragraph (b), and

(b) subsection (5B) has effect with the omission of the words 'or (b)'.

(8) Schedule 1 shall have effect as respects the application of this section to trustees.

4   Rates of capital gains tax

(1) Subject to the provisions of this section, the rate of capital gains tax in respect of gains accruing to a person in a year of assessment shall be equivalent to the lower rate of income tax for the year.

(1AA) The rate of capital gains tax in respect of gains accruing to –

(a) the trustees of a settlement, or

(b) the personal representatives of a deceased person,

in a year of assessment shall be equivalent to the rate which for that year is the rate applicable to trusts under section 686 of the Taxes Act.

(1AB) If (after allowing for any deductions in accordance with the Income Tax Acts) an individual has no income for a year of assessment or his total income for the year is less than the starting rate limit, then –

(a) if the amount on which he is chargeable to capital gains tax does not exceed the unused part of his starting rate band, the rate of capital gains tax in respect of gains accruing to him in the year shall be equivalent to the starting rate;

(b) if the amount on which he is chargeable to capital gains tax exceeds the unused part of his starting rate band, the rate of capital gains tax in respect of such gains accruing to him in the year as correspond to the unused part shall be equivalent to the starting rate.

(1AC) The references in subsection (1AB) above to the unused part of an individual's starting rate band are to the amount by which the starting rate limit exceeds his total income (as reduced by any deductions made in accordance with the Income Tax Acts).

(2) If income tax is chargeable at the higher rate or the Schedule F upper rate in respect of any part of the income of an individual for a year of assessment, the rate of capital gains tax in respect of gains accruing to him in the year shall be equivalent to the higher rate.

(3) If no income tax is chargeable at the higher rate or the Schedule F upper rate in respect of the income of an individual for a year of assessment, but the amount on which he is chargeable to capital gains tax exceeds the unused part of his basic rate band, the rate of capital gains tax on the excess shall be equivalent to the higher rate of income tax for the year.

(4) The reference in subsection (3) above to the unused part of an individual's basic rate band is a reference to the amount by which the basic rate limit exceeds his total income (as reduced by any deductions made in accordance with the Income Tax Acts).

PART II

GENERAL PROVISIONS RELATING TO COMPUTATION OF GAINS AND ACQUISITIONS AND DISPOSALS OF ASSETS

CHAPTER I

INTRODUCTORY

15 Computation of gains

(1) The amount of the gains accruing on the disposal of assets shall be computed in accordance with this Part, subject to the other provisions of this Act.

(2) Every gain shall, except as otherwise expressly provided, be a chargeable gain.

16 Computation of losses

(1) Subject to section 72 of the Finance Act 1991 [deduction of trading losses] and except as otherwise expressly provided, the amount of a loss accruing on a disposal of an asset shall be computed in the same way as the amount of a gain accruing on a disposal is computed.

(2) Except as otherwise expressly provided, all the provisions of this Act which distinguish gains which are chargeable gains from those which are not, or which make part of a gain a chargeable gain, and part not, shall apply also to distinguish losses which are allowable losses from those which are not, and to make part of a loss an allowable loss, and part not; and references in this Act to an allowable loss shall be construed accordingly.

(2A) A loss accruing to a person in a year of assessment shall not be an allowable loss for the purposes of this Act unless, in relation to that year, he gives a notice to an officer of the Board quantifying the amount of that loss; and sections 42 and 43 of the Management Act shall apply in relation to such a notice as if it were a claim for relief. ...

17 Disposals and acquisitions treated as made at market value

(1) Subject to the provisions of this Act, a person's acquisitions or disposal of an asset shall for the purposes of this Act be deemed to be for a consideration equal to the market value of the asset –

(a) where he acquires or, as the case may be, disposes of the asset otherwise than by way of a bargain made at arm's length, and in particular where he acquires or disposes of it by way of gift or on a transfer into settlement by a settlor or by way of distribution from a company in respect of shares in the company, or

(b) where he acquires or, as the case may be, disposes of the asset wholly or partly for a consideration that cannot be valued, or in connection with his own or another's loss of office or employment or diminution of emoluments, or otherwise in consideration for or recognition of his or another's services or past services in any office or employment or of any other service rendered or to be rendered by him or another.

(2) Subsection (1) shall not apply to the acquisition of an asset if –

(a) there is no corresponding disposal of it, and

(b) there is no consideration in money or money's worth or the consideration is of an amount or value lower than the market value of the asset.

18   Transactions between connected persons

(1) This section shall apply where a person acquires an asset and the person making the disposal is connected with him.

(2) Without prejudice to the generality of section 17(1) the person acquiring the asset and the person making the disposal shall be treated as parties to a transaction otherwise than by way of a bargain made at arm's length.

(3) Subject to subsection (4) below, if on the disposal a loss accrued to the person making the disposal, it shall not be deductible except from a chargeable gain accruing to him on such other disposal of an asset to the person acquiring the asset mentioned in subsection (1) above, being a disposal made at a time when they are connected persons.

(4) Subsection (3) above shall not apply to a disposal by way of gift in settlement if the gift and the income from it is wholly or primarily applicable for educational, cultural or recreational purposes, and the persons benefiting from the application for those purposes are confined to members of an association of persons for whose benefit the gift was made, not being persons all or most of whom are connected persons.

(5) Where the asset mentioned in subsection (1) above is an option to enter into a sale or other transaction given by the person making the disposal a loss accruing to the person acquiring the asset shall not be an allowable loss unless it accrues on a disposal of the option at arm's length to a person who is not connected with him.

(6) Subject to subsection (7) below, in a case where the asset mentioned in subsection (1) above is subject to any right or restriction enforceable by the person making the disposal, or by a person connected with him, then (where the amount of the consideration for the acquisition is, in accordance with subsection (2) above, deemed to be equal to the market value of the asset) that market value shall be –

  (a) what its market value would be if not subject to the right or restriction, minus –

  (b) the market value of the right or restriction or the amount by which its extinction would enhance the value of the asset to its owner, whichever is the less.

(7) If the right or restriction is of such a nature that its enforcement would or might effectively destroy or substantially impair the value of the asset without bringing any countervailing advantage either to the person making the disposal or a person connected with him or is an option or other right to acquire the asset or, in the case of incorporeal property, is a right to extinguish the asset in the hands of the person giving the consideration by

forfeiture or merger or otherwise, the market value of the asset shall be determined, and the amount of the gain accruing on the disposal shall be computed, as if the right or restriction did not exist.

(8) Subsections (6) and (7) above shall not apply to a right of forfeiture or other right exercisable on breach of a covenant contained in a lease of land or other property, and shall not apply to any right or restriction under a mortgage or other charge.

CHAPTER II

ASSETS AND DISPOSALS OF ASSETS

21   Assets and disposals

(1) All forms of property shall be assets for the purposes of this Act, whether situated in the United Kingdom or not, including –

(a) options, debts and incorporeal property generally, and

(b) any currency other than sterling, and

(c) any form of property created by the person disposing of it, or otherwise coming to be owned without being acquired.

(2) For the purposes of this Act –

(a) references to a disposal of an asset include, except where the context otherwise requires, references to a part disposal of an asset, and

(b) there is a part disposal of an asset where an interest or right in or over the asset is created by the disposal, as well as where it subsists before the disposal, and generally, there is a part disposal of an asset where, on a person making a disposal, any description of property derived from the asset remains undisposed of.

22   Disposal where capital sums derived from assets

(1) Subject to sections 23 and 26(1), and to any other exceptions in this Act, there is for the purposes of this Act a disposal of assets by their owner where any capital sum is derived from assets notwithstanding that no asset is acquired by the person paying the capital sum, and this subsection applies in particular to –

(a) capital sums received by way of compensation for any kind of damage or injury to assets or for the loss, destruction or dissipation of assets or for any depreciation or risk of depreciation of an asset,

(b) capital sums received under a policy of insurance of the risk of any kind of damage or injury to, or the loss or depreciation of, assets,

(c) capital sums received in return for forfeiture or surrender of rights, or for refraining from exercising rights, and

(d) capital sums received as consideration for use or exploitation of assets.

(2) In the case of a disposal within paragraph (a), (b), (c) or (d) of subsection (1) above, the time of the disposal shall be the time when the capital sum is received as described in that subsection.

(3) In this section 'capital sum' means any money or money's worth which is not excluded from the consideration taken into account in the computation of the gain.

23 Receipt of compensation and insurance money not treated as a disposal

(1) If the recipient so claims, receipt of a capital sum within paragraph (a), (b), (c) or (d) of section 22(1) derived from an asset which is not lost or destroyed shall not be treated for the purposes of this Act as a disposal of the asset if –

(a) the capital sum is wholly applied in restoring the asset, or

(b) (subject to subsection (2) below), the capital sum is applied in restoring the asset except for a part of the capital sum which is not reasonably required for the purpose and which is small as compared with the whole capital sum, or

(c) (subject to subsection (2) below), the amount of the capital sum is small, as compared with the value of the asset,

but, if the receipt is not treated as a disposal, all sums which would, if the receipt had been so treated, have been brought into account as consideration for that disposal in the computation of the gain shall be deducted from any expenditure allowable under Chapter III of this Part as a deduction in computing a gain on the subsequent disposal of the asset.

(2) If the allowable expenditure is less than the consideration for the disposal constituted by the receipt of the capital sum (or is nil) –

(a) paragraphs (b) and (c) of subsection (1) above shall not apply, and

(b) if the recipient so elects (and there is any allowable expenditure) –

(i) the amount of the consideration for the disposal shall be reduced by the amount of the allowable expenditure, and

(ii) none of that expenditure shall be allowable as a deduction in computing a gain accruing on the occasion of the disposal or any subsequent occasion.

In this subsection 'allowable expenditure' means expenditure which, immediately before the disposal, was attributable to the asset under paragraphs (a) and (b) of section 38(1).

(3) If, in a case not falling within subsection (1)(b) above, a part of a capital sum within paragraph (a) or paragraph (b) of section 22(1) derived from an asset which is not lost or destroyed is applied in restoring the asset, then if the recipient so claims, that part of the capital sum shall not be treated as consideration for the disposal deemed to be effected on receipt of the capital sum but shall be deducted from any expenditure allowable under Chapter III of this Part as a deduction in computing a gain on the subsequent disposal of the asset.

(4) If an asset is lost or destroyed and a capital sum received by way of compensation for the loss or destruction, or under a policy of insurance of the risk of the loss or destruction, is within one year of receipt, or such longer period as the inspector may allow, applied in acquiring an asset in replacement of the asset lost or destroyed the owner shall if he so claims be treated for the purposes of this Act –

(a) as if the consideration for the disposal of the old asset were (if otherwise of a greater amount) of such amount as would secure that on the disposal neither a gain nor a loss accrues to him, and

(b) as if the amount of the consideration for the acquisition of the new asset were reduced by the excess of the amount of the capital sum received by way of compensation or under the policy of insurance, together with any residual or scrap value, over the amount of the consideration which he is treated as receiving under paragraph (a) above.

(5) A claim shall not be made under subsection (4) above if part only of the capital sum is applied in acquiring the new asset but if all of that capital sum except for a part which is less than the amount of the gain (whether all chargeable gain or not) accruing on the disposal of the old asset is so applied, then the owner shall if he so claims be treated for the purposes of this Act –

(a) as if the amount of the gain so accruing were reduced to the amount of the said part (and, if not all chargeable gain, with a proportionate reduction in the amount of the chargeable gain), and

(b) as if the amount of the consideration for the acquisition of the new asset were reduced by the amount by which the gain is reduced under paragraph (a) of this subsection.

(6) If a building ('the old building') is destroyed or irreparably damaged, and all or part of a capital sum received by way of compensation for the destruction or damage, or under a policy of insurance of the risk of the destruction or damage, is applied by the recipient in constructing or otherwise acquiring a replacement building situated on other land ('the new building'), then for the purposes of subsections (4) and (5) above each of the old building and new building shall be regarded as an asset separate from the land on which it is or was situated and the old building shall be treated as lost or destroyed.

(7) For the purposes of subsection (6) above:

(a) references to a building include references to any permanent or semi-permanent structure in the nature of a building; and

(b) the reference to a sum applied in acquiring the new building does not include a reference to a sum applied in acquiring the land on which the new building is situated; and

(c) all necessary apportionments shall be made of any expenditure, compensation or consideration, and the method of apportionment shall be such as is just and reasonable.

(8) This section shall apply in relation to a wasting asset with the following modifications:

(a) paragraphs (b) and (c) of subsection (1) above, and subsection (2) above, shall not apply; and

(b) in subsections (1) and (3) above, the amount of the expenditure from which the deduction is to be made shall be the amount which would have been allowable under Chapter III of this Part if the asset had been disposed of immediately after the application of the capital sum.

24 Disposals where assets lost or destroyed, or become of negligible value

(1) Subject to the provisions of this Act and, in particular to section 144, the occasion of the entire loss, destruction, dissipation or extinction of an asset shall, for the purposes of this Act, constitute a disposal of the asset whether or not any capital sum by way of compensation or otherwise is received in respect of the destruction, dissipation or extinction of the asset.

(2) Where the owner of an asset which has become of negligible value makes a claim to that effect:

(a) This Act shall apply as if the claimant had sold, and immediately reacquired, the asset at the time of the claim or (subject to paragraphs (b) and (c) below) at any earlier time specified in the claim, for a consideration of an amount equal to the value specified in the claim.

(b) An earlier time may be specified in the claim if:

(i) the claimant owned the asset at the earlier time; and

(ii) the asset had become of negligible value at the earlier time; and either

(iii) for capital gains tax purposes the earlier time is not more than two years before the beginning of the year of assessment in which the claim is made; or

(iv) for corporation tax purposes the earlier time is on or after the first day of the earliest accounting period ending not more than two years before the time of the claim.

(c) Section 93 of and Schedule 12 to the Finance Act 1994 (indexation losses and transitional relief) shall have effect in relation to an asset to which this section applies as if the sale and reacquisition occurred at the time of the claim and not at any earlier time.

(3) For the purposes of subsections (1) and (2) above, a building and any permanent or semi-permanent structure in the nature of a building may be regarded as an asset separate from the land on which it is situated, but where either of those subsections applies in accordance with this subsection, the person deemed to make the disposal of the building or structure shall be treated as if he had also sold, and immediately reacquired, the site of the building or structure (including in the site any land occupied for purposes ancillary to the use of the building or structure) for a consideration equal to its market value at that time.

26   Mortgages and charges not to be treated as disposals

(1) The conveyance or transfer by way of security of an asset or of an interest or right in or over it, or transfer of a subsisting interest or right by way of security in or over an asset (including a retransfer on redemption of the security), shall not be treated for the purposes of this Act as involving any acquisition or disposal of the asset. ...

27   Disposals in cases of hire-purchase and similar transactions

A hire-purchase or other transaction under which the use and enjoyment of an asset is obtained by a person for a period at the end of which the property in the asset will or may pass to that person shall be treated for the purposes of this Act, both in relation to that person and in relation to the person from whom he obtains the use and enjoyment of the asset, as if it amounted to an entire disposal of the asset to that person at the beginning of the period for which he obtains the use and enjoyment of the asset, but subject to such adjustments of tax, whether by way of repayment or discharge of tax or otherwise, as may be required where the period for which that person has the use and enjoyment of the asset terminates without the property in the asset passing to him.

28 Time of disposal and acquisition where asset disposed of under contract

(1) Subject to section 22(2), and subsection (2) below, where an asset is disposed of and acquired under a contract the time at which the disposal and acquisition is made is the time the contract is made (and not, if different, the time at which the asset is conveyed or transferred).

(2) If the contract is conditional (and in particular if it is conditional on the exercise of an option) the time at which the disposal and acquisition is made is the time when the condition is satisfied.

CHAPTER III

COMPUTATION OF GAINS: GENERAL PROVISIONS

35 Assets held on 31st March 1982 (including assets held on 6th April 1965)

(1) This section applies to a disposal of an asset which was held on 31st March 1982 by the person making the disposal.

(2) Subject to the following provisions of this section, in computing for the purpose of this Act the gain or loss accruing on the disposal it shall be assumed that the asset was on 31st March 1982 sold by the person making the disposal, and immediately reacquired by him, at its market value on that date.

(3) Subject to subsections (5) below, subsection (2) above shall not apply to a disposal –

    (a) where a gain would accrue on the disposal to the person making the disposal if that subsection did apply, and either a smaller gain or a loss would so accrue if it did not,

    (b) where a loss would so accrue if that subsection did apply, and either a smaller loss or a gain would accrue if it did not,

(c) where, either on the facts of the case or by virtue of Schedule 2, neither a gain nor a loss would accrue if that subsection did not apply; or

(d) where neither a gain nor a loss would accrue by virtue of any of –

(i) sections 58, 73, 139 [reconstruction or amalgamation involving transfer of business], 140A [transfer of a UK trade], 171 [transfers within a group: general provisions], 215 [disposal of assets on amalgamation of building societies, etc], 216 [assets transferred from society to company], 217A [transfer of assets on incorporation of registered friendly society], 218 to 221 [The Housing Corporation, Housing for Wales, housing associations and harbour authorities], 257(3), 258(4), 264 [relied for local constituency associations of political parties on reorganisation of constituencies] and 267(2) [sharing of transmission facilities] of this Act; ...

(4) Where in the case of a disposal of an asset –

(a) the effect of subsection (2) above would be to substitute a loss for a gain or a gain for a loss, but

(b) the application of subsection (2) is excluded by subsection (3),

it shall be assumed in relation to the disposal that the asset was acquired by the person making the disposal for a consideration such that, on the disposal, neither a gain nor a loss accrues to him.

(5) If a person so elects, disposals made by him (including any made by him before the election) shall fall outside subsection (3) above (so that subsection (2) above is not excluded by that subsection).

(6) An election by a person under subsection (5) above shall be irrevocable and shall be made by notice to an officer of the Board at any time before 6th April 1990 or at any time during the period beginning with the day of the first relevant disposal and ending –

(a) in the case of an election for the purposes of capital gains tax, with the first anniversary of the 31st January next following the year of assessment in which the disposal is made;

(aa) in the case of an election for the purposes of corporation tax, 2 years after the end of the accounting period in which the disposal is made; or

(b) in either case, at such later time as the Board may allow;

and 'the first relevant disposal' means the first disposal to which this section applies which is made by the person making the election.

(7) An election made by a person under subsection (5) above in one capacity does not cover disposals made by him in another capacity.

(8) All such adjustments shall be made, whether by way of discharge or repayment of tax, the making of assessments or otherwise, as are required to give effect to an election under subsection (5) above. ...

37   Consideration chargeable to tax on income

(1) There shall be excluded from the consideration for a disposal of assets taken into account in the computation of the gain any money or money's worth charged to income tax as income of, or taken into account as a receipt in computing income or profits or gains or losses of, the person making the disposal for the purposes of the Income Tax Acts. ...

38   Acquisition and disposal costs, etc

(1) Except as otherwise expressly provided, the sums allowable as a deduction from the consideration in the computation of the gain accruing to a person on the disposal of an asset shall be restricted to –

> (a) the amount or value of the consideration, in money or money's worth, given by him or on his behalf wholly and exclusively for the acquisition of the asset, together with the incidental costs to him of the acquisition or, if the asset was not acquired by him, any expenditure wholly and exclusively incurred by him in providing the asset.

> (b) the amount of any expenditure wholly and exclusively incurred on the asset by him or on his behalf for the purpose of enhancing the value of the asset, being expenditure reflected in the state or nature of the asset at the time of the disposal, and any expenditure wholly and exclusively incurred by him in establishing, preserving or defending his title to, or to a right over, the asset,

> (c) the incidental costs to him of making the disposal.

(2) For the purposes of this section and for the purposes of all other provisions of this Act, the incidental costs to the person making the disposal of the acquisition of the asset or of its disposal shall consist of expenditure wholly and exclusively incurred by him for the purposes of the acquisition or, as the case may be, the disposal, being fees, commission or remuneration paid for the professional services of any surveyor or valuer, or auctioneer, or accountant, or agent or legal adviser and costs of transfer or conveyance (including stamp duty or stamp duty land tax) together –

> (a) in the case of the acquisition of an asset, with costs of advertising to find a seller, and

> (b) in the case of a disposal, with costs of advertising to find a buyer and costs reasonably incurred in making any valuation or

apportionment required for the purposes of the computation of the gain, including in particular expenses reasonably incurred in ascertaining market value where required by this Act.

(3) Except as provided by section 40, no payment of interest shall be allowable under this section.

(4) Any provision in this Act introducing the assumption that assets are sold and immediately reacquired shall not imply that any expenditure is incurred as incidental to the sale or reacquisition.

39   Exclusion of expenditure by reference to tax on income

(1) There shall be excluded from the sums allowable under section 38 as a deduction in the computation of the gain any expenditure allowable as a deduction in computing the profits or losses of a trade, profession or vocation for the purposes of income tax or allowable as a deduction in computing any other income or profits or gains or losses for the purposes of the Income Tax Acts and any expenditure which, although not so allowable as a deduction in computing any losses, would be so allowable but for an insufficiency of income or profits or gains; and this subsection applies irrespective of whether effect is or would be given to the deduction in computing the amount of tax chargeable or by discharge or repayment of tax or in any other way.

(2) Without prejudice to the provisions of subsection (1) above, there shall be excluded from the sums allowable under section 38 as a deduction in the computation of the gain any expenditure which, if the assets, or all the assets to which the computation relates, were, and had at all times been, held or used as part of the fixed capital of a trade the profits of which were (irrespective of whether the person making the disposal is a company or not) chargeable to income tax would be allowable as a deduction in computing the profits or losses of the trade for the purposes of income tax. ...

42   Part disposals

(1) Where a person disposes of an interest or right in or over an asset, and generally wherever on the disposal of an asset any description of property derived from that asset remains undisposed of, the sums which under paragraphs (a) and (b) of section 38(1) are attributable to the asset shall, both for the purposes of the computation of the gain accruing on the disposal and for the purposes of applying this Part in relation to the property which remains undisposed of, be apportioned.

(2) The apportionment shall be made by reference –

(a) to the amount or value of the consideration for the disposal on the one hand (call that amount or value A), and

(b) to the market value of the property which remains undisposed of on the other hand (call that market value B),

and accordingly the fraction of the said sums allowable as a deduction in the computation of the gain accruing on the disposal shall be –

$$\frac{A}{A + B}$$

and the remainder shall be attributed to the property which remains undisposed of.

(3) Any apportionment to be made in pursuance of this section shall be made before operating the provisions of section 41 and if, after a part disposal, there is a subsequent disposal of an asset the capital allowance or renewals allowances to be taken into account in pursuance of that section in relation to the subsequent disposal shall, subject to subsection (4) below, be those referable to the sums which under paragraphs (a) and (b) of section 38(1) are attributable to the asset whether before or after the part disposal, but those allowances shall be reduced by the amount if any) by which the loss on the earlier disposal was restricted under the provisions of section 41.

(4) This section shall not be taken as requiring the apportionment of any expenditure which, on the facts, is wholly attributable to what is disposed of, or wholly attributable to what remains undisposed of.

(5) It is hereby declared that this section, and all other provisions for apportioning on a part disposal expenditure which is deductible in computing a gain, are to be operated before the operation of, and without regard to, section 58(1), sections 152 to 158 (but without prejudice to section 152(10)), section 171(1) or any other enactment making an adjustment to secure that neither a gain nor a loss occurs on a disposal.

43   Assets derived from other assets

If and so far as, in a case where assets have been merged or divided or have changed their nature or rights or interests in or over assets have been created or extinguished, the value of an asset is derived from any other asset in the same ownership, an appropriate proportion of the sums allowable as a deduction in the computation of a gain in respect of the other asset under paragraphs (a) and (b) of section 38(1) shall, both for the purpose of the computation of a gain accruing on the disposal of the first-mentioned asset and, if the other asset remains in existence, on a disposal of that other asset, be attributed to the first-mentioned asset.

44 Meaning of 'wasting asset'

(1) In this Chapter 'wasting asset' means an asset with a predictable life not exceeding 50 years but so that –

(a) freehold land shall not be a wasting asset whatever its nature, and whatever the nature of the buildings or works on it;

(b) 'life', in relation to any tangible movable property, means useful life, having regard to the purpose for which the tangible assets were acquired or provided by the person making the disposal;

(c) plant and machinery shall in every case be regarded as having a predictable life of less than 50 years, and in estimating that life it shall be assumed that its life will end when it is finally put out of use as being unfit for further use, and that it is going to be used in the normal manner and to the normal extent and is going to be so used throughout its life as so estimated;

(d) a life interest in settled property shall not be a wasting asset until the predictable expectation of life of the life tenant is 50 years or less, and the predictable life of life interests in settled property and of annuities shall be ascertained from actuarial tables approved by the Board.

(2) In this Chapter 'the residual or scrap value', in relation to a wasting asset, means the predictable value, if any, which the wasting asset will have at the end of its predictable life as estimated in accordance with this section.

(3) The question what is the predictable life of an asset, and the question what is its predictable residual or scrap value at the end of that life, if any, shall, so far as those questions are not immediately answered by the nature of the asset, be taken, in relation to any disposal of the asset, as they were known or ascertainable at the time when the asset was acquired or provided by the person making the disposal.

45 Exemption for certain wasting assets

(1) Subject to the provisions of this section, no chargeable gain shall accrue on the disposal of, or of an interest in, an asset which is tangible movable property and which is a wasting asset.

(2) Subsection (1) above shall not apply to a disposal of, or of an interest in, an asset –

(a) if, from the beginning of the period of ownership of the person making the disposal to the time when the disposal is made, the asset has been used and used solely for the purposes of a trade, profession or vocation and if that person has claimed or could have claimed any capital allowance in respect of any expenditure attributable to the asset or interest under paragraph (a) or paragraph (b) of section 38(1); or

(b) if the person making the disposal has incurred any expenditure on the asset or interest which has otherwise qualified in full for any capital allowance.

(3) In the case of the disposal of, or of an interest in, an asset which, in the period of ownership of the person making the disposal, has been used partly for the purposes of a trade, profession or vocation and partly for other purposes, or has been used for the purposes of a trade, profession or vocation for part of that period, or which has otherwise qualified in part only for capital allowances –

(a) the consideration for the disposal, and any expenditure attributable to the asset or interest by virtue of section 38(1)(a) and (b), shall be apportioned by reference to the extent to which that expenditure qualified for capital allowances, and

(b) the computation of the gain shall be made separately in relation to the apportioned parts of the expenditure and consideration, and

(c) subsection (1) above shall not apply to any gain accruing by reference to the computation in relation to the part of the consideration apportioned to use for the purposes of the trade, profession or vocation, or to the expenditure qualifying for capital allowances.

(4) Subsection (1) above shall not apply to a disposal of commodities of any description by a person dealing on a terminal market or dealing with or through a person ordinarily engaged in dealing on a terminal market.

51   Exemption for winnings and damages, etc

(1) It is hereby declared that winnings from betting, including pool betting, or lotteries or games with prizes are not chargeable gains, and no chargeable gain or allowable loss shall accrue on the disposal of rights to winnings obtained by participating in any pool betting or lottery or game with prizes.

(2) It is hereby declared that sums obtained by way of compensation or damages for any wrong or injury suffered by an individual in his person or in his profession or vocation are not chargeable gains.

PART III

INDIVIDUALS, PARTNERSHIPS, TRUSTS AND
COLLECTIVE INVESTMENT SCHEMES

CHAPTER I

MISCELLANEOUS PROVISIONS

58   Husband and wife

(1) If, in any year of assessment, and in the case of a woman who in that year of assessment is a married woman living with her husband, the man disposes of an asset to the wife, or the wife disposes of an asset to the man, both shall be treated as if the asset was acquired from the one making the disposal for a consideration of such amount as would secure that on the disposal neither a gain nor a loss would accrue to the one making the disposal.

(2) This section shall not apply –

(a) if until the disposal the asset formed part of trading stock of a trade carried on by the one making the disposal, or if the asset is acquired as trading stock for the purposes of a trade carried on by the one acquiring the asset, or

(b) if the disposal is by way of donatio mortis causa,

but this section shall have effect notwithstanding the provisions of section 18 or 161 [appropriations to and from stock], or of any other provisions of this Act fixing the amount of the consideration deemed to be given on a disposal or acquisition.

59   Partnerships

Where 2 or more persons carry on a trade or business in partnership –

(a) tax in respect of chargeable gains accruing to them on the disposal of any partnership assets shall ... be assessed and charged on them separately, and

(b) any partnership dealings shall be treated as dealings by the partners and not by the firm as such.

59A Limited liability partnerships

(1) Where a limited liability partnership carries on a trade or business with a view to profit –

(a) assets held by the limited liability partnership are treated for the purposes of tax in respect of chargeable gains as held by its members as partners, and

(b) any dealings by the limited liability partnership are treated for those purposes as dealings by its members in partnership (and not by the limited liability partnership as such);

and tax in respect of chargeable gains accruing to the members of the limited liability partnership on the disposal of any of its assets shall be assessed and charged on them separately.

(2) For all purposes, except as otherwise provided, in the enactments relating to tax in respect of chargeable gains –

(a) references to a partnership include a limited liability partnership in relation to which subsection (1) above applies,

(b) references to members of a partnership include members of such a limited liability partnership,

(c) references to a company do not include such a limited liability partnership, and

(d) references to members of a company do not include members of such a limited liability partnership. ...

(6) Neither the commencement of the application of subsection (1) above nor the cessation of its application in relation to a limited liability partnership shall be taken as giving rise to the disposal of any assets by it or any of its members.

60   Nominees and bare trustees

(1) In relation to assets held by a person as nominee for another person, or as trustee for another person absolutely entitled as against the trustee, or for any person who would be so entitled as against the trustee, or for any person who would be so entitled but for being an infant or other person under disability (or for 2 or more persons who are or would be jointly so entitled), this Act shall apply as if the property were vested in, and the acts of the nominee or trustee in relation to the assets were the acts of, the person or persons for whom he is the nominee or trustee (acquisitions from or disposals to him by that person or persons being disregarded accordingly).

(2) It is hereby declared that references in this Act to any asset held by a person as trustee for another person absolutely entitled as against the trustee are references to a case where that other person has the exclusive right, subject only to satisfying any outstanding charge, lien or other right of the trustees to resort to the asset for payment of duty, taxes, costs or other outgoings, to direct how that asset shall be dealt with.

62   Death: general provisions

(1) For the purposes of this Act the assets of which a deceased person was competent to dispose –

(a) shall be deemed to be acquired on his death by the personal representatives or other person on whom they devolve for a consideration equal to their market value at the date of the death, but

(b) shall not be deemed to be disposed of by him on his death (whether or not they were the subject of a testamentary disposition).

(2) Allowable losses sustained by an individual in the year of assessment in which he dies may, so far as they cannot be deducted from chargeable gains accruing in that year, be deducted from chargeable gains accruing to the deceased in the 3 years of assessment preceding the year of assessment in which the death occurs, taking chargeable gains accruing in a later year before those accruing in an earlier year.

(2A) Amounts deductible from chargeable gains for any year in accordance with subsection (2) above shall not be so deductible from any such gains so far as they are gains that are brought into account for that year by virtue of section 2(5)(b).

(2B) Where deductions under subsection (2) above fall to be made from the chargeable gains for any year, the provisions of this Act relating to taper relief shall have effect as if those deductions were deductions under section 2(2)(a) and (b) and, accordingly, as if –

(a) those deductions were to be made (before the application of the relief) in computing for that year the excess (if any) mentioned in section 2A(1) [taper relief]; and

(b) for the purposes of determining the gains represented in that excess, the gains for that year from which those deductions are treated as made were to be ascertained in accordance with section 2A(6).

(3) In relation to property forming part of the estate of a deceased person the personal representatives shall for the purposes of this Act be treated as being a single and continuing body of persons (distinct from the persons who

may from time to time be the personal representatives), and that body shall be treated as having the deceased's residence, ordinary residence, and domicile at the date of death.

(4) On a person acquiring any asset as legatee (as defined in section 64) –

(a) no chargeable gain shall accrue to the personal representatives, and

(b) the legatee shall be treated as if the personal representatives' acquisition of the asset had been his acquisition of it.

(5) Notwithstanding section 17(1) no chargeable gain shall accrue to any person on his making a disposal by way of donatio mortis causa.

(6) Subject to subsections (7) and (8) below, where within the period of 2 years after a person's death any of the dispositions (whether effected by will, under the law relating to intestacy or otherwise) of the property of which he was competent to dispose are varied, or the benefit conferred by any of those dispositions is disclaimed, by an instrument in writing made by the persons or any of the persons who benefit or would benefit under the dispositions –

(a) the variation or disclaimer shall not constitute a disposal for the purposes of this Act, and

(b) this section shall apply as if the variation had been effected by the deceased or, as the case may be, the disclaimed benefit had never been conferred.

(7) Subsection (6) above does not apply to a variation unless the instrument contains a statement by the persons making the instrument to the effect that they intend the subsection to apply to the variation.

(8) Subsection (6) above does not apply to a variation or disclaimer made for any consideration in money or money's worth other than consideration consisting of the making of a variation or disclaimer in respect of another of the dispositions.

(9) Subsection (6) above applies whether or not the administration of the estate is complete or the property has been distributed in accordance with the original dispositions.

(10) In this section references to assets of which a deceased person was competent to dispose are references to assets of the deceased which (otherwise than in right of a power of appointment or of the testamentary power conferred by statute to dispose of entailed interests) he could, if of full age and capacity, have disposed of by his will, assuming that all the assets were situated in England and, if he was not domiciled in the United Kingdom, that he was domiciled in England, and include references to his

severable shares in any assets to which, immediately before his death, he was beneficially entitled as a joint tenant.

64   Expenses in administration of estates and trusts

(1) In the case of a gain accruing to a person on the disposal of, or of a right or interest in or over, an asset to which he became absolutely entitled as legatee or as against the trustees of settled property –

> (a) any expenditure within section 38(2) incurred by him in relation to the transfer of the asset to him by the personal representatives or trustees, and
>
> (b) any such expenditure incurred in relation to the transfer of the asset by the personal representatives or trustees,

shall be allowable as a deduction in the computation of the gain accruing to that person on the disposal.

(2) In this Act, unless the context otherwise requires, 'legatee' includes any person taking under a testamentary disposition or on an intestacy or partial intestacy, whether he takes beneficially or as trustee, and a person taking under a donatio mortis causa shall be treated (except for the purposes of section 62) as a legatee and his acquisition as made at the time of the donor's death.

(3) For the purposes of the definition of 'legatee' above, and of any reference in this Act to a person acquiring an asset 'as legatee', property taken under a testamentary disposition or on an intestacy or partial intestacy includes any asset appropriated by the personal representatives in or towards satisfaction of a pecuniary legacy or any other interest or share in the property devolving under the disposition or intestacy.

65   Liability for tax of trustees or personal representatives

(1) Subject to subsection (3) below, capital gains tax chargeable in respect of chargeable gains accruing to the trustees of a settlement or capital gains tax due from the personal representatives of a deceased person may be assessed and charged on and in the name of any one or more of the relevant trustees or the relevant personal representatives.

(2) Subject to section 60 and any other express provision to the contrary, chargeable gains accruing to the trustees of a settlement or to the personal representatives of a deceased person, and capital gains tax chargeable on or in the name of such trustees or personal representatives, shall not be regarded for the purposes of this Act as accruing to, or chargeable on, any

other person, nor shall any trustee or personal representative be regarded for the purposes of this Act as an individual. ...

(4) In this section – ...

'the relevant trustees', in relation to any chargeable gains, means the trustees in the year of assessment in which the chargeable gains accrue and any subsequent trustees of the settlement, and 'the relevant personal representatives' has a corresponding meaning.

CHAPTER II

SETTLEMENTS

68 Meaning of 'settled property'

In this Act, unless the context otherwise requires, 'settled property' means any property held in trust other than property to which section 60 applies.

69 Trustees of settlements

(1) In relation to settled property, the trustees of the settlement shall for the purposes of this Act be treated as being a single and continuing body of persons (distinct from the persons who may from time to time be the trustees), and that body shall be treated as being resident and ordinarily resident in the United Kingdom unless the general administration of the trusts is ordinarily carried on outside the United Kingdom and the trustees or a majority of them for the time being are not resident or not ordinarily resident in the United Kingdom.

(2) Notwithstanding subsection (1) above, a person carrying on a business which consists of or includes the management of trusts, and acting as trustee of a trust in the course of that business, shall be treated in relation to that trust as not resident in the United Kingdom if the whole of the settled property consists of or derives from property provided by a person not at the time (or, in the case of a trust arising under a testamentary disposition or on an intestacy or partial intestacy, at his death) domiciled, resident or ordinarily resident in the United Kingdom, and if in such a case the trustees or a majority of them are or are treated in relation to that trust as not resident in the United Kingdom, the general administration of the trust shall be treated as ordinarily carried on outside the United Kingdom.

(3) For the purposes of this section, and of sections 71(1) and 72(1), where part of the property comprised in a settlement is vested in one trustee or set of trustees and part in another (and in particular where settled land

within the meaning of the Settled Land Act 1925 is vested in the tenant for life and investments representing capital money are vested in the trustees of the settlement), they shall be treated as together constituting and, in so far as they act separately, as acting on behalf of a single body of trustees.

(4) If tax assessed on the trustees, or anyone trustee, of a settlement in respect of a chargeable gain accruing to the trustees is not paid within 6 months from the date when it becomes payable by the trustees or trustee, and before or after the expiration of that period of 6 months the asset in respect of which the chargeable gain accrued, or any part of the proceeds of sale of that asset, is transferred by the trustees to a person who as against the trustees is absolutely entitled to it, that person may at any time within 2 years from the time when the tax became payable be assessed and charged (in the name of the trustees) to an amount of capital gains tax not exceeding tax chargeable on an amount equal to the amount of the chargeable gain and, where part only of the asset or of the proceeds was transferred, not exceeding a proportionate part of that amount.

70   Transfers into settlement

A transfer into settlement, whether revocable or irrevocable, is a disposal of the entire property thereby becoming settled property notwithstanding that the transferor has some interest as a beneficiary under the settlement and notwithstanding that he is a trustee, or the sole trustee, of the settlement.

71   Person becoming absolutely entitled to settled property

(1) On the occasion when a person becomes absolutely entitled to any settled property as against the trustee all the assets forming part of the settled property to which he becomes so entitled shall be deemed to have been disposed of by the trustee, and immediately reacquired by him in his capacity as a trustee within section 60(1), for a consideration equal to their market value.

(2) Where, in any case in which a person ('the beneficiary') becomes absolutely entitled to any settled property as against the trustee, an allowable loss would (apart from this subsection) have accrued to the trustee on the deemed disposal under subsection (1) above of an asset comprised in that property –

(a) that loss shall be treated, to the extent only that it cannot be deducted from pre-entitlement gains of the trustee, as an allowable loss accruing to the beneficiary (instead of to the trustee); but

(b) any allowable loss treated as accruing to the beneficiary under this subsection shall be deductible under this Act from chargeable gains accruing to the beneficiary to the extent only that it can be deducted from gains accruing to the beneficiary on the disposal by him of –

(i) the asset on the deemed disposal of which the loss accrued; or

(ii) where that asset is an estate, interest or right in or over land, that asset or any asset deriving from that asset.

(2A) In subsection (2) above 'pre-entitlement gain', in relation to an allowable loss accruing to a trustee on the deemed disposal of any asset comprised in any settled property, means a chargeable gain accruing to that trustee on –

(a) a disposal which, on the occasion on which the beneficiary becomes absolutely entitled as against the trustee to that property, is deemed under subsection (1) above to have taken place; or

(b) any other disposal taking place before that occasion but in the same year of assessment.

(2B) For the purposes of subsection (2)(b)(ii) above an asset ('the relevant asset') derives from another if, in a case where –

(a) assets have merged,

(b) an asset has divided or otherwise changed its nature, or

(c) different rights or interests in or over any asset have been created or extinguished at different times,

the value of the relevant asset is wholly or partly derived (through one or more successive events falling within paragraphs (a) to (c) above but not otherwise) from the other asset.

(2C) The rules set out in subsection (2D) below shall apply (notwithstanding any other rules contained in this Act or in section 113(2) of the Finance Act 1995 (order of deduction)) –

(a) for determining for the purposes of this section whether an allowable loss accruing to the trustee, or treated as accruing to the beneficiary, can be deducted from particular chargeable gains for any year of assessment; and

(b) for the making of deductions of allowable losses from chargeable gains in cases where it has been determined that such an allowable loss can be deducted from particular chargeable gains.

(2D) Those rules are as follows –

(a) allowable losses accruing to the trustee on a deemed disposal under subsection (1) above shall be deducted before any deduction is made in respect of any other allowable losses accruing to the trustee in that year;

(b) allowable losses treated as accruing to the beneficiary under this section, so far as they cannot be deducted in a year of assessment as mentioned in subsection (2)(b) above, may be carried forward from year to year until they can be so deducted; and

(c) allowable losses treated as accruing to the beneficiary for any year of assessment under this section, and allowable losses carried forward to any year of assessment under paragraph (b) above –

(i) shall be deducted before any deduction is made in respect of any allowable losses accruing to the beneficiary in that year otherwise than by virtue of this section; and

(ii) in the case of losses carried forward to any year, shall be deductible as if they were losses actually accruing in that year.

(3) References in this section to the case where a person becomes absolutely entitled to settled property as against the trustee shall be taken to include references to the case where a person would become so entitled but for being an infant or other person under disability.

72 Termination of ... interest on death of person entitled

(1) On the termination, on the death of the person entitled to it, of an interest in possession in all or any part of settled property –

(a) the whole or a corresponding part of each of the assets forming part of the settled property and not ceasing at that time to be settled property shall be deemed for the purposes of this Act at that time to be disposed of and immediately reacquired by the trustee for a consideration equal to the whole or a corresponding part of the market value of the asset; but

(b) no chargeable gain shall accrue on that disposal.

For the purposes of this subsection an interest which is a right to part of the income of settled property shall be treated as an interest in a corresponding part of the settled property.

(2) Subsection (1) above shall apply where the person entitled to an interest in possession in all or any part of settled property dies (although the interest does not then terminate) as it applies on the termination of such an interest.

(3) This section shall apply on the death of the person entitled to any annuity payable out of, or charged on, settled property or the income of

settled property as it applies on the death of a person whose interest in possession in the whole or any part of settled property terminates on his death.

(4) Where, in the case of any entitlement to an annuity created by a settlement some of the settled property is appropriated by the trustees as a fund out of which the annuity is payable, and there is no right to recourse to, or to the income of, settled property not so appropriated, then without prejudice to subsection (5) below, the settled property so appropriated shall, while the annuity is payable, and on the occasion of the death of the person entitled to the annuity, be treated for the purposes of this section as being settled property under a separate settlement.

(5) If there is an interest in a part of the settled property and, where that is an interest in income, there is no right of recourse to, or to the income of, the remainder of the settled property, the part of the settled property in which the interest subsists shall while it subsists be treated for the purposes of this section as being settled property under a separate settlement.

73 Death of [person entitled]: exclusion of chargeable gain

(1) Where, by virtue of section 71(1), the assets forming part of any settled property are deemed to be disposed of and reacquired by the trustee on the occasion when a person becomes (or would but for a disability become) absolutely entitled thereto as against the trustee, then, if that occasion is the death of a person entitled to an interest in possession in the settled property –

(a) no chargeable gain shall accrue on the disposal, and

(b) if on the death the property reverts to the disponer, the disposal and reacquisition under that subsection shall be deemed to be for such consideration as to secure that neither a gain nor a loss accrues to the trustee, and shall, if the trustee had first acquired the property at a date earlier than 6th April 1965, be deemed to be at that earlier date.

(2) Where the interest referred to in subsection (1) above is an interest in part only of the settled property to which section 71 applies, subsection (1)(a) above shall not apply but any chargeable gain accruing on the disposal shall be reduced by a proportion corresponding to that represented by the part.

(3) The last sentence of subsection (1) of section 72 and subsections (3) to (5) of that section shall apply for the purposes of this section as they apply for the purposes of section 72(1).

74   Effect on sections 72 and 73 of relief under section 165 or 260

(1) This section applies where –

(a) a claim for relief was made under section 165 or 260 in respect of the disposal of an asset to a trustee, and

(b) the trustee is deemed to have disposed of the asset, or part of it, by virtue of section 71(1) or 72(1)(a).

(2) Sections 72(1)(b) and 73(1)(a) shall not apply to the disposal of the asset or part by the trustee, but any chargeable gain accruing to the trustee on the disposal shall be restricted to the amount of the held-over gain (or a corresponding part of it) on the disposal of the asset to him.

(3) Subsection (2) above shall not have effect in a case within section 73(2) but in such a case the reduction provided for by section 73(2) shall be diminished by an amount equal to the proportion there mentioned of the held-over gain.

(4) In this section 'held-over gain' has the same meaning as in section 165 or as the case may be, 260.

76   Disposal of interests in settled property

(1) Subject to subsection (1A) below, no chargeable gain shall accrue on the disposal of an interest created by or arising under a settlement (including, in particular, an annuity or life interest, and the reversion to an annuity or life interest) by the person for whose benefit the interest was created by the terms of the settlement or by any other person except one who acquired, or derives his title from one who acquired, the interest for a consideration in money or money's worth, other than consideration consisting of another interest under the settlement.

(1A) Subject to subsection (3) below, subsection (1) above does not apply if –

(a) the settlement falls within subsection (1B) below; or

(b) the property comprised in the settlement is or includes property deriving directly or indirectly from a settlement falling within that subsection.

(1B) A settlement falls within this subsection if there has been a time when the trustees of that settlement –

(a) were not resident or ordinarily resident in the United Kingdom; or

(b) fell to be regarded for the purposes of any double taxation relief arrangements as resident in a territory outside the United Kingdom.

(2) Subject to subsection (1) above, where a person who has acquired an interest in settled property (including in particular the reversion to an annuity or life interest) becomes, as the holder of that interest, absolutely entitled as against the trustee to any settled property, he shall be treated as disposing of the interest in consideration of obtaining that settled property (but without prejudice to any gain accruing to the trustee on the disposal of that property deemed to be effected by him under section 71(1)).

(3) Subsection (1A) above shall not prevent subsection (1) above from applying where the disposal in question is a disposal in consideration of obtaining settled property that is treated as made under subsection (2) above.

76A Disposal of interest in settled property: deemed disposal of underlying assets

Schedule 4A to this Act has effect with respect to disposals for consideration of an interest in settled property.

77   Charge on settlor with interest in settlement

(1) Where in a year of assessment –

(a) chargeable gains accrue to the trustees of a settlement from the disposal of any or all of the settled property,

(b) after making any deduction provided for by section 2(2) in respect of disposals of the settled property there remains an amount on which the trustees would be chargeable to tax for the year in respect of those gains if –

(i) the gains were not eligible for taper relief, but section 2(2) applied as if they were (so that the order of deducting losses provided for by section 2A(6) applied), and

(ii) section 3 were disregarded,

and

(c) at any time during the year the settlor has an interest in the settlement,

the trustees shall not be chargeable to tax in respect of those but instead chargeable gains of an amount equal to that referred to in paragraph (b) shall be treated as accruing to the settlor in that year.

(2) Subject to the following provisions of this section, a settlor shall be regarded as having an interest in a settlement if –

(a) any property which may at any time be comprised in the settlement, or any derived property is, or will or may become, payable to or applicable for the benefit of the settlor or his spouse in any circumstances whatsoever, or

(b) the settlor or his spouse enjoys a benefit deriving directly or indirectly from any property which is comprised in the settlement or any derived property.

(3) The references in subsection (2)(a) and (b) above to the spouse of the settlor do not include –

(a) a person to whom the settlor is not for the time being married but may later marry, or

(b) a spouse from whom the settlor is separated under an order of a court, or under a separation agreement or in such circumstances that the separation is likely to be permanent, or

(c) the widow or widower of the settlor.

(4) A settlor shall not be regarded as having an interest in a settlement by virtue of subsection (2)(a) above if and so long as none of the property which may at any time be comprised in the settlement, and no derived property, can become payable or applicable as mentioned in that provision except in the event of –

(a) the bankruptcy of some person who is or may become beneficially entitled to the property or any derived property, or

(b) an assignment of or charge on the property or any derived property being made or given by some such person, or

(c) in the case of a marriage settlement, the death of both parties to the marriage and of all or any of the children of the marriage, or

(d) the death of a child of the settlor who had become beneficially entitled to the property or any derived property at an age not exceeding 25.

(5) A settlor shall not be regarded as having an interest in a settlement by virtue of subsection (2)(a) above if and so long as some person is alive and under the age of 25 during whose life the property or any derived property cannot become payable or applicable as mentioned in that provision except in the event of that person becoming bankrupt or assigning or charging his interest in that property.

(6) This section does not apply –

(a) where the settlor dies during the year; or

(b) in a case where the settlor is regarded as having an interest in the settlement by reason only of –

(i) the fact that property is, or will or may become, payable to or applicable for the benefit of his spouse, or

(ii) the fact that a benefit is enjoyed by his spouse,

where the spouse dies, or the settlor and the spouse cease to be married, during the year.

(7) This section does not apply unless the settlor is, and the trustees are, either resident in the United Kingdom during any part of the year or ordinarily resident in the United Kingdom during the year.

(8) In this section 'derived property', in relation to any property, means income from that property or any other property directly or indirectly representing proceeds of, or of income from, that property or income therefrom.

78   Right of recovery

(1) Where any tax becomes chargeable on and is paid by a person in respect of gains treated as accruing to him under section 77 he shall be entitled –

(a) to recover the amount of the tax from any trustee of the settlement, and

(b) for that purpose to require an inspector to give him a certificate specifying –

(i) the amount of the gains accruing to the trustees in respect of which he has paid tax; and

(ii) the amount of tax paid;

and any such certificate shall be conclusive evidence of the facts stated in it.

(2) In order to ascertain for the purposes of subsection (1) above the amount of tax chargeable for any year by virtue of section 77 in respect of gains treated as accruing to any person, those gains shall be regarded as forming the highest part of the amount on which he is chargeable to capital gains tax for the year. ...

79   Provisions supplemental to sections 77 and 78

(1) For the purposes of this section and sections 77 and 78 a person is a settlor in relation to a settlement if the settled property consists of or includes property originating from him.

(2) In this section and sections 77 and 78 –

(a) references to settled property (and to property comprised in a settlement), in relation to any settlor, are references only to property originating from that settlor.

(3) References in this section to property originating from a settlor are references to –

(a) property which that settlor has provided directly or indirectly for the purposes of the settlement,

(b) property representing that property, and

(c) so much of any property which represents both property so provided and other property as, on a just apportionment, represents the property so provided.

(5) In subsection (3) –

(a) references to property which a settlor has provided directly or indirectly include references to property which has been provided directly or indirectly by another person in pursuance of reciprocal arrangements with that settlor, but do not include references to property which that settlor has provided directly or indirectly in pursuance of reciprocal arrangements with another person, and

(b) references to property which represents other property include references to property which represents accumulated income from that other property.

(6) An inspector may by notice require any person who is or has been a trustee of, a beneficiary under, or a settlor in relation to, a settlement to give him within such time as he may direct, not being less than 28 days, such particulars as he thinks necessary for the purposes of this section and sections 77 and 78.

(7) The reference in section 77(1)(a) to gains accruing to trustees from the disposal of settled property incudes a reference to gains treated as accruing to them under section 13 and the reference in section 77(1)(b) to deductions on account of losses treated under section 13 as accruing to the trustees.

(8) Where the trustees of a settlement have elected that section 691(2) of the Taxes Act (certain income of maintenance funds for historic buildings not to be income of settlor, etc) shall have effect in the case of any settlement or part of a settlement in relation to a year of assessment, sections 77 and 78 and subsections (1) to (7) above shall not apply in relation to the settlement or part for the year.

PART IV

SHARES, SECURITIES, OPTIONS, ETC

CHAPTER I

GENERAL

115 Exemptions for gilt-edged securities and qualifying corporate bonds, etc

(1) A gain which accrues on the disposal by any person of –

(a) gilt-edged securities or qualifying corporate bonds, or

(b) any option or contract to acquire or dispose of gilt-edged securities or qualifying corporate bonds,

shall not be a chargeable gain. ...

121 Exemption for government non-market securities

(1) Savings certificates and non-marketable securities issued under the National Loans Act 1968 or the National Loans Act 1939 ... shall not be chargeable assets, and accordingly no chargeable gain shall accrue on their disposal.

(2) In this section –

(a) 'savings certificates' means savings certificates issued under section 12 of the National Loans Act 1968, or section 7 of the National Debt Act 1958, or section 59 of the Finance Act 1920, and any war savings certificates as defined in section 9(3) of the National Debt Act 1972 ..., and

(b) 'non-marketable securities' means securities which are not transferable, or which are transferable only with the consent of some Minister of the Crown ... or only with the consent of the National Debt Commissioners.

CHAPTER III

MISCELLANEOUS PROVISIONS RELATING TO COMMODITIES,
FUTURES, OPTIONS AND OTHER SECURITIES

151 Personal equity plans

(1) The Treasury may make regulations providing that an individual who invests under a plan shall be entitled to relief from capital gains tax in respect of the investments. ...

151A Venture capital trusts: reliefs

(1) A gain or loss accruing to an individual on a qualifying disposal of any ordinary shares in a company which –

(a) was a venture capital trust at the time when he acquired the shares, and

(b) is still such a trust at the time of the disposal,

shall not be a chargeable gain or, as the case may be, an allowable loss.

(2) For the purposes of this section a disposal of shares is a qualifying disposal in so far as –

(a) it is made by an individual who has attained the age of eighteen years;

(b) the shares disposed of were not acquired in excess of the permitted maximum for any year of assessment; and

(c) that individual acquired those shares for bona fide commercial purposes and not as part of a scheme or arrangement the main purpose of which, or one of the main purposes of which, is the avoidance of tax. ...

PART VI

COMPANIES, OIL, INSURANCE, ETC

CHAPTER III

INSURANCE

210 Life assurance and deferred annuities

(1) This section has effect in relation to any policy of insurance or contract for a deferred annuity on the life of any person.

(2) A gain accruing on a disposal of, or of an interest in, the rights conferred by the policy of insurance or contract for a deferred annuity is not a chargeable gain unless subsection (3) below applies.

(3) This subsection applies if –

(a) (in the case of a disposal of the rights) the rights or any interest in the rights, or

(b) (in the case of a disposal of an interest in the rights) the rights, the interest or any interest from which the interest directly or indirectly derives (in whole or in part),

have or has at any time been acquired by any person for actual consideration (as opposed to consideration deemed to be given by any enactment relating to the taxation of chargeable gains).

(4) For the purposes of subsection (3) above –

(a) (in the case of a policy of insurance) amounts paid under the policy by way of premiums, and

(b) (in the case of a contract for a deferred annuity) amounts paid under the contract, whether by way of premiums or as lump sum consideration,

do not constitute actual consideration.

(5) And for those purposes actual consideration for –

(a) a disposal which is made by one spouse to the other or is an approved post-marriage disposal, or

(b) a disposal to which section 171(1) [transfers within a group] applies,

is to be treated as not constituting actual consideration.

(6) For the purposes of subsection (5)(a) above a disposal is an approved post-marriage disposal if –

(a) it is made in consequence of the dissolution or annulment of a marriage by one person who was a party to the marriage to the other,

(b) it is made with the approval, agreement or authority of a court (or other person or body) having jurisdiction under the law of any country or territory or pursuant to an order of such a court (or other person or body), and

(c) the rights disposed of were, or the interest disposed of was, held by the person by whom the disposal is made immediately before the marriage was dissolved or annulled.

(7) Subsection (8) below applies for the purposes of tax on chargeable gains where –

(a) (if that subsection did not apply) a loss would accrue on a disposal of, or of an interest in, the rights conferred by the policy of insurance or contract for a deferred annuity, but

(b) if sections 37 and 39 were disregarded, there would accrue on the disposal a loss of a smaller amount, a gain or neither a loss nor a gain.

(8) If (disregarding those sections) a loss of a smaller amount would accrue, that smaller amount is to be taken to be the amount of the loss accruing on the disposal; and in any other case, neither a loss nor a gain is to be taken to accrue on the disposal.

(9) But subsection (8) above does not affect the treatment for the purposes of tax on chargeable gains of the person who acquired rights, or an interest in rights, on the disposal.

(10) The occasion of –

(a) the receipt of the sum or sums assured by the policy of insurance,

(b) the transfer of investments or other assets to the owner of the policy of insurance in accordance with the policy, or

(c) the surrender of the policy of insurance,

is for the purposes of tax on chargeable gains an occasion of a disposal of the rights (or of all of the interests in the rights) conferred by the policy of insurance.

(11) The occasion of –

(a) the receipt of the first instalment of the annuity under the contract for a deferred annuity, or

(b) the surrender of the rights conferred by the contract for a deferred annuity,

is for the purposes of tax on chargeable gains an occasion of a disposal of the rights (or of all of the interests in the rights) conferred by the contract for a deferred annuity.

(12) Where there is a disposal on the occasion of the receipt of the first instalment of the annuity under the contract for a deferred annuity –

(a) in the case of a disposal of the rights conferred by the contract, the consideration for the disposal is the aggregate of the amount or value of the first instalment and the market value at the time of the disposal of the right to receive the further instalments of the annuity, and

(b) in the case of a disposal of an interest in the rights, the consideration for the disposal is such proportion of that aggregate as is just and reasonable;

and no gain accruing on any subsequent disposal of, or of any interest in, the rights is a chargeable gain (even if subsection (3) above applies).

(13) In this section 'interest', in relation to rights conferred by a policy of insurance or contract for a deferred annuity, means an interest as a co-owner of the rights (whether the rights are owned jointly or in common and whether or not the interests of the co-owners are equal).

PART VII

OTHER PROPERTY, BUSINESS, INVESTMENTS, ETC

222 Relief on disposal of private residence

(1) This section applies to a gain accruing to an individual so far as attributable to the disposal of, or of an interest in –

(a) a dwelling-house or part of a dwelling-house which is, or has at any time in his period of ownership been, his only or main residence, or

(b) land which he has for his own occupation and enjoyment with that residence as its garden or grounds up to the permitted area.

(2) In this section 'the permitted area' means, subject to subsections (3) and (4) below, an area (inclusive of the site of the dwelling-house) of 0.5 of a hectare.

(3) Where the area required for the reasonable enjoyment of the dwelling-house (or of the part in question) as a residence, having regard to the size and character of the dwelling-house, is larger than 0.5 of a hectare, that larger area shall be the permitted area.

(4) Where part of the land occupied with a residence is and part is not within subsection (1) above, then (up to the permitted area) that part shall be taken to be within subsection (1) above which, if the remainder were separately occupied, would be the most suitable for occupation and enjoyment with the residence.

(5) So far as is necessary for the purposes of this section to determine which of 2 or more residences is an individual's main residence for any period –

(a) the individual may conclude that question by notice to the inspector given within 2 years from the beginning of that period but subject to a right to vary that notice by a further notice to the inspector as respects any period beginning not earlier than 2 years before the giving of the further notice.

(6) In the case of a man and his wife living with him –

(a) there can only be one residence or main residence for both, so long as living together and, where a notice under subsection (5)(a) above affects both the husband and the wife, it must be given by both.

(7) In this section and sections 223 to 226, 'the period of ownership' where the individual has had different interests at different times shall be taken to begin from the first acquisition taken into account in arriving at the expenditure which under Chapter III of Part II is allowable as a deduction in the computation of the gain to which this section applies, and in the case of a man and his wife living with him –

(a) if the one disposes of, or of his or her interest in, the dwelling-house or part of a dwelling-house which is their only or main residence to the other, and in particular if it passes on death to the other as legatee, the other's period of ownership shall begin with the beginning of the period of ownership of the one making the disposal, and

(b) if paragraph (a) above applies, but the dwelling-house or part of a dwelling-house was not the only or main residence of both throughout the period of ownership of the one making the disposal, account shall be taken of any part of that period during which it was his only or main residence as if it was also that of the other.

(8) If at any time during an individual's period of ownership of a dwelling-house or part of a dwelling-house he –

(a) resides in living accommodation which is for him job-related, and

(b) intends in due course to occupy the dwelling-house or part of a dwelling-house as his only or main residence,

this section and sections 223 to 226 shall apply as if the dwelling-house or part of a dwelling-house were at that time occupied by him as a residence.

(8A) Subject to subsections (8B), (8C) and (9) below, for the purposes of subsection (8) above living accommodation is job-related for a person if –

(a) it is provided for him by reason of his employment, or for his spouse by reason of her employment, in any of the following cases –

(i) where it is necessary for the proper performance of the duties of the employment that the employee should reside in that accommodation;

(ii) where the accommodation is provided for the better performance of the duties of the employment, and it is one of the kinds of employment in the case of which it is customary for employers to provide living accommodation for employees;

(iii) where, there being a special threat to the employee's security, special security arrangements are in force and the employee resides in the accommodation as part of those arrangements;

or

(b) under a contract entered into at arm's length and requiring him or his spouse to carry on a particular trade, profession or vocation, he or his spouse is bound –

(i) to carry on that trade, profession or vocation on premises or other land provided by another person (whether under a tenancy or otherwise); and

(ii) to live either on those premises or on other premises provided by that other person.

(8B) If the living accommodation is provided by a company and the employee is a director of that or an associated company, subsection (8A)(a)(i) or (ii) above shall not apply unless –

(a) the company of which the employee is a director is one in which he or she has no material interest; and

(b) either –

(i) the employment is as a full-time working director, or

(ii) the company is non-profit making, that is to say, it does not carry on a trade nor do its functions consist wholly or mainly in the holding of investments or other property, or

(iii) the company is established for charitable purposes only.

(8C) Subsection (8A)(b) above does not apply if the living accommodation concerned is in whole or in part provided by –

(a) a company in which the borrower or his spouse has a material interest; or

(b) any person or persons together with whom the borrower or his spouse carries on a trade or business in partnership.

(8D) For the purposes of this section –

(a) a company is an associated company of another if one of them has control of the other or both are under the control of the same person; and

(b) 'employment', 'director', 'full-time working director', 'material interest' and 'control', in relation to a body corporate, have the meanings given by Chapter 2 of Part 3 of [the Income Tax (Earnings and Pensions) Act] 2003.

(9) Subsections (8A)(b) and (8C) above shall apply for the purposes of subsection (8) above only in relation to residence on or after 6th April 1983 in living accommodation which is job-related for the purposes of that subsection.

(10) Apportionments of consideration shall be made wherever required by this section or sections 223 to 226 and, in particular, where a person disposes of a dwelling-house only part of which is his only or main residence.

223 Amount of relief

(1) No part of a gain to which section 222 applies shall be a chargeable gain if the dwelling-house or part of a dwelling-house has been the individual's only or main residence throughout the period of ownership, or throughout the period of ownership except for all or any part of the last 36 months of that period.

(2) Where subsection (1) above does not apply, a fraction of the gain shall not be a chargeable gain, and that fraction shall be –

(a) the length of the part or parts of the period of ownership during which the dwelling-house or the part of the dwelling-house was the individual's only or main residence, but inclusive of the last 36 months of the period of ownership in any event, divided by

(b) the length of the period of ownership.

(3) For the purposes of subsections (1) and (2) above –

(a) a period of absence not exceeding 3 years (or periods of absence which together did not exceed 3 years), and in addition

(b) any period of absence throughout which the individual worked in an employment or office all the duties of which were performed outside the United Kingdom, and in addition

(c) any period of absence not exceeding 4 years (or periods of absence which together did not exceed 4 years) throughout which the individual was prevented from residing in the dwelling-house or part of the dwelling-house in consequence of the situation of his place of work or in consequence of any condition imposed by his employer requiring him to reside elsewhere, being a condition reasonably imposed to secure the effective performance by the employee of his duties, shall be treated as if in that period of absence the dwelling-house or the part of the dwelling-house was the individual's only or main residence if both before and after the period there was a time when the dwelling-house was the individual's only or main residence.

(4) Where a gain to which section 222 applies accrues to any individual and the dwelling-house in question or any part of it is or has at any time in his period of ownership been wholly or partly let by him as residential accommodation, the part of the gain, if any, which (apart from this subsection) would be a chargeable gain by reason of the letting, shall be such a gain only to the extent, if any, to which it exceeds whichever is the lesser of –

(a) the part of the gain which is not a chargeable gain by virtue of the provisions of subsection (1) to (3) above or those provisions as applied by section 225; and

(b) £40,000.

(5) Where at any time the number of months specified in subsections (1) and (2)(a) above is 36, the Treasury may by order amend those subsections by substituting references to 24 for the references to 36 in relation to disposals on or after such date as is specified in the order.

(6) Subsection (5) above shall also have effect as if 36 (in both places) read 24 and as if 24 read 36.

(7) In this section –

'period of absence' means a period during which the dwelling-house or the part of the dwelling-house was not the individual's only or main residence and throughout which he had no residence or main residence eligible for relief under this section; and

'period of ownership' does not include any period before 31st March 1982.

224 Amount of relief: further provisions

(1) If the gain accrues from the disposal of a dwelling-house or part of a dwelling-house part of which is used exclusively for the purpose of a trade or business, or of a profession or vocation, the gain shall be apportioned and section 223 shall apply in relation to the part of the gain apportioned to the part which is not exclusively used for those purposes.

(2) If at any time in the period of ownership there is a change in what is occupied as the individual's residence, whether on account of a reconstruction or conversion of a building or for any other reason, or there

have been changes as regards the use of part of the dwelling-house for the purpose of a trade or business, or of a profession or vocation, or for any other purpose, the relief given by section 223 may be adjusted in a manner which is just and reasonable.

(3) Section 223 shall not apply in relation to a gain if the acquisition of, or of the interest in, the dwelling-house or the part of a dwelling-house was made wholly or partly for the purpose of realising a gain from the disposal of it, and shall not apply in relation to a gain so far as attributable to any expenditure which was incurred after the beginning of the period of ownership and was incurred wholly or partly for the purpose of realising a gain from the disposal.

225 Private residence occupied under terms of settlement

Sections 222 to 224 shall also apply in relation to a gain accruing to a trustee on a disposal of settled property being a asset within section 222(1) where, during the period of ownership of the trustee, the dwelling-house or part of the dwelling-house mentioned in that subsection has been the only or main residence of a person entitled to occupy it under the terms of the settlement, and in those sections as so applied –

(a) references to the individual shall be taken as references to the trustee except in relation to the occupation of the dwelling-house or part of the dwelling-house, and

(b) the notice which may be given to the inspector under section 222(5)(a) shall be a joint notice by the trustee and the person entitled to occupy the dwelling-house or part of the dwelling-house.

237 Superannuation funds, annuities and annual payments

No chargeable gain shall accrue to any person on the disposal of a right to, or to any part of–

(a) any allowance, annuity or capital sum payable out of any superannuation fund, or under any superannuation scheme, established solely or mainly for persons employed in a profession, trade, undertaking or employment, and their dependants,

(b) an annuity granted otherwise than under a contract for a deferred annuity by a company as part of its business of granting annuities on human life, whether or not including instalments of capital, or an annuity granted or deemed to be granted under the Government Annuities Act 1929, or

(c) annual payments which are due under a covenant made by any person and which are not secured on any property.

250 Woodlands

(1) Consideration for the disposal of trees standing or felled or cut on woodlands managed by the occupier on a commercial basis and with a view to the realisation of profits shall be excluded from the computation of the gain if the person making the disposal is the occupier.

(2) Capital sums received under a policy of insurance in respect of the destruction of or damage or injury to trees by fire or other hazard on such woodlands shall be excluded from the computation of the gain if the person making the disposal is the occupier.

(3) Subsection (2) above shall have effect notwithstanding section 22(1).

(4) In the computation of the gain so much of the cost of woodland in the United Kingdom shall be disregarded as is attributable to trees growing on the land.

(5) In the computation of the gain accruing on a disposal of woodland in the United Kingdom so much of the consideration for the disposal as is attributable to trees growing on the land shall be excluded.

(6) References in this section to trees include references to saleable underwood.

251 General provisions

(1) Where a person incurs a debt to another, whether in sterling or in some other currency, no chargeable gain shall accrue to that (that is the original) creditor or his personal representative or legatee on a disposal of the debt, except in the case of the debt on a security (as defined in section 132 [ie 'security' includes any loan stock or similar security whether of the Government of the United Kingdom or of any other government, or of any public or local authority in the United Kingdom or elsewhere, or of any company, and whether secured or unsecured]). ...

256 Charities

(1) Subject to section 505(3) of the Taxes Act [restriction on relief where excess income and gains do not exceed non-qualifying expenditure] and subsection (2) below, a gain shall not be a chargeable gain if it accrues to a charity and is applicable and applied for charitable purposes.

(2) If property held on charitable trusts ceases to be subject to charitable trusts –

(a) the trustees shall be treated as if they had disposed of, and immediately reacquired, the property for a consideration equal to its market value, any gain on the disposal being treated as not accruing to a charity, and

(b) if and so far as any of that property represents, directly or indirectly, the consideration for the disposal of assets by the trustees, any gain accruing on that disposal shall be treated as not having accrued to a charity,

and an assessment to capital gains tax chargeable by virtue of paragraph (b) above may be made at any time not more than 3 years after the end of the year of assessment in which the property ceases to be subject to charitable trusts.

257 Gifts to charities, etc

(1) Subsection (2) below shall apply where a disposal of an asset is made otherwise than under a bargain at arm's length –

(a) to a charity, or

(b) to any bodies mentioned in Schedule 3 to the Inheritance Tax Act 1984 (gifts for national purposes, etc),

and the disposal is not one in relation to which section 151A(1) [venture capital trusts] has effect.

(2) Sections 17(1) and 258(3) shall not apply; but if the disposal is by way of gift (including a gift in settlement) or for a consideration not exceeding the sums allowable as a deduction under section 38, then –

(a) the disposal and acquisition shall be treated for the purposes of this Act as being made for such consideration as to secure that neither a gain nor a loss accrues on the disposal, and

(b) where, after the disposal, the asset is disposed of by the person who acquired it under the disposal, its acquisition by the person making the earlier disposal shall be treated for the purposes of this Act as the acquisition of the person making the later disposal.

(3) Where –

(a) otherwise than on the termination of a life interest (within the meaning of section 72) by the death of the person entitled thereto, any asset or parts of any assets forming part of settled property are, under section 71, deemed to be disposed of and reacquired by the trustee, and

(b) the person becoming entitled as mentioned in section 71(1) is a charity, or a body mentioned in Schedule 3 to the Inheritance Tax Act 1984 (gifts for national purposes, etc),

then, if no consideration is received by any person for or in connection with any transaction by virtue of which the charity or other body becomes so entitled, the disposal and reacquisition of the assets to which the charity or other body becomes so entitled shall, notwithstanding section 71, be treated for the purposes of this Act as made for such consideration as to secure that neither a gain nor a loss accrues on the disposal.

258 Works of art, etc

(2) A gain shall not be a chargeable gain if it accrues on the disposal of an asset with respect to which an inheritance tax undertaking or an undertaking under the following provisions of this section has been given and –

(a) the disposal is by way of sale by private treaty to a body mentioned in Schedule 3 to the Inheritance Tax Act 1984 ('the 1984 Act') (museums, etc), or is to such a body otherwise than by sale, or

(b) the disposal is to the Board in pursuance of section 230 of the 1984 Act or in accordance with directions given by the Treasury under section 50 or 51 of the Finance Act 1946 (acceptance of property in satisfaction of tax).

(3) Subsection (4) below shall have effect in respect of the disposal of any asset which is property which has been or could be designated under section 31 of the 1984 Act, being –

(a) a disposal by way of gift, including a gift in settlement, or

(b) a disposal of settled property by the trustee on an occasion when, under section 71(1), the trustee is deemed to dispose of and immediately reacquire settled property (other than any disposal on which by virtue of section 73 no chargeable gain or allowable loss accrues to the trustee),

if the requisite undertaking described in section 31 of the 1984 Act (maintenance, preservation and access) is given by such person as the Board think appropriate in the circumstances of the case.

(4) The person making a disposal to which subsection (3) above applies and the person acquiring the asset on the disposal shall be treated for all the purposes of this Act as if the asset was acquired from the one making the

disposal for a consideration of such an amount as would secure that on the disposal neither a gain nor a loss would accrue to the one making the disposal.

(5) If –

(a) there is a sale of the asset and inheritance tax is chargeable under section 32 of the 1984 Act (or would be chargeable if an inheritance tax undertaking as well as an undertaking under this section had been given), or

(b) the Board are satisfied that at any time during the period for which any such undertaking was given it has not been observed in a material respect,

the person selling that asset or, as the case may be, the owner of the asset shall be treated for the purposes of this Act as having sold the asset for a consideration equal to its market value, and, in the case of a failure to comply with the undertaking, having immediately reacquired it for a consideration equal to its market value.

(6) The period for which an undertaking under this section is given shall be until the person beneficially entitled to the asset dies or it is disposed of, whether by sale or gift or otherwise; and if the asset subject to the undertaking is disposed of –

(a) otherwise than on sale, and

(b) without a further undertaking being given under this section,

subsection (5) above shall apply as if the asset had been sold to an individual.

References in this subsection to a disposal shall be construed without regard to any provision of this Act under which an asset is deemed to be disposed of.

(7) Where under subsection (5) above a person is treated as having sold for a consideration equal to its market value any asset within section 31(1)(c), (d) or (e) of the 1984 Act, he shall also be treated as having sold and immediately reacquired for a consideration equal to its market value any asset associated with it; but the Board may direct that the preceding provisions of this subsection shall not have effect in any case in which it appears to them that the entity consisting of the asset and any assets associated with it has not been materially affected.

For the purposes of this subsection 2 or more assets are associated with each other if one of them is a building falling within section 31(1)(c) of the 1984

Act and the other or others such land or objects as, in relation to that building, fall within section 31(1)(d) or (e) of the 1984 Act.

(8) If in pursuance of subsection (5) above a person is treated as having on any occasion sold an asset and inheritance tax becomes chargeable on the same occasion, then, in determining the value of the asset for the purposes of that tax, an allowance shall be made for the capital gains tax chargeable on any chargeable gain accruing on that occasion.

(8A) Section 35A of the 1984 Act (variation of undertakings) shall have effect in relation to an undertaking given under this section as it has effect in relation to an undertaking given under section 30 of that Act.

(9) In this section 'inheritance tax undertaking' means an undertaking under Chapter II of Part II or section 78 of, or Schedule 5 to, the 1984 Act.

259 Gifts to housing associations

(1) Subsection (2) below shall apply where –

> (a) a disposal of an estate or interest in land in the United Kingdom is made to a relevant housing association otherwise than under a bargain at arm's length, and

> (b) a claim for relief under this section is made by the transferor and the association.

(2) Section 17(1) shall not apply; but if the disposal is by way of gift or for a consideration not exceeding the sums allowable as a deduction under section 38, then –

> (a) the disposal and acquisition shall be treated for the purposes of this Act as being made for such consideration as to secure that neither a gain nor a loss accrues on the disposal, and

> (b) where, after the disposal, the estate or interest is disposed of by the association, its acquisition by the person making the earlier disposal shall be treated for the purposes of this Act as the acquisition of the association.

(3) In this section 'relevant housing association' means –

> (a) a registered social landlord within the meaning of Part I of the Housing Act 1996, ...

260 Gifts on which inheritance tax is chargeable, etc

(1) If –

(a) an individual or the trustees of a settlement ('the transferor') make a disposal within subsection (2) below of an asset,

(b) the asset is acquired by an individual or the trustees of a settlement ('the transferee'), and

(c) a claim for relief under this section is made by the transferor and the transferee or, where the trustees of a settlement are the transferee, by the transferor alone,

then, subject to subsection (6) below and sections 169 [gifts into dual resident trusts] and 261 [section 260 relief: gifts to non-residents], subsection (3) below shall apply in relation to the disposal.

(2) A disposal is within this subsection if it is made otherwise than under a bargain at arm's length and –

(a) is a chargeable transfer within the meaning of the Inheritance Tax Act 1984 (or would be but for section 19 of that Act) and is not a potentially exempt transfer (within the meaning of that Act),

(b) is an exempt transfer by virtue of –

(i) section 24 of that Act (transfers to political parties),

(iii) section 27 of that Act (transfers to maintenance funds for historic buildings etc), or

(iv) section 30 of that Act (transfers of designated property),

(c) is a disposition to which section 57A of that Act [relief where property enters maintenance fund] applies and by which the property disposed of becomes held on trusts of the kind referred to in subsection (1)(b) of that section (maintenance funds for historic buildings etc),

(d) by virtue of subsection (4) of section 71 of that Act (accumulation and maintenance trusts) does not constitute an occasion on which inheritance tax is chargeable under that section,

(e) by virtue of section 78(1) of that Act (transfers of works of art etc) does not constitute an occasion on which tax is chargeable under Chapter III of Part III of that Act, or

(f) is a disposal of an asset comprised in a settlement where, as a result of the asset or part of it becoming comprised in another settlement, there is no charge, or a reduced charge, to inheritance tax by virtue of paragraph 9, 16 or 17 of Schedule 4 to that Act (transfers to maintenance funds for historic buildings etc).

(3) Where this subsection applies in relation to a disposal –

(a) the amount of any chargeable gain which, apart from this section, would accrue to the transferor on the disposal, and

(b) the amount of the consideration for which, apart from this section, the transferee would be regarded for the purposes of capital gains tax as having acquired the asset in question,

shall each be reduced by an amount equal to the held-over gain on the disposal.

(4) Subject to subsection (5) below, the reference in subsection (3) above to the held-over gain on a disposal is a reference to the exchange gain which would have accrued on that disposal apart from this section.

(5) In any case where –

(a) there is actual consideration (as opposed to the consideration equal to the market value which is deemed to be given by virtue of any provision of this Act) for a disposal in respect of which a claim for relief is made under this section, and

(b) that actual consideration exceeds the sums allowable as a deduction under section 38,

the held-over gain on the disposal shall be reduced by the excess referred to in paragraph (b) above. ...

(7) In the case of a disposal within subsection (2)(a) above there shall be allowed as a deduction in computing the chargeable gain accruing to the transferee on the disposal of the asset in question an amount equal to whichever is the lesser of –

(a) the inheritance tax attributable to the value of the asset; and

(b) the amount of the chargeable gain as computed apart from this subsection. ...

262 Chattel exemption

(1) Subject to this section a gain accruing on a disposal of an asset which is tangible movable property shall not be a chargeable gain if the amount or value of the consideration for the disposal does not exceed £6,000.

(2) Where the amount or value of the consideration for the disposal of an asset which is tangible movable property exceeds £6,000, there shall be excluded from any chargeable gain accruing on the disposal so much of it as exceeds five-thirds of the difference between –

(a) the amount or value of the consideration, and

(b) £6,000.

(3) Subsections (1) and (2) above shall not affect the amount of an allowable

loss accruing on the disposal of an asset, but for the purposes of computing under this Act the amount of a loss accruing on the disposal of tangible movable property the consideration for the disposal shall, if less than £6,000, be deemed to be £6,000 and the losses which are allowable losses shall be restricted accordingly.

(4) If 2 or more assets which have formed part of a set of articles of any description all owned at one time by one person are disposed of by that person, and –

(a) to the same person, or

(b) to persons who are acting in concert or who are connected persons,

whether on the same or different occasions, the 2 or more transactions shall be treated as a single transaction disposing of a single asset, but with any necessary apportionments of the reductions in chargeable gains, and in allowable losses, under subsections (2) and (3) above.

(5) If the disposal is of a right or interest in or over tangible movable property –

(a) in the first instance subsections (1), (2) and (3) above shall be applied in relation to the asset as a whole, taking the consideration as including the market value of what remains undisposed of, in addition to the actual consideration,

(b) where the sum of the actual consideration and that market value exceeds £6,000, the part of any chargeable gain that is excluded from it under subsection (2) above shall be so much of the gain as exceeds five-thirds of the difference between that sum and £6,000 multiplied by the fraction equal to the actual consideration divided by the said sum, and

(c) where that sum is less than £6,000 any loss shall be restricted under subsection (3) above by deeming the consideration to be the actual consideration plus the said fraction of the difference between the said sum and £6,000.

(6) This section shall not apply –

(a) in relation to a disposal of commodities of any description by a person dealing on a terminal market or dealing with or through a person ordinarily engaged in dealing on a terminal market, or

(b) in relation to a disposal of currency of any description.

263 Passenger vehicles

A mechanically propelled road vehicle constructed or adapted for the carriage of passengers, except for a vehicle of a type not commonly used as a private vehicle and unsuitable to be so used, shall not be a chargeable asset; and accordingly no chargeable gain or allowable loss shall accrue on its disposal.

268 Decorations for valour or gallant conduct

A gain shall not be a chargeable gain if accruing on the disposal by any person of a decoration awarded for valour or gallant conduct which he acquired otherwise than for consideration in money or money's worth.

269 Foreign currency for personal expenditure

A gain shall not be a chargeable gain if accruing on the disposal by an individual of currency of any description acquired by him for the personal expenditure outside the United Kingdom of himself or his family or dependants (including expenditure on the provision or maintenance of any residence outside the United Kingdom).

PART VIII

SUPPLEMENTAL

272 Valuation: general

(1) In this Act 'market value' in relation to any assets means the price which those assets might reasonably be expected to fetch on a sale in the open market.

(2) In estimating the market value of any assets no reduction shall be made in the estimate on account of the estimate being made on the assumption that the whole of the assets is to be placed on the market at one and the same time.

(3) Subject to subsection (4) below, the market value of shares or securities quoted in The Stock Exchange Daily Official List shall, except where in consequence of special circumstances prices quoted in that List are by themselves not a proper measure of market value, be as follows –

   (a) the lower of the 2 prices shown in the quotations for the shares or securities in The Stock Exchange Daily Official List on the relevant date plus one-quarter of the difference between those 2 figures, or

   (b) halfway between the highest and lowest prices at which bargains other than bargains done at special prices, were recorded in the shares or securities for the relevant date, choosing the amount under paragraph (a), if less than that under paragraph (b), or if no such bargains were recorded for the relevant date, and choosing the amount under paragraph (b) if less than that under paragraph (a).

(4) Subsection (3) shall not apply to shares or securities for which The Stock Exchange provides a more active market elsewhere than on the London trading floor; and, if the London trading floor is closed on the relevant date, the market value shall be ascertained by reference to the latest previous date or earliest subsequent date on which it is open, whichever affords the lower market value.

(5) In this Act 'market value' in relation to any rights of unit holders in any unit trust scheme the buying and selling prices of which are published regularly by the managers of the scheme shall mean an amount equal to the buying price (that is the lower price) so published on the relevant date, or if none were published on that date, on the latest date before.

(6) The provisions of this section, with sections 273 and 274, have effect subject to Part I of Schedule 11 [valuation].

273 Unquoted shares and securities

(1) The provisions of subsection (3) below shall have effect in any case where, in relation to an asset to which this section applies, there falls to be determined by virtue of section 272(1) the price which the asset might reasonably be expected to fetch on a sale in the open market.

(2) The assets to which this section applies are shares and securities which are not quoted on a recognised stock exchange at the time as at which their market value for the purposes of tax on chargeable gains falls to be determined.

(3) For the purposes of a determination falling within subsection (1) above, it shall be assumed that, in the open market which is postulated for the purposes of that determination, there is available to any prospective purchaser of the asset in question all the information which a prudent prospective purchaser of the asset might reasonably require if he were proposing to purchase it from a willing vendor by private treaty and at arm's length.

274 Value determined for inheritance tax

Where on the death of any person inheritance tax is chargeable on the value of his estate immediately before his death and the value of an asset forming part of that estate has been ascertained (whether in any proceedings or otherwise) for the purposes of that tax, the value so ascertained shall be taken for the purposes of this Act to be the market value of that asset at the date of the death.

275 Location of assets

For the purposes of this Act –

(a) the situation of rights or interests (otherwise than by way of security) in or over immovable property is that of the immovable property,

(b) subject to the following provisions of this subsection, the situation of rights or interests (otherwise than by way of security) in or over tangible movable property is that of the tangible movable property,

(c) subject to the following provisions of this subsection, a debt, secured or unsecured, is situated in the United Kingdom if and only if the creditor is resident in the United Kingdom,

(d) shares or securities issued by any municipal or governmental authority, or by any body created by such an authority, are situated in the country of that authority,

(e) subject to paragraph (d) above, registered shares or securities are situated where they are registered and, if registered in more than one register, where the principal register is situated,

(f) a ship or aircraft is situated in the United Kingdom if and only if the owner is then resident in the United Kingdom, and an interest or right in or over a ship or aircraft is situated in the United Kingdom if and only if the person entitled to the interest or right is resident in the United Kingdom,

(g) the situation of goodwill as a trade, business or professional asset is at the place where the trade, business or profession is carried on.

(h) patents, trade marks and registered designs are situated where they are registered, and if registered in more than one register, where each register is situated, and rights or licences to use a patent, trade mark or registered design are situated in the United Kingdom if they or any right derived from them are exercisable in the United Kingdom,

(j) copyright, design rights and franchises, and rights or licences to use any copyright work or design in which design rights subsists, are situated in the United Kingdom if they or any right derived from them are exercisable in the United Kingdom,

(k) a judgment debt is situated where the judgment is recorded,

(l) a debt which –

(i) is owed by a bank, and

(ii) is not in sterling, and

(iii) is represented by a sum standing to the credit of an account in the bank of an individual who is not domiciled in the United Kingdom,

is situated in the United Kingdom if and only if that individual is resident in the United Kingdom and the branch or other place of business of the bank at which the account is maintained is itself situated in the United Kingdom.

276 The territorial sea and the continental shelf

(1) The territorial sea of the United Kingdom shall for all purposes of the taxation of chargeable gains ... be deemed to be part of the United Kingdom. ...

280 Consideration payable by instalments

If the consideration, or part of the consideration, taken into account in the computation of the gain is payable by instalments over a period beginning not earlier than the time when the disposal is made, being a period exceeding 18 months, then, at the option of the person making the disposal, the tax on a chargeable gain accruing on the disposal may be paid by such instalments as the Board may allow over a period not exceeding 8 years and ending not later than the time at which the last of the first-mentioned instalments is payable.

282 Recovery of tax from donee

(1) If in any year of assessment a chargeable gain accrues to any person on the disposal of an asset by way of gift and any amount of capital gains tax assessed on that person for that year of assessment is not paid within 12 months from the date when the tax becomes payable, the donee may, by an assessment made not later than 2 years from the date when the tax became payable, be assessed and charged (in the name of the donor) to capital gains tax on an amount not exceeding the amount of the chargeable gain so accruing, and not exceeding the grossed up amount of that capital gains tax unpaid at the time when he is so assessed, grossing up at the marginal rate of tax, that is to say, taking capital gains tax on a chargeable gain at the amount which would not have been chargeable but for that chargeable gain.

(2) A person paying any amount of tax in pursuance of this section shall be entitled to recover a sum of that amount from the donor.

(3) References in this section to a donor include, in the case of an individual who has died, references to his personal representatives.

(4) In this section references to a gift include references to any transaction otherwise than by way of a bargain made at arm's length so far as money or money's worth passes under the transaction without full consideration in money or money's worth, and 'donor' and 'donee' shall be construed accordingly; and this section shall apply in relation to a gift made by 2 or more donors with the necessary modifications and subject to any necessary apportionments.

286 Connected persons: interpretation

(1) Any questions whether a person is connected with another shall for the purposes of this Act be determined in accordance with the following subsections of this section (any provision that one person is connected with another being taken to mean that they are connected with one another).

(2) A person is connected with an individual if that person is the individual's husband or wife, or is a relative, or the husband or wife of a relative, of the individual or of the individual's husband or wife.

(3) A person, in his capacity as trustee of a settlement, is connected with –

   (a) any individual who in relation to the settlement is a settlor,
   (b) any person who is connected with such an individual, and
   (c) any body corporate which is connected with that settlement.

In this subsection 'settlement' and 'settlor' have the same meaning as in Chapter IA of Part XV of the Taxes Act (see section 660G(1) and (2) of that Act).

(3A) For the purposes of subsection (3) above a body corporate is connected with a settlement if –

   (a) it is a close company (or only not a close company because it is not resident in the United Kingdom) and the participators include the trustees of the settlement; or
   (b) it is controlled (within the meaning of section 840 of the Taxes Act) by a company falling within paragraph (a) above.

(4) Except in relation to acquisitions or disposals of partnership assets pursuant to bona fide commercial arrangements, a person is connected with any person with whom he is in partnership, and with the husband or wife or a relative of any individual with whom he is in partnership.

(5) A company is connected with another company –

   (a) if the same person has control of both, or a person has control of one and persons connected with him, or he and persons connected with him, have control of the other, or

(b) if a group of 2 or more persons has control of each company, and the groups either consist of the same persons or could be regarded as consisting of the same persons by treating (in one or more cases) a member of either group as replaced by a person with whom he is connected.

(6) A company is connected with another person, if that person has control of it or if that person and persons connected with him together have control of it.

(7) Any 2 or more persons acting together to secure or exercise control of a company shall be treated in relation to that company as connected with one another and with any person acting on the directions of any of them to secure or exercise control of the company.

(8) In this section 'relative' means brother, sister, ancestor or lineal descendant.

NB Extra-statutory concession D5 *Private residence exemption: property held by personal representatives*: Section 225, TCGA 1992 extends the exemption from capital gains tax given for private residences to cases where a trustee disposes of a house which has been the only or main residence of an individual entitled to occupy it under the terms of a settlement. Relief is also given where personal representatives dispose of a house which before and after the deceased's death has been used as their only or main residence by individuals who under the will or intestacy are entitled to the whole or substantially the whole of the proceeds of the house either absolutely or for life.

As amended by the Finance (No 2) Act 1992 ss35(1), 46(1), (2), 56, 77, 82, Schedule 9, para 21(1), (2), Schedule 12, para 5(b); Finance Act 1993, ss79, 83, 208(2), (4), Schedule 6, paras 22, 23, Schedule 23, Pt III(6); Finance Act 1994, ss91, 93(1), 258, Schedule 11, para 2, Schedule 26, Pt V(7); Trade Marks Act 1994, s106(2), Schedule 5; Finance Act 1995, ss72(1), (3), (5), (8), 74, 103(7), 113(1), 114, 162, Schedule 17, Pt III, paras 27–29, 31, Schedule 29, Pt VIII(8), (16); Finance Act 1996, ss73(4), 134(1), (2), 135(1), (2), 199, 201, 205, Schedule 20, paras 59, 60, 65, Schedule 21, para 35, Schedule 38, para 12(1), (3), Schedule 39, Pt II, paras 3–6, Schedule 41, Pts V(10), VIII(4); Housing Act 1996 (Consequential Provisions) Order 1996, art 5, Schedule 2, para 20(1), (3); Finance Act 1997, s113, Schedule 18, Pt VI(7); Finance (No 2) Act 1997, s34, Schedule 4, para 24; Finance Act 1998, ss46(3), 120, 121(1), (3), (4), 128, 142, 143(7), 165, Schedule 7, para 7, Schedule 21, paras 1–3, 5, 6(1), Schedule 25, paras 1, 9, Schedule 27, Pt III(29), (31), Pt IV; Finance Act 1999, ss26, 38(8), 75, 139, Schedule 4, paras 17, 18(4), Schedule 20, Pt III(1), (7); Finance Act 2000, ss37, 66(1), (2), 90(2), 91(1), 156, Schedule 40, Pt II(12); Finance Act 2001, s75(2), (6); Finance Act 2002, s46, 51, 52, 141, Schedule 11, paras 1–3, 7, 8, Schedule 4, Pt 3(4); Income Tax (Earnings and Pensions) Act 2003, s732, Schedule 6, Pt 2, paras 207, 213; Finance Act 2003, ss123, 157, 159, Schedule 18, para 5, Schedule 28, paras 3, 7, 8, Schedule 43, Pt 3(7); Capital Gains Tax (Annual Exempt Amount) Order 2004.

LAW OF PROPERTY (MISCELLANEOUS PROVISIONS) ACT 1994
(1994 c 36)

PART II

MATTERS ARISING IN CONNECTION WITH DEATH

14   Vesting of estate in case of intestacy or lack of executors

(1) [Substitutes s9 of the Administration of Estates Act 1925]

(2) Any real or personal estate of a person dying before the commencement of this section shall, if it is property to which this subsection applies, vest in the Public Trustee on the commencement of this section.

(3) Subsection (2) above applies to any property –

(a) if it was vested in the Probate Judge under section 9 of the Administration of Estates Act 1925 immediately before the commencement of this section, or

(b) if it was not so vested but as at commencement there has been no grant of representation in respect of it and there is no executor with power to obtain such a grant.

(4) Any property vesting in the Public Trustee by virtue of subsection (2) above shall –

(a) if the deceased died intestate, be treated as vesting in the Public Trustee under section 9(1) of the Administration of Estates Act 1925 (as substituted by subsection (1) above); and

(b) otherwise be treated as vesting in the Public Trustee under section 9(2) of that Act (as so substituted).

(5) Anything done by or in relation to the Probate Judge with respect to property vested in him as mentioned in subsection (3)(a) above shall be treated as having been done by or in relation to the Public Trustee.

(6) So far as may be necessary in consequence of the transfer to the Public

Trustee of the functions of the Probate Judge under section 9 of the Administration of Estates Act 1925, any reference in an enactment or instrument to the Probate Judge shall be construed as a reference to the Public Trustee.

16 Concurrence of personal representatives in dealings with interests in land

(1) [Amends s2(2) of the Administration of Estates Act 1925]

(3) The amendments made by subsection (1) apply to contracts made after the commencement of this section.

NB These sections came into force on 1 July 1995.

As amended by the Trusts of Land and Appointment of Trustees Act 1996, s25(2), Schedule 4.

FINANCE ACT 1995
(1995 c 4)

154 Short rotation coppice

(1) The cultivation of short rotation coppice shall be regarded for the purposes of the Tax Acts and the Taxation of Chargeable Gains Act 1992 as farming (and, where relevant, as husbandry or agriculture) and not as forestry; and land in the United Kingdom on which the activity is carried on shall accordingly be regarded for those purposes as farm land or agricultural land, as the case may be, and not as woodlands.

(2) For the purposes of the Inheritance Tax Act 1984 the cultivation of short rotation coppice shall be regarded as agriculture; and accordingly for those purposes –

(a) land on which short rotation coppice is cultivated shall be regarded as agricultural land, and

(b) buildings used in connection with the cultivation of short rotation coppice shall be regarded as farm buildings.

(3) In subsections (1) and (2) 'short rotation coppice' means a perennial crop of tree species planted at high density, the stems of which are harvested above ground level at intervals of less than ten years. ...

LAW REFORM (SUCCESSION) ACT 1995
(1995 c 41)

1 Intestacy and partial intestacy

(1) [Inserts s46(2A) of the Administration of Estates Act 1925 ('the 1925 Act')]

(2) [Repeals ss47(1)(iii) and 49(1)(aa), (a), (2), (3), of the 1925 Act]

(3) Subsections (1) and (2) above have effect as respects an intestate dying on or after 1st January 1996.

(4) In section 50 of the 1925 Act (construction of documents), the references in subsection (1) to Part IV of that Act and to the foregoing provisions of that Part shall, in relation to an instrument inter vivos made or a will or codicil coming into operation on or after 1st January 1996 (but not in relation to instruments inter vivos made or wills or codicils coming into operation earlier), be construed as including references to this section.

(5) In this section 'intestate' shall be construed in accordance with section 55(1)(vi) of the 1925 Act.

2 Application for financial provision by person who lived with deceased as husband or wife

[Inserts ss1(1)(ba), (1A), 3(2A) of the Inheritance (Provision for Family and Dependants) Act 1975]

3 Effect of dissolution or annulment of marriage on will

(1) [Substitutes s18A(1)(a), (b) of the Wills Act 1837]

(2) Subsection (1) above has effect as respects a will made by a person dying on or after 1st January 1996 (regardless of the date of the will and the date of the dissolution or annulment).

4 Effect of dissolution or annulment of marriage on appointment of guardian

(1) [Inserts s6(3A) of the Children Act 1989]

(2) Subsection (1) above has effect as respects an appointment made by a person dying on or after 1st January 1996 (regardless of the date of the appointment and the date of the dissolution or annulment).

TRUSTS OF LAND AND APPOINTMENT OF TRUSTEES ACT 1996

(1996 c 47)

PART I

TRUSTS OF LAND ...

6   General powers of trustees

(1) For the purpose of exercising their functions as trustees, the trustees of land have in relation to the land subject to the trust all the powers of an absolute owner.

(2) Where in the case of any land subject to a trust of land each of the beneficiaries interested in the land is a person of full age and capacity who is absolutely entitled to the land, the powers conferred on the trustees by subsection (1) include the power to convey the land to the beneficiaries even though they have not required the trustees to do so; and where land is conveyed by virtue of this subsection –

(a) the beneficiaries shall do whatever is necessary to secure that it vests in them, and

(b) if they fail to do so, the court may make an order requiring them to do so.

(3) The trustees of land have power to acquire land under the power conferred by section 8 of the Trustee Act 2000.

(5) In exercising the powers conferred by this section trustees shall have regard to the rights of the beneficiaries.

(6) The powers conferred by this section shall not be exercised in contravention of, or of any order made in pursuance of, any other enactment or any rule of law or equity.

(7) The reference in subsection (6) to an order includes an order of any court or of the Charity Commissioners.

(8) Where any enactment other than this section confers on trustees authority to act subject to any restriction, limitation or condition, trustees of land may not exercise the powers conferred by this section to do any act which they are prevented from doing under the other enactment by reason of the restriction, limitation or condition.

(9) The duty of care under section 1 of the Trustee Act 2000 applies to trustees of land when exercising the powers conferred by this section.

7 Partition by trustees

(1) The trustees of land may, where beneficiaries of full age are absolutely entitled in undivided shares to land subject to the trust, partition the land, or any part of it, and provide (by way of mortgage or otherwise) for the payment of any equality money.

(2) The trustees shall give effect to any such partition by conveying the partitioned land in severalty (whether or not subject to any legal mortgage created for raising equality money), either absolutely or in trust, in accordance with the rights of those beneficiaries.

(3) Before exercising their powers under subsection (2) the trustees shall obtain the consent of each of those beneficiaries.

(4) Where a share in the land is affected by an incumbrance, the trustees may either give effect to it or provide for its discharge from the property allotted to that share as they think fit.

(5) If a share in the land is absolutely vested in a minor, subsections (1) to (4) apply as if he were of full age, except that the trustees may act on his behalf and retain land or other property representing his share in trust for him.

8 Exclusion and restriction of powers

(1) Sections 6 and 7 do not apply in the case of a trust of land created by a disposition in so far as provision to the effect that they do not apply is made by the disposition.

(2) If the disposition creating such a trust makes provision requiring any consent to be obtained to the exercise of any power conferred by section 6 or 7, the power may not be exercised without that consent.

(3) Subsection (1) does not apply in the case of charitable, ecclesiastical or public trusts.

(4) Subsections (1) and (2) have effect subject to any enactment which

prohibits or restricts the effect of provision of the description mentioned in them.

9 Delegation by trustees

(1) The trustees of land may, by power of attorney, delegate to any beneficiary or beneficiaries of full age and beneficially entitled to an interest in possession in land subject to the trust any of their functions as trustees which relate to the land.

(2) Where trustees purport to delegate to a person by a power of attorney under subsection (1) functions relating to any land and another person in good faith deals with him in relation to the land, he shall be presumed in favour of that other person to have been a person to whom the functions could be delegated unless that other person has knowledge at the time of the transaction that he was not such a person. And it shall be conclusively presumed in favour of any purchaser whose interest depends on the validity of that transaction that that other person dealt in good faith and did not have such knowledge if that other person makes a statutory declaration to that effect before or within three months after the completion of the purchase.

(3) A power of attorney under subsection (1) shall be given by all the trustees jointly and (unless expressed to be irrevocable and to be given by way of security) may be revoked by any one or more of them; and such a power is revoked by the appointment as a trustee of a person other than those by whom it is given (though not by any of those persons dying or otherwise ceasing to be a trustee).

(4) Where a beneficiary to whom functions are delegated by a power of attorney under subsection (1) ceases to be a person beneficially entitled to an interest in possession in land subject to the trust –

(a) if the functions are delegated to him alone, the power is revoked,

(b) if the functions are delegated to him and to other beneficiaries to be exercised by them jointly (but not separately), the power is revoked if each of the other beneficiaries ceases to be so entitled (but otherwise functions exercisable in accordance with the power are so exercisable by the remaining beneficiary or beneficiaries), and

(c) if the functions are delegated to him and to other beneficiaries to be exercised by them separately (or either separately or jointly), the power is revoked in so far as it relates to him.

(5) A delegation under subsection (1) may be for any period or indefinite.

(6) A power of attorney under subsection (1) cannot be an enduring power within the meaning of the Enduring Powers of Attorney Act 1985.

(7) Beneficiaries to whom functions have been delegated under subsection (1) are, in relation to the exercise of the functions, in the same position as trustees (with the same duties and liabilities); but such beneficiaries shall not be regarded as trustees for any other purposes (including, in particular, the purposes of any enactment permitting the delegation of functions by trustees or imposing requirements relating to the payment of capital money).

(9) Neither this section nor the repeal by this Act of section 29 of the Law of Property Act 1925 (which is superseded by this section) affects the operation after the commencement of this Act of any delegation effected before that commencement.

9A   Duties of trustees in connection with delegation, etc

(1) The duty of care under section 1 of the Trustee Act 2000 applies to trustees of land in deciding whether to delegate any of their functions under section 9.

(2) Subsection (3) applies if the trustees of land –

(a) delegate any of their functions under section 9, and

(b) the delegation is not irrevocable.

(3) While the delegation continues, the trustees –

(a) must keep the delegation under review,

(b) if circumstances make it appropriate to do so, must consider whether there is a need to exercise any power of intervention that they have, and

(c) if they consider that there is a need to exercise such a power, must do so.

(4) 'Power of intervention' includes –

(a) a power to give directions to the beneficiary;

(b) a power to revoke the delegation.

(5) The duty of care under section 1 of the 2000 Act applies to trustees in carrying out any duty under subsection (3).

(6) A trustee of land is not liable for any act or default of the beneficiary, or beneficiaries, unless the trustee fails to comply with the duty of care in

deciding to delegate any of the trustees' functions under section 9 or in carrying out any duty under subsection (3).

(7) Neither this section nor the repeal of section 9(8) by the Trustee Act 2000 affects the operation after the commencement of this section of any delegation effected before that commencement.

12   The right to occupy

(1) A beneficiary who is beneficially entitled to an interest in possession in land subject to a trust of land is entitled by reason of his interest to occupy the land at any time if at that time –

   (a) the purposes of the trust include making the land available for his occupation (or for the occupation of beneficiaries of a class of which he is a member or of beneficiaries in general), or

   (b) the land is held by the trustees so as to be so available.

(2) Subsection (1) does not confer on a beneficiary a right to occupy land if it is either unavailable or unsuitable for occupation by him.

(3) This section is subject to section 13.

13   Exclusion and restriction of right to occupy

(1) Where two or more beneficiaries are (or apart from this subsection would be) entitled under section 12 to occupy land, the trustees of land may exclude or restrict the entitlement of any one or more (but not all) of them.

(2) Trustees may not under subsection (1) –

   (a) unreasonably exclude any beneficiary's entitlement to occupy land, or

   (b) restrict any such entitlement to an unreasonable extent.

(3) The trustees of land may from time to time impose reasonable conditions on any beneficiary in relation to his occupation of land by reason of his entitlement under section 12.

(4) The matters to which trustees are to have regard in exercising the powers conferred by this section include –

   (a) the intentions of the person or persons (if any) who created the trust,

   (b) the purposes for which the land is held, and

   (c) the circumstances and wishes of each of the beneficiaries who is (or apart from any previous exercise by the trustees of those powers would be) entitled to occupy the land under section 12.

(5) The conditions which may be imposed on a beneficiary under subsection (3) include, in particular, conditions requiring him –

(a) to pay any outgoings or expenses in respect of the land, or

(b) to assume any other obligation in relation to the land or to any activity which is or is proposed to be conducted there.

(6) Where the entitlement of any beneficiary to occupy land under section 12 has been excluded or restricted, the conditions which may be imposed on any other beneficiary under subsection (3) include, in particular, conditions requiring him to –

(a) make payments by way of compensation to the beneficiary whose entitlement has been excluded or restricted, or

(b) forgo any payment or other benefit to which he would otherwise be entitled under the trust so as to benefit that beneficiary.

(7) The powers conferred on trustees by this section may not be exercised –

(a) so as to prevent any person who is in occupation of land (whether or not by reason of an entitlement under section 12) from continuing to occupy the land, or

(b) in a manner likely to result in any such person ceasing to occupy the land,

unless he consents or the court has given approval.

(8) The matters to which the court is to have regard in determining whether to give approval under subsection (7) include the matters mentioned in subsection (4)(a) to (c).

15   Matters relevant in determining applications

(1) The matters to which the court is to have regard in determining an application for an order under section 14 include –

(a) the intentions of the person or persons (if any) who created the trust,

(b) the purposes for which the property subject to the trust is held,

(c) the welfare of any minor who occupies or might reasonably be expected to occupy any land subject to the trust as his home, and

(d) the interests of any secured creditor of any beneficiary.

(2) In the case of an application relating to the exercise in relation to any land of the powers conferred on the trustees by section 13, the matters to which the court is to have regard also include the circumstances and wishes

of each of the beneficiaries who is (or apart from any previous exercise by the trustees of those powers would be) entitled to occupy the land under section 12.

(3) In the case of any other application, other than one relating to the exercise of the power mentioned in section 6(2), the matters to which the court is to have regard also include the circumstances and wishes of any beneficiaries of full age and entitled to an interest in possession in property subject to the trust or (in case of dispute) of the majority (according to the value of their combined interests).

(4) This section does not apply to an application if section 335A of the Insolvency Act 1986 (which is inserted by Schedule 3 and relates to applications by a trustee of a bankrupt) applies to it.

16   Protection of purchasers

(1) A purchaser of land which is or has been subject to a trust need not be concerned to see that any requirement imposed on the trustees by section 6(5), 7(3) or 11(1) has been complied with.

(2) Where –

(a) trustees of land who convey land which (immediately before it is conveyed) is subject to the trust contravene section 6(6) or (8), but

(b) the purchaser of the land from the trustees has no actual notice of the contravention,

the contravention does not invalidate the conveyance.

(3) Where the powers of trustees of land are limited by virtue of section 8 –

(a) the trustees shall take all reasonable steps to bring the limitation to the notice of any purchaser of the land from them, but

(b) the limitation does not invalidate any conveyance by the trustees to a purchaser who has no actual notice of the limitation.

(4) Where trustees of land convey land which (immediately before it is conveyed) is subject to the trust to persons believed by them to be beneficiaries absolutely entitled to the land under the trust and of full age and capacity –

(a) the trustees shall execute a deed declaring that they are discharged from the trust in relation to that land, and

(b) if they fail to do so, the court may make an order requiring them to do so.

(5) A purchaser of land to which a deed under subsection (4) relates is entitled to assume that, as from the date of the deed, the land is not subject to the trust unless he has actual notice that the trustees were mistaken in their belief that the land was conveyed to beneficiaries absolutely entitled to the land under the trust and of full age and capacity.

(6) Subsections (2) and (3) do not apply to land held on charitable, ecclesiastical or public trusts.

(7) This section does not apply to registered land.

17 Application of provisions to trusts of proceeds of sale ...

(3) In this section 'trust of proceeds of sale of land' means (subject to subsection (5)) any trust of property (other than a trust of land) which consists of or includes –

(a) any proceeds of a disposition of land held in trust (including settled land), or

(b) any property representing any such proceeds.

(4) The references in subsection (3) to a trust –

(a) are to any description of trust (whether express, implied, resulting or constructive), including a trust for sale and a bare trust, and

(b) include a trust created, or arising, before the commencement of this Act.

(5) A trust which (despite section 2 [trusts in place of settlements]) is a settlement for the purposes of the Settled Land Act 1925 cannot be a trust of proceeds of sale of land.

(6) In subsection (3) –

(a) 'disposition' includes any disposition made, or coming into operation, before the commencement of this Act, and

(b) the reference to settled land includes personal chattels to which section 67(1) of the Settled Land Act 1925 (heirlooms) applies.

18 Application of Part to personal representatives

(1) The provisions of this Part relating to trustees, other than sections 10, 11 and 14, apply to personal representatives, but with appropriate modifications and without prejudice to the functions of personal representatives for the purposes of administration.

(2) The appropriate modifications include –

(a) the substitution of references to persons interested in the due administration of the estate for references to beneficiaries, and

(b) the substitution of references to the will for references to the disposition creating the trust.

(3) Section 3(1) [abolition of doctrine of conversion] does not apply to personal representatives if the death occurs before the commencement of this Act.

PART III

SUPPLEMENTARY

22   Meaning of 'beneficiary'

(1) In this Act 'beneficiary', in relation to a trust, means any person who under the trust has an interest in property subject to the trust (including a person who has such an interest as a trustee or a personal representative).

(2) In this Act references to a beneficiary who is beneficially entitled do not include a beneficiary who has an interest in property subject to the trust only by reason of being a trustee or personal representative.

(3) For the purposes of this Act a person who is a beneficiary only by reason of being an annuitant is not to be regarded as entitled to an interest in possession in land subject to the trust.

23   Other interpretation provisions

(1) In this Act 'purchaser' has the same meaning as in Part I of the Law of Property Act 1925.

(2) Subject to that, where an expression used in this Act is given a meaning by the Law of Property Act 1925 it has the same meaning as in that Act unless the context otherwise requires.

(3) In this Act 'the court' means –

(a) the High Court, or
(b) a county court.

25 Amendments, repeals, etc ...

(4) The amendments and repeals made by this Act do not affect any entailed interest created before the commencement of this Act.

(5) The amendments and repeals made by this Act in consequence of section 3 [abolition of doctrine of conversation] –

(a) do not affect a trust created by a will if the testator died before the commencement of this Act, and

(b) do not affect personal representatives of a person who died before that commencement;

and the repeal of section 22 of the Partnership Act 1890 does not apply in any circumstances involving the personal representatives of a partner who died before that commencement.

27 Short title, commencement and extent ...

(2) This Act comes into force on such day as the Lord Chancellor appoints by order made by statutory instrument. ...

NB This Act came into force on 1st January 1997.

As amended by the Trustee Act 2000, s40, Schedule 2, paras 45–47, Schedule 4, Pt II.

TRUSTEE ACT 2000
(2000 c 29)

PART I

THE DUTY OF CARE

1   The duty of care

(1) Whenever the duty under this subsection applies to a trustee, he must exercise such care and skill as is reasonable in the circumstances, having regard in particular –

(a) to any special knowledge or experience that he has or holds himself out as having, and

(b) if he acts as trustee in the course of a business or profession, to any special knowledge or experience that it is reasonable to expect of a person acting in the course of that kind of business or profession.

(2) In this Act the duty under subsection (1) is called 'the duty of care'.

2   Application of duty of care

Schedule 1 makes provision about when the duty of care applies to a trustee.

PART II

INVESTMENT

3   General power of investment

(1) Subject to the provisions of this Part, a trustee may make any kind of investment that he could make if he were absolutely entitled to the assets of the trust.

(2) In this Act the power under subsection (1) is called 'the general power of investment'.

(3) The general power of investment does not permit a trustee to make investments in land other than in loans secured on land (but see also section 8).

(4) A person invests in a loan secured on land if he has rights under any contract under which –

(a) one person provides another with credit, and

(b) the obligation of the borrower to repay is secured on land.

(5) 'Credit' includes any cash loan or other financial accommodation.

(6) 'Cash' includes money in any form.

4 Standard investment criteria

(1) In exercising any power of investment, whether arising under this Part or otherwise, a trustee must have regard to the standard investment criteria.

(2) A trustee must from time to time review the investments of the trust and consider whether, having regard to the standard investment criteria, they should be varied.

(3) The standard investment criteria, in relation to a trust, are –

(a) the suitability to the trust of investments of the same kind as any particular investment proposed to be made or retained and of that particular investment as an investment of that kind, and

(b) the need for diversification of investments of the trust, in so far as is appropriate to the circumstances of the trust.

5 Advice

(1) Before exercising any power of investment, whether arising under this Part or otherwise, a trustee must (unless the exception applies) obtain and consider proper advice about the way in which, having regard to the standard investment criteria, the power should be exercised.

(2) When reviewing the investments of the trust, a trustee must (unless the exception applies) obtain and consider proper advice about whether, having regard to the standard investment criteria, the investments should be varied.

(3) The exception is that a trustee need not obtain such advice if he reasonably concludes that in all the circumstances it is unnecessary or inappropriate to do so.

(4) Proper advice is the advice of a person who is reasonably believed by the trustee to be qualified to give it by his ability in and practical experience of financial and other matters relating to the proposed investment.

6   Restriction or exclusion of this Part, etc

(1) The general power of investment is –

(a) in addition to powers conferred on trustees otherwise than by this Act, but

(b) subject to any restriction or exclusion imposed by the trust instrument or by any enactment or any provision of subordinate legislation.

(2) For the purposes of this Act, an enactment or a provision of subordinate legislation is not to be regarded as being, or as being part of, a trust instrument.

(3) In this Act 'subordinate legislation' has the same meaning as in the Interpretation Act 1978.

7   Existing trusts

(1) This Part applies in relation to trusts whether created before or after its commencement.

(2) No provision relating to the powers of a trustee contained in a trust instrument made before 3rd August 1961 is to be treated (for the purposes of section 6(1)(b)) as restricting or excluding the general power of investment.

(3) A provision contained in a trust instrument made before the commencement of this Part which –

(a) has effect under section 3(2) of the Trustee Investments Act 1961 as a power to invest under that Act, or

(b) confers power to invest under that Act,

is to be treated as conferring the general power of investment on a trustee.

PART III

ACQUISITION OF LAND

8   Power to acquire freehold and leasehold land

(1) A trustee may acquire freehold or leasehold land in the United Kingdom –

  (a) as an investment,
  (b) for occupation by a beneficiary, or
  (c) for any other reason.

(2) 'Freehold or leasehold land' means –

  (a) in relation to England and Wales, a legal estate in land,
  (b) in relation to Scotland –

   (i) the estate or interest of the proprietor of the dominium utile or, in the case of land not held on feudal tenure, the estate or interest of the owner, or
   (ii) a tenancy, and

  (c) in relation to Northern Ireland, a legal estate in land, including land held under a fee farm grant.

(3) For the purpose of exercising his functions as a trustee, a trustee who acquires land under this section has all the powers of an absolute owner in relation to the land.

9   Restriction or exclusion of this Part, etc

The powers conferred by this Part are –

  (a) in addition to powers conferred on trustees otherwise than by this Part, but

  (b) subject to any restriction or exclusion imposed by the trust instrument or by any enactment or any provision of subordinate legislation.

10   Existing trusts

(1) This Part does not apply in relation to –

  (a) a trust of property which consists of or includes land which (despite section 2 of the Trusts of Land and Appointment of Trustees Act 1996) is settled land, or

(b) a trust to which the Universities and College Estates Act 1925 applies.

(2) Subject to subsection (1), this Part applies in relation to trusts whether created before or after its commencement.

PART IV

AGENTS, NOMINEES AND CUSTODIANS

11 Power to employ agents

(1) Subject to the provisions of this Part, the trustees of a trust may authorise any person to exercise any or all of their delegable functions as their agent.

(2) In the case of a trust other than a charitable trust, the trustees' delegable functions consist of any function other than –

(a) any function relating to whether or in what way any assets of the trust should be distributed,

(b) any power to decide whether any fees or other payment due to be made out of the trust funds should be made out of income or capital,

(c) any power to appoint a person to be a trustee of the trust, or

(d) any power conferred by any other enactment or the trust instrument which permits the trustees to delegate any of their functions or to appoint a person to act as a nominee or custodian. ...

12 Persons who may act as agents

(1) Subject to subsection (2), the persons whom the trustees may under section 11 authorise to exercise functions as their agent include one or more of their number.

(2) The trustees may not authorise two (or more) persons to exercise the same function unless they are to exercise the function jointly.

(3) The trustees may not under section 11 authorise a beneficiary to exercise any function as their agent (even if the beneficiary is also a trustee).

(4) The trustees may under section 11 authorise a person to exercise functions as their agent even though he is also appointed to act as their nominee or custodian (whether under section 16, 17 or 18 or any other power).

13   Linked functions, etc

(1) Subject to subsections (2) and (5), a person who is authorised under section 11 to exercise a function is (whatever the terms of the agency) subject to any specific duties or restrictions attached to the function.

For example, a person who is authorised under section 11 to exercise the general power of investment is subject to the duties under section 4 in relation to that power.

(2) A person who is authorised under section 11 to exercise a power which is subject to a requirement to obtain advice is not subject to the requirement if he is the kind of person from whom it would have been proper for the trustees, in compliance with the requirement, to obtain advice.

(3) Subsections (4) and (5) apply to a trust to which section 11(1) of the Trusts of Land and Appointment of Trustees Act 1996 (duties to consult beneficiaries and give effect to their wishes) applies.

(4) The trustees may not under section 11 authorise a person to exercise any of their functions on terms that prevent them from complying with section 11(1) of the 1996 Act.

(5) A person who is authorised under section 11 to exercise any function relating to land subject to the trust is not subject to section 11(1) of the 1996 Act.

14   Terms of agency

(1) Subject to subsection (2) and sections 15(2) and 29 to 32, the trustees may authorise a person to exercise functions as their agent on such terms as to remuneration and other matters as they may determine.

(2) The trustees may not authorise a person to exercise functions as their agent on any of the terms mentioned in subsection (3) unless it is reasonably necessary for them to do so.

(3) The terms are –

   (a) a term permitting the agent to appoint a substitute;

   (b) a term restricting the liability of the agent or his substitute to the trustees or any beneficiary;

   (c) a term permitting the agent to act in circumstances capable of giving rise to a conflict of interest.

15   Asset management: special restrictions

(1) The trustees may not authorise a person to exercise any of their asset management functions as their agent except by an agreement which is in or evidenced in writing.

(2) The trustees may not authorise a person to exercise any of their asset management functions as their agent unless –

   (a) they have prepared a statement that gives guidance as to how the functions should be exercised ('a policy statement'), and

   (b) the agreement under which the agent is to act includes a term to the effect that he will secure compliance with –

   (i) the policy statement, or

   (ii) if the policy statement is revised or replaced under section 22, the revised or replacement policy statement.

(3) The trustees must formulate any guidance given in the policy statement with a view to ensuring that the functions will be exercised in the best interests of the trust.

(4) The policy statement must be in or evidenced in writing.

(5) The asset management functions of trustees are their functions relating to –

   (a) the investment of assets subject to the trust,

   (b) the acquisition of property which is to be subject to the trust, and

   (c) managing property which is subject to the trust and disposing of, or creating or disposing of an interest in, such property.

21   Application of sections 22 and 23

(1) Sections 22 and 23 apply in a case where trustees have, under section 11, 16, 17 or 18 –

   (a) authorised a person to exercise functions as their agent, or

   (b) appointed a person to act as a nominee or custodian.

(2) Subject to subsection (3), sections 22 and 23 also apply in a case where trustees have, under any power conferred on them by the trust instrument or by any enactment or any provision of subordinate legislation –

   (a) authorised a person to exercise functions as their agent, or

   (b) appointed a person to act as a nominee or custodian.

(3) If the application of section 22 or 23 is inconsistent with the terms of the trust instrument or the enactment or provision of subordinate legislation, the section in question does not apply.

22   Review of agents, nominees and custodians, etc

(1) While the agent, nominee or custodian continues to act for the trust, the trustees –

(a) must keep under review the arrangements under which the agent, nominee or custodian acts and how those arrangements are being put into effect,

(b) if circumstances make it appropriate to do so, must consider whether there is a need to exercise any power of intervention that they have, and

(c) if they consider that there is a need to exercise such a power, must do so.

(2) If the agent has been authorised to exercise asset management functions, the duty under subsection (1) includes, in particular –

(a) a duty to consider whether there is any need to revise or replace the policy statement made for the purposes of section 15,

(b) if they consider that there is a need to revise or replace the policy statement, a duty to do so, and

(c) a duty to assess whether the policy statement (as it has effect for the time being) is being complied with.

(3) Subsections (3) and (4) of section 15 apply to the revision or replacement of a policy statement under this section as they apply to the making of a policy statement under that section.

(4) 'Power of intervention' includes –

(a) a power to give directions to the agent, nominee or custodian;

(b) a power to revoke the authorisation or appointment.

23   Liability for agents, nominees and custodians, etc

(1) A trustee is not liable for any act or default of the agent, nominee or custodian unless he has failed to comply with the duty of care applicable to him, under paragraph 3 of Schedule 1 –

(a) when entering into the arrangements under which the person acts as agent, nominee or custodian, or

(b) when carrying out his duties under section 22.

(2) If a trustee has agreed a term under which the agent, nominee or custodian is permitted to appoint a substitute, the trustee is not liable for any act or default of the substitute unless he has failed to comply with the duty of care applicable to him, under paragraph 3 of Schedule 1 –

(a) when agreeing that term, or

(b) when carrying out his duties under section 22 in so far as they relate to the use of the substitute.

24   Effect of trustees exceeding their powers

A failure by the trustees to act within the limits of the powers conferred by this Part –

(a) in authorising a person to exercise a function of theirs as an agent, or

(b) in appointing a person to act as a nominee or custodian,

does not invalidate the authorisation or appointment.

25   Sole trustees

(1) Subject to subsection (2), this Part applies in relation to a trust having a sole trustee as it applies in relation to other trusts (and references in this Part to trustees – except in sections 12(1) and (3) and 19(5) – are to be read accordingly).

(2) Section 18 does not impose a duty on a sole trustee if that trustee is a trust corporation.

26   Restriction or exclusion of this Part, etc

The powers conferred by this Part are –

(a) in addition to powers conferred on trustees otherwise than by this Act, but

(b) subject to any restriction or exclusion imposed by the trust instrument or by any enactment or any provision of subordinate legislation.

27 Existing trusts

This Part applies in relation to trusts whether created before or after its commencement.

PART V

REMUNERATION

28 Trustee's entitlement to payment under trust instrument

(1) Except to the extent (if any) to which the trust instrument makes inconsistent provision, subsections (2) to (4) apply to a trustee if –

(a) there is a provision in the trust instrument entitling him to receive payment out of trust funds in respect of services provided by him to or on behalf of the trust, and

(b) the trustee is a trust corporation or is acting in a professional capacity.

(2) The trustee is to be treated as entitled under the trust instrument to receive payment in respect of services even if they are services which are capable of being provided by a lay trustee.

(3) Subsection (2) applies to a trustee of a charitable trust who is not a trust corporation only –

(a) if he is not a sole trustee, and

(b) to the extent that a majority of the other trustees have agreed that it should apply to him.

(4) Any payments to which the trustee is entitled in respect of services are to be treated as remuneration for services (and not as a gift) for the purposes of –

(a) section 15 of the Wills Act 1837 (gifts to an attesting witness to be void), and

(b) section 34(3) of the Administration of Estates Act 1925 (order in which estate to be paid out).

(5) For the purposes of this Part, a trustee acts in a professional capacity if he acts in the course of a profession or business which consists of or includes the provision of services in connection with –

(a) the management or administration of trusts generally or a particular kind of trust, or

(b) any particular aspect of the management or administration of trusts generally or a particular kind of trust,

and the services he provides to or on behalf of the trust fall within that description.

(6) For the purposes of this Part, a person acts as a lay trustee if he –

(a) is not a trust corporation, and

(b) does not act in a professional capacity.

29   Remuneration of certain trustees

(1) Subject to subsection (5), a trustee who –

(a) is a trust corporation, but

(b) is not a trustee of a charitable trust,

is entitled to receive reasonable remuneration out of the trust funds for any services that the trust corporation provides to or on behalf of the trust.

(2) Subject to subsection (5), a trustee who –

(a) acts in a professional capacity, but

(b) is not a trust corporation, a trustee of a charitable trust or a sole trustee,

is entitled to receive reasonable remuneration out of the trust funds for any services that he provides to or on behalf of the trust if each other trustee has agreed in writing that he may be remunerated for the services.

(3) 'Reasonable remuneration' means, in relation to the provision of services by a trustee, such remuneration as is reasonable in the circumstances for the provision of those services to or on behalf of that trust by that trustee and for the purposes of subsection (1) includes, in relation to the provision of services by a trustee who is an authorised institution under the Banking Act 1987 and provides the services in that capacity, the institution's reasonable charges for the provision of such services.

(4) A trustee is entitled to remuneration under this section even if the services in question are capable of being provided by a lay trustee.

(5) A trustee is not entitled to remuneration under this section if any provision about his entitlement to remuneration has been made –

(a) by the trust instrument, or

(b) by any enactment or any provision of subordinate legislation.

(6) This section applies to a trustee who has been authorised under a power conferred by Part IV or the trust instrument –

(a) to exercise functions as an agent of the trustees, or

(b) to act as a nominee or custodian,

as it applies to any other trustee.

31   Trustees' expenses

(1) A trustee –

(a) is entitled to be reimbursed from the trust funds, or

(b) may pay out of the trust funds,

expenses properly incurred by him when acting on behalf of the trust.

(2) This section applies to a trustee who has been authorised under a power conferred by Part IV or any other enactment or any provision of subordinate legislation, or by the trust instrument –

(a) to exercise functions as an agent of the trustees, or

(b) to act as a nominee or custodian,

as it applies to any other trustee.

32   Remuneration and expenses of agents, nominees and custodians

(1) This section applies if, under a power conferred by Part IV or any other enactment or any provision of subordinate legislation, or by the trust instrument, a person other than a trustee has been –

(a) authorised to exercise functions as an agent of the trustees, or

(b) appointed to act as a nominee or custodian.

(2) The trustees may remunerate the agent, nominee or custodian out of the trust funds for services if –

(a) he is engaged on terms entitling him to be remunerated for those services, and

(b) the amount does not exceed such remuneration as is reasonable in the circumstances for the provision of those services by him to or on behalf of that trust.

(3) The trustees may reimburse the agent, nominee or custodian out of the

trust funds for any expenses properly incurred by him in exercising functions as an agent, nominee or custodian.

33 Application

(1) Subject to subsection (2), sections 28, 29, 31 and 32 apply in relation to services provided to or on behalf of, or (as the case may be) expenses incurred on or after their commencement on behalf of, trusts whenever created.

(2) Nothing in section 28 or 29 is to be treated as affecting the operation of –

(a) section 15 of the Wills Act 1837, or

(b) section 34(3) of the Administration of Estates Act 1925,

in relation to any death occurring before the commencement of section 28 or (as the case may be) section 29.

PART VI

MISCELLANEOUS AND SUPPLEMENTARY

35 Personal representatives

(1) Subject to the following provisions of this section, this Act applies in relation to a personal representative administering an estate according to the law as it applies to a trustee carrying out a trust for beneficiaries.

(2) For this purpose this Act is to be read with the appropriate modifications and in particular –

(a) references to the trust instrument are to be read as references to the will,

(b) references to a beneficiary or to beneficiaries, apart from the reference to a beneficiary in section 8(1)(b), are to be read as references to a person or the persons interested in the due administration of the estate, and

(c) the reference to a beneficiary in section 8(1)(b) is to be read as a reference to a person who under the will of the deceased or under the law relating to intestacy is beneficially interested in the estate.

(3) Remuneration to which a personal representative is entitled under section 28 or 29 is to be treated as an administration expense for the purposes of –

(a) section 34(3) of the Administration of Estates Act 1925 (order in which estate to be paid out), and

(b) any provision giving reasonable administration expenses priority over the preferential debts listed in Schedule 6 to the Insolvency Act 1986.

(4) Nothing in subsection (3) is to be treated as affecting the operation of the provisions mentioned in paragraphs (a) and (b) of that subsection in relation to any death occurring before the commencement of this section.

39   Interpretation

(1) In this Act –

'asset' includes any right or interest; ...

'custodian trustee' has the same meaning as in the Public Trustee Act 1906;

'enactment' includes any provision of a Measure of the Church Assembly or of the General Synod of the Church of England; ...

'functions' includes powers and duties;

'legal mortgage' has the same meaning as in the Law of Property Act 1925;

'personal representative' has the same meaning as in the Trustee Act 1925;

'settled land' has the same meaning as in the Settled Land Act 1925;

'trust corporation' has the same meaning as in the Trustee Act 1925;

'trust funds' means income or capital funds of the trust. ...

40   Minor and consequential amendments, etc

[Where appropriate, these have been included in the text.]

41   Power to amend other Acts

(1) A Minister of the Crown may by order make such amendments of any Act, including an Act extending to places outside England and Wales, as appear to him appropriate in consequence of or in connection with Part II or III.

(2) Before exercising the power under subsection (1) in relation to a local, personal or private Act, the Minister must consult any person who appears to him to be affected by any proposed amendment.

(3) An order under this section may –

(a) contain such transitional provisions and savings as the Minister thinks fit;

(b) make different provision for different purposes.

(4) The power to make an order under this section is exercisable by statutory instrument which shall be subject to annulment in pursuance of a resolution of either House of Parliament.

(5) 'Minister of the Crown' has the same meaning as in the Ministers of the Crown Act 1975.

42   Commencement and extent

(1) Section 41, this section and section 43 shall come into force on the day on which this Act is passed.

(2) The remaining provisions of this Act shall come into force on such day as the Lord Chancellor may appoint by order made by statutory instrument; and different days may be so appointed for different purposes. ...

SCHEDULE 1

APPLICATION OF DUTY OF CARE

INVESTMENT

1. The duty of care applies to a trustee –

(a) when exercising the general power of investment or any other power of investment, however conferred;

(b) when carrying out a duty to which he is subject under section 4 or 5 (duties relating to the exercise of a power of investment or to the review of investments).

ACQUISITION OF LAND

2. The duty of care applies to a trustee –

(a) when exercising the power under section 8 to acquire land;

(b) when exercising any other power to acquire land, however conferred;

(c) when exercising any power in relation to land acquired under a power mentioned in sub-paragraph (a) or (b).

AGENTS, NOMINEES AND CUSTODIANS

3. (1) The duty of care applies to a trustee –

(a) when entering into arrangements under which a person is authorised under section 11 to exercise functions as an agent; ...

(d) when entering into arrangements under which, under any other power, however conferred, a person is authorised to exercise functions as an agent or is appointed to act as a nominee or custodian;

(e) when carrying out his duties under section 22 (review of agent, nominee or custodian, etc.). ...

COMPOUNDING OF LIABILITIES

4. The duty of care applies to a trustee –

(a) when exercising the power under section 15 of the Trustee Act 1925 to do any of the things referred to in that section;

(b) when exercising any corresponding power, however conferred.

INSURANCE

5. The duty of care applies to a trustee –

(a) when exercising the power under section 19 of the Trustee Act 1925 to insure property;

(b) when exercising any corresponding power, however conferred.

REVERSIONARY INTERESTS, VALUATIONS AND AUDIT

6. The duty of care applies to a trustee –

(a) when exercising the power under section 22(1) or (3) of the Trustee Act 1925 to do any of the things referred to there;

(b) when exercising any corresponding power, however conferred.

EXCLUSION OF DUTY OF CARE

7. The duty of care does not apply if or in so far as it appears from the trust instrument that the duty is not meant to apply.

NB Sections 41–43 came into force on 23 November 2000 (the date of Royal Assent), the remaining provisions on 1 February 2001.

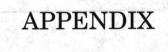

APPENDIX

ADMINISTRATION OF JUSTICE ACT 1982
(1982 c 53)

27 The form of an international will

(1) The Annex to the Convention on International Wills shall have the force of law in the United Kingdom.

(2) The Annex is set out in Schedule 2 to this Act.

(3) In this Part of this Act –

'international will' means a will made in accordance with the requirements of the Annex, as set out in Schedule 2 to this Act; and

'the Convention on International Wills' means the Convention providing a Uniform Law on the Form of an International Will concluded at Washington on 26th October 1973.

28 International wills – procedure

(1) The persons authorised to act in the United Kingdom in connection with international wills are –

(a) solicitors; and
(b) notaries public.

(2) A person who is authorised under section 6(1) of the Commissioners for Oaths Act 1889 to do notarial acts in any foreign country or place is authorised to act there in connection with international wills.

(3) An international will certified by virtue of subsection (1) or (2) above may be deposited in a depository provided under section 23 above.

(4) Section 23 above shall accordingly have effect in relation to such international wills.

(5) Subject to subsection (6) below, regulations under section 25 above shall have effect in relation to such international wills as they have effect in relation to wills deposited under section 23 above.

(6) Without prejudice to the generality of section 25 above, regulations under that section may make special provision with regard to such international wills. ...

SCHEDULE 2

THE ANNEX TO THE CONVENTION ON INTERNATIONAL WILLS

UNIFORM LAW ON THE FORM OF AN INTERNATIONAL WILL

ARTICLE 1

1. A will shall be valid as regards form, irrespective particularly of the place where it is made, of the location of the assets and of the nationality, domicile or residence of the testator, if it is made in the form of an international will complying with the provisions set out in Articles 2 to 5 hereinafter.

2. The invalidity of the will as an international will shall not affect its formal validity as a will of another kind.

ARTICLE 2

This law shall not apply to the form of testamentary dispositions made by two or more persons in one instrument.

ARTICLE 3

1. The will shall be made in writing.

2. It need not be written by the testator himself.

3. It may be written in any language, by hand or by an other means.

ARTICLE 4

1. The testator shall declare in the presence of two witnesses and of a person authorised to act in connection with international wills that the document is his will and that he knows the contents thereof.

2. The testator need not inform the witnesses, or the authorised person, of the contents of the will.

ARTICLE 5

1. In the presence of the witnesses and of the authorised person, the testator shall sign the will or, if he has previously signed it, shall acknowledge his signature.

2. When the testator is unable to sign, he shall indicate the reason therefor to the authorised person who shall make note of this on the will. Moreover, the testator may be authorised by the law under which the authorised person was designated to direct another person to sign on his behalf.

3. The witnesses and the authorised person shall there and then attest the will by signing in the presence of the testator.

ARTICLE 6

1. The signatures shall be placed at the end of the will.

2. If the will consists of several sheets, each sheet shall be signed by the testator or, if he is unable to sign, by the person signing on his behalf or, if there is no such person, by the authorised person. In addition, each sheet shall be numbered.

ARTICLE 7

1. The date of the will shall be the date of its signature by the authorised person.

2. This date shall be noted at the end of the will by the authorised person.

ARTICLE 8

In the absence of any mandatory rule pertaining to the safekeeping of the will, the authorised person shall ask the testator whether he wishes to make a declaration concerning the safekeeping of his will. If so and at the express request of the testator the place where he intends to have his will kept shall be mentioned in the certificate provided for in Article 9.

ARTICLE 9

The authorised person shall attach to the will a certificate in the form prescribed in Article 10 establishing that the obligations of this law have been complied with.

ARTICLE 10

The certificate drawn up by the authorised person shall be in the following form or in a substantially similar form:

CERTIFICATE

(Convention of October 26th, 1973)

1. I, ... (name, address and capacity), a person authorised to act in connection with international wills

2. Certify that on .... (date) at .... place

3. (testator) .... (name, address, date and place of birth) in my presence and that of the witnesses

4. (a) .... (name, address, date and place of birth)

   (b) .... (name, address, date and place of birth) has declared that the attached document is his will and that he knows the contents thereof.

5. I furthermore certify that:

6. (a) in my presence and in that of the witnesses

   (1) the testator has signed the will or has acknowledged his signature previously affixed.

   *(2) following a declaration of the testator stating that he was unable to sign his will for the following reason ....

      – I have mentioned this declaration on the will
      * – the signature has been affixed by .... (name, address)

7. (b) the witnesses and I have signed the will;

8. *(c) each page of the will has been signed by .... and numbered:

9. (d) I have satisfied myself as to the identity of the testator and of the witnesses as designated above;

10. (e) the witnesses met the conditions requisite to act as such according to the law under which I am acting;

11. *(f) the testator has requested me to include the following statement concerning the safekeeping of his will:

....

....

12. PLACE

13. DATE

14. SIGNATURE and, if necessary, SEAL

* To be completed if appropriate.

ARTICLE 11

The authorised person shall keep a copy of the certificate and deliver another to the testator.

ARTICLE 12

In the absence of evidence to the contrary, the certificate of the authorised person shall be conclusive of the formal validity of the instrument as a will under this Law.

ARTICLE 13

The absence or irregularity of a certificate shall not affect the formal validity of a will under this Law.

ARTICLE 14

The international will shall be subject to the ordinary rules of revocation of wills.

ARTICLE 15

In interpreting and applying the provisions of this law, regard shall be had to its international origin and to the need for uniformity in its interpretation.

INDEX

Revision Aids

Designed for the undergraduate, the 101 Questions & Answers series and the Suggested Solutions series are for all those who have a positive commitment to passing their law examinations. Each series covers a different examinable topic and comprises a selection of answers to examination questions and, in the case of the 101 Questions and Answers, interrograms. The majority of questions represent examination 'bankers' and are supported by full-length essay solutions. These titles will undoubtedly assist you with your research and further your understanding of the subject in question.

101 Questions & Answers Series

Only £7.95 Published December 2003

Constitutional Law
ISBN: 1 85836 522 8

Criminal Law
ISBN: 1 85836 432 9

Land Law
ISBN: 1 85836 515 5

Law of Contract
ISBN: 1 85836 517 1

Law of Tort
ISBN: 1 85836 516 3

Suggested Solutions to Past Examination Questions 2001–2002 Series

Only £6.95 Published December 2003

Company Law
ISBN: 1 85836 519 8

Employment Law
ISBN: 1 85836 520 1

European Union Law
ISBN: 1 85836 524 4

Evidence
ISBN: 1 85836 521 X

Family Law
ISBN: 1 85836 525 2

For further information or to place an order, please contact:

Mail Order
Old Bailey Press at Holborn College
Woolwich Road
Charlton
London
SE7 8LN

Telephone: 020 8317 6039
Fax: 020 8317 6004
Website: www.oldbaileypress.co.uk
E-Mail: mailorder@oldbaileypress.co.uk

Old Bailey Press

The Old Bailey Press Integrated Student Law Library is tailor-made to help you at every stage of your studies, from the preliminaries of each subject through to the final examination. The series of Textbooks, Revision WorkBooks, 150 Leading Cases and Cracknell's Statutes are interrelated to provide you with a comprehensive set of study materials.

You can buy Old Bailey Press books from your University Bookshop, your local Bookshop, directly using this form, or you can order a free catalogue of our titles from the address shown overleaf.

The following subjects each have a Textbook, 150 Leading Cases, Revision WorkBook and Cracknell's Statutes unless otherwise stated.

Administrative Law
Commercial Law
Company Law
Conflict of Laws
Constitutional Law
Conveyancing (Textbook and 150 Leading Cases)
Criminal Law
Criminology (Textbook and Sourcebook)
Employment Law (Textbook and Cracknell's Statutes)
English and European Legal Systems
Equity and Trusts
Evidence
Family Law
Jurisprudence: The Philosophy of Law (Textbook, Sourcebook and
    Revision WorkBook)
Land: The Law of Real Property
Law of International Trade
Law of the European Union
Legal Skills and System
    (Textbook)
Obligations: Contract Law
Obligations: The Law of Tort
Public International Law
Revenue Law (Textbook,
    Revision WorkBook and
    Cracknell's Statutes)
Succession (Textbook, Revision
    WorkBook and Cracknell's
    Statutes)

Mail order prices:	
Textbook	£15.95
150 Leading Cases	£12.95
Revision WorkBook	£10.95
Cracknell's Statutes	£11.95
Suggested Solutions 1999–2000	£6.95
Suggested Solutions 2000–2001	£6.95
Suggested Solutions 2001–2002	£6.95
101 Questions and Answers	£7.95
Law Update 2004	£10.95

Please note details and prices are subject to alteration.

To complete your order, please fill in the form below:

Module	Books required	Quantity	Price	Cost
		Postage		
		TOTAL		

For the UK and Europe, add £4.95 for the first book ordered, then add £1.00 for each subsequent book ordered for postage and packing.
For the rest of the world, add 50% for airmail.

ORDERING

By telephone to Mail Order at 020 8317 6039, with your credit card to hand.

By fax to 020 8317 6004 (giving your credit card details).

Website: www.oldbaileypress.co.uk
E-Mail: mailorder@oldbaileypress.co.uk

By post to: Mail Order, Old Bailey Press at Holborn College, Woolwich Road, Charlton, London, SE7 8LN.

When ordering by post, please enclose full payment by cheque or banker's draft, or complete the credit card details below. You may also order a free catalogue of our complete range of titles from this address.

We aim to despatch your books within 3 working days of receiving your order. All parts of the form must be completed.

Name
Address

E-Mail
Postcode   Telephone

Total value of order, including postage: £
I enclose a cheque/banker's draft for the above sum, or

charge my   ☐ Access/Mastercard   ☐ Visa   ☐ American Express

Cardholder: ....
Card number

☐☐☐☐ ☐☐☐☐ ☐☐☐☐ ☐☐☐☐

Expiry date   ☐☐☐☐

Signature: ....Date: ....